Law, Ethics and Society

Law, Ethics and Society: Historical and Contemporary Perspectives

Edited by
Stephan U. Breu
Craig Paterson

Miami, Florida
Johann Heinrich Pestalozzi University Press
2019

This collection reflects the result of interactive academic work initiated by Johann Heinrich Pestalozzi University Inc., Miami, Florida, during the academic year 2018, and also the scholarly work of academics supporting our University. The authors include international academics from the United States of America, Great Britain, Croatia, Bosnia-Herzegovina, Switzerland, Austria, Serbia, and Macedonia.

Keywords
law, ethics, international law, geopolitics, geostrategy, civil society, philosophy of law, legal history, education, heraldry, political theory

ISBN: 978-1-7335371-0-0 (Hardback)
ISBN: 978-1-7335371-1-7 (Paperback)

Volume Editors

Stephan U. Breu

President of Johann Heinrich Pestalozzi University, Miami, Florida, USA; Doctorate in Business Administration; Secretary General of Swiss Centre for International Humanitarian Law, Zuerich, Switzerland; Secretary General of Internationale Pestalozzi Gesellschaft, Taegerschen, Switzerland; Chairman of Advisory Board of East-West Bridge, Geneva, Switzerland.

Craig Paterson

Provost of Johann Heinrich Pestalozzi University, Miami, Florida, USA; PhD in Ethics from Saint Louis University, Missouri, USA; Honorary Research Professor with the Concilium Research Group, Complutense University of Madrid, Spain; previously held university teaching appointments at Saint Louis University, Missouri, USA and Providence College, Rhode Island, USA.

Foreword

The collected papers contained in this volume are the inaugural series of papers commissioned by *Johann Heinrich Pestalozzi University* (JHPU) in collaboration with *The Swiss Centre for International Humanitarian Law* (SCIHL). We are pleased to collate and publish these papers as part of a new publishing program under the JHPU Press imprint.

The papers are reflective of the array of scholarly interests sponsored by JHPU and SCIHL over the past two years. We look forward to the issuance of future volumes highlighting sponsored research.

We thank the authors for their consent to publish the papers together in this inaugural monograph.

JHPU was founded as a non-profit educational corporation in Miami, State of Florida, in 2017. The Members of the prior Steering Committee became the University's Board of Directors upon incorporation. In 2016, after a feasibility study, the Steering Committee decided to create and develop a small selective studium based university inspired by the visionary educational philosophy of Johann Heinrich Pestalozzi, the enlightened early 19th century Swiss pedagogist and reformer.

After appropriate filings, in January of 2018, the University was granted permission by the Florida State Commission on Independent Education to award University degrees based on the enlightened educational mission of Pestalozzi. The University is authorized by its governing regulations to publish scholarly monographs, journals and papers under the JHPU Press imprint.

The University's motto is Pestalozzi's celebrated phrase "Das Leben bildet"—It is life itself that educates. The present design of the University's shield is influenced by Pestalozzi's own historic personal shield and pays homage to his great educational legacy.

SCIHL was founded as Association in 2017 in Zürich, Switzerland. It is an international think-tank aiming at observing, researching and training in developments concerning international humanitarian law in co-operation with governments, universities, NGO's, civil society partners and other entities concerned with international law. SCIHL is registered with the EU Transparency Register and as a Civil Society Partner with UN Department of Economic and Social Affairs.

We hope you will benefit from reading the articles written by our staff, friends and partners.

Editors
Prof. Stephan U. Breu, DBA
Prof. Craig Paterson, PhD

February 2019.

Contents

About the Authors

Sanja Angelovska is a PhD candidate in International Relations and Conflict Management. She has been a peace advocate for many years and a member of several global peace organizations. Her academic interest is in the psychological dimensions of inter-group conflicts.

Darko Bekić is an historian, author and freelance analyst & consultant. He is former Assistant Foreign Minister and Ambassador of Croatia to the OSCE in Vienna and the UN in Geneva, as well as to Portugal and Morocco. He is a past Rockefeller post-doctoral Fellow at the Woodrow Wilson International Centre for Scholars and a lecturer at the Foreign Service Institute, Rosslyn, VA. Inter alia, he authored the first-ever History of Croatian Diplomacy published in 2016 by Skolska Knjiga, Zagreb.

Hatidža Beriša is a Professor at the School of National Defence, Ministry of Defence, Serbia.

Paul Borrow-Longain holds an advanced degree in physics from Cardiff University, Wales. He is a fellow of several learned societies in the UK and overseas. He is an acknowledged expert in the field of heraldry and serves on the board of several heraldry bodies. He is Chairman of Terrestres Servo Coronas, a charity that promotes good works within the Commonwealth. He is a Feeeman of the City of London and a Liveryman of The Worshipful Company of Scriveners.

Stephan U. Breu is President of Johann Heinrich Pestalozzi University, Miami, Florida, USA. He holds a doctorate in Business Administration. He is an Honorary Research Professor with the Concilium Research Group, Complutense University of Madrid. He is Secretary General of Swiss Centre for International Humanitarian Law, Zuerich, Switzerland; Secretary General of Internationale Pestalozzi Gesellschaft, Taegerschen, Switzerland; Chairman of Advisory Board of East-West Bridge, Geneva, Switzerland.

Joseph P. Garske writes and speaks on topics of legal culture, technology, convergence, and globalization. He holds a bachelor's degree in history from Harvard University and serves as Chairman of The Global Conversation.

Parvis Hanson is President of Manor Group, Switzerland, consulting with leading corporations and governments from Asia, Europe and North America. He was Senior Manager of the World Economic Forum, Asia; ICT corporations and New Asian Leaders. He is President, East-West Bridge, Switzerland; President of Swiss-China Partnership, Switzerland, Founder of The Princess Carina Organization, Switzerland, and a senior advisor to the United Nations, INTERPOL, Brookings Institute, WIPO, WCO, ICC, and Horasis.

Elmar Kuhn is an external Associate Professor for Religious Science and European Advisor of the Johann Heinrich Pestalozzi University, Florida, USA. Dr Kuhn has studied in Munich, Buenos Aires, Vienna, and Salzburg, specializing in Religious Studies. In 2012 he was elected Dean of "World Religions" at the European Academy of Sciences and Arts. He is also founding member of European Academy of Religions, Correspondent of Academia de Artes e Letras de Portugal and honorary member of Academia delle Science d´Abruzzo. His main research projects are the intercultural influence of religions and interreligious dialogue in general. Since 2011 he has served as CEO and Secretary General of "Christians in Need", an international working NGO for interreligious dialogue.

Orlando Mardner is the CEO of Professional Security Academy (PSA) a training company that offers a comprehensive range of training programs for security and allied professionals. He has presented academic papers at the International scientific conference organised by the Strategic Research Institute and the Department of Strategy of the National Defence School in Belgrade, Serbia, as well as at international conferences. He is a member of the East-West Bridge International (EWB).

Craig Paterson serves as the Provost of Johann Heinrich Pestalozzi University, Miami, Florida. He was educated at universities in Scotland, England and the USA. He holds an LLB law degree with distinction from the University of Edinburgh, Scotland, an MA degree in philosophy for the University of York, England and a PhD degree in Ethics from Saint Louis University, Missouri, USA. He is currently an independent consultant as Paterson Consulting and Honorary Research Professor with the Concilium Research Group, Complutense University of Madrid, Spain. He has previously held university teaching appointments at Saint Louis University, Missouri, USA and Providence College, Rhode Island, USA. He has published two books with Routledge on Ethics and Philosophy.

Milka Ristova is a Judge of the Supreme Court of Macedonia and current lecturer at the Academy for Judges and Public Prosecutors "Pavel Satev" Skopje. She is also a Member of the Board in the HWPL and Women's Organization IWPG. She has been participated in several judicial reform projects, regarding Chapter 23 of the Accession Negotiations for the EU. She is the author of a number of expert and scientific papers.

Manisha Sharma is the former chairperson and is engaged in Post-Graduate teaching and research at Panjab University, Chandigarh. His specialism is Gandhian Peace Studies. He is in-charge of the Gandhi Bhawan Project with Getty Foundation, USA, and Chair Holder of UNESCO Network Chair on "Global Peace and Non-Violence". He is Co-Secretary General of The Asia-Pacific Peace Research Association (APPRA).

Zoran R. Vitorovic is a Visiting Professor at the Euro-Balkan University, Macedonia. He is also President of the Association Swiss Morning Star, an NGO active in the promotion of culture and knowledge. He has been honoured by academic bodies in the USA, Latin America and Europe with honorary awards recognizing his contributions to diplomacy and global processes.

CONTEXTUALISM AND THE HISTORY OF PHILOSOPHY

Craig Paterson

Introduction

Philosophy, as a discipline, often tends to view its subject matter in abstract and ahistorical terms. Concepts are often assumed to be 'fixed' in meaning across many centuries of thought, and their historical change is often neglected. The transmission and reception of ideas is commonly conceived of in terms of a chain of connected dialogue that revolves around an established canon of great intellectual thinkers discussing great philosophical works, divorced from contextual-historical influences. While there has been, in the wider academy, a movement for the 'history of ideas' as an approach to intellectual history, this movement has tended to function as a separate discipline and has failed to make much of an impression in the interpretative methodology typically pursued by philosophers in analytical philosophy departments. Attention to historical inquiry, it is often thought, tends to 'dilute' or 'corrupt' the genuine spirit of philosophical inquiry by corrosively attacking its dedication to the universal (perennial validity), the abstract (departicularization), and the heroic (philosopher *contra mundi*).[1] The minds of several generations of students of philosophy, raised in the Anglo-American analytical tradition, are marked with a lesson from the 18th century idealist philosopher Immanuel Kant who castigated those "scholarly men, to whom the history of philosophy (both ancient and modern) is philosophy itself."[2] For Kant, the search for the transcendental foundations of all reality necessitated

---

[1] This, for example, is very much the kind of position taken by Bertrand Russell, a leading influence in contemporary analytical philosophy. See Russell on *Metaphysics: Selections from the Writings of Bertrand Russell*. Stephen Mumford ed. (London: Routledge, 2003). For another example typical of this kind of de-contextualized approach to philosophical history, see also Anthony Flew's, *An Introduction to Western Philosophy: Ideas and Argument from Plato to Popper* (London: Thames and Hudson, 1989).
[2] Immanuel Kant, *Prolegomena*, trans. Paul Carus (Chicago: Open Court, 1993), p. 1.

discounting concerns about how a proposition came to be formed as a mere distraction from a proposition's epistemological status (a concern shared by contemporary analytical philosophy—philosophers are not mere "curators in the museum of ideas").[3]

The above picture is, of course, something of a distortion of my own creation. Most philosophers are aware that ideas do not just spring forth miraculously from the mind of a philosopher, and therefore accord to philosophy the need for some kind of historical connectivity. But the attention to historical context is one that is often understood in terms of a kind of history that we may call 'idealized history.' Idealized history is the history of great minds battling with the perennial ideas of other great minds, in one long continuous great and noble conversation, removed from the taint of more particular concerns. The kind of historical understanding operative here often amounts to little more than a discussion of broad philosophical doctrines organized into chronological time slots allotted to the great philosophers, and fleshed out, for good measure, with some 'human interest' stories. History of philosophy, in short, is often viewed as something amounting to hagiography.

This tendency towards ahistoricism (even anti-historicism), still very prevalent in the mindset of contemporary analytical philosophy, needs, I think, to be challenged by a form of approach that stresses the 'contextually mediated' nature of much philosophical thinking and writing. We need, in short, to focus upon an approach to understanding human thought processes that channels our attention to how the human mind is strongly influenced by, and reacts to, the 'ideational ecology' it inhabits—a complex web made up of various kinds of intellectual, cultural, and social networks that are closely woven into the thought processes of any given thinker.

In this paper, I seek to advance the thesis that if we are to come to a better appreciation of the historical rootedness of philosophical thinking, we must strive to encourage the

---

[3] D.S. Hutchinson, *The Virtues of Aristotle* (London: Routledge, 1986), p. 12.

contextualization of philosophical texts and support this goal by developing methods and tools for research that are facilitative of this contextualist goal.

In my analysis of this thesis, I will first turn to a discussion of some of the conceptual issues that underpin the need for philosophers to understand, and apply to the history of philosophy, better interpretative practices. The analysis will draw upon helpful developments that have occurred in ordinary language philosophy, a 'post-analytical' philosophical approach conceptually more amenable to contextualist historical interpretation. I will also draw upon helpful developments in literary theory that offer useful insights into the analysis of texts that also seem applicable to the study of philosophical texts.

Secondly, I will then seek to advance the case for the thesis by focusing on a case example, John Locke and his *Two Treatises of Government*, that illustrates, by way of a *via negativa*, the problems of distortion and error in attempting to interpret philosophical texts with little regard for context.

Thirdly, I will address the question of why unhistorical forms of approach to the history of philosophy continue to be perpetuated within the ranks of contemporary practitioners of philosophy, tracing this problem to the inculturation practices that typify the academy bound profession of Anglo-American philosophy.

Lastly, by way of conclusion, I will set about the task of examining some issues pertaining to the development of resource-based initiatives designed to better facilitate historical based scholarship in philosophy, resources that will furnish the philosopher with a better array of tools for the development of their research, for example, digital libraries of primary source documents.

The Significance of Contextualism

While I do not intend this paper to be an exercise in philosophy, I wish to illustrate some conceptual ways in which philosophy itself may fruitfully respond to the kinds of concern that I have highlighted in my introduction. This legacy has now been coming under fire for a number of years, in particular, with the retreat of the hitherto very dominant influences of

Law, Ethics & Society

both empiricism and positivism in analytical philosophy. In a forthright essay by Stephen Turner, the author berates modern analytical philosophy for its lack of historical character, arguing that a contextualist understanding of philosophy's own history is itself an indispensable part of any adequate philosophy. Turner identifies two helpful turns in philosophy, the turn away from empiricism, and the turn away from positivism, as offering some weak rays of hope in support of his plea for a broad contextualist approach to the study of the history of philosophy.[4]

Firstly, the anti-empiricist turn. Empiricism, the belief in sense data which are capable of being directly perceived and embodied in a non-interpretative observation language, has been undermined by, amongst others, W.V.O. Quine, and Paul Feyerabend. Quine, and Feyerabend have deeply challenged the belief that we can gather a structure of empirical knowledge that is independent of our own evaluative judgments that mediates the interaction of the human mind with the word around it.

Secondly, the anti-positivist turn. Another helpful turn has been the questioning of the credo of positivism that meaningful statements must refer to facts, and that the meaning of a sentence must be demonstrated by its method of verification in order to establish its truth content. The main challenge to this key idea of logical positivism was the later work of the Cambridge philosopher Ludwig Wittgenstein in his *Philosophical Investigations*.[5] In the *Investigations*, he asserted the famous injunction not to ask directly about the abstract meaning of propositions but rather about how they are used in particular "language games."[6] The underlying assumption of this approach—that the analysis of meaning needs to be connected with the use of language for purposes of communication—has been further refined by the Cambridge ordinary language philosopher John Austin and his theory of

---

[4] Stephen Turner, "Teaching Subtlety of Thought: The Lessons of Contextualism," *Argumentation* 15(1) (2001): 77-95.
[5] Ludwig Wittgenstein, *Philosophical Investigations*, trans. G.E.M. Anscombe (London: Macmillan, 1958).
[6] Wittgenstein's earlier work, for example, his *Tracatus Logico-Philosophicus*, was highly positivistic.

"speech acts." Austin, in developing his theory of speech acts, proposed that the "utterance itself," whether verbal or written, in short, the words divorced from their context, is a "locution," and a locution can only be understood by exploring the locution in context.[7]

Contribution of Literary Theory

Literary theorists seem to have embraced some of the subtler lessons of ordinary language philosophy more fully that many writers in the history of philosophy. In consequence, literary theory has, on the whole, been more directly aware of, and keener to apply, ways of textual analysis that meaningfully relate the text to a wider context of conventions and assumptions. These conventions and assumptions shape a text, and give a text a context which serves to relate the parts of the text, its utterances, patterns, and forms of words, to a meaningful frame of reference that does not seek to divorce the text from the social, political, and cultural contexts that influence its ideational content.

Unlike much writing in the history of philosophy that has been produced (though not without some notable exceptions), it is common for literary theory to delve into the different senses in which it is possible to flesh out the background of a given text, and to make it clear that their main concern is with a weaved context of meanings. There is, consequently, more awareness of, and resistance to, the problem of *post-hoc* rationalizations of contemporary concepts being stamped onto the past writings of a given thinker in what amounts to the 'cookie-cutter' fashioning of a text.

It is not possible to find out what a philosopher meant simply by studying his or her written statements (a 'just look at the text' approach) in isolation from the milieu of the author of the text. The kinds of questions that the author is addressing and communicating to the reader need to be examined. In other words, it is not possible to understand what has been said in a text until the detailed and specific questions being engaged by a text, and by the author's agenda in writing it,

---

[7] J.L. Austin, *How to Do Things with Words* (Oxford: Clarendon Press, 1975).

are scrutinized. The emphasis, however, needs to be on the detailed and specific questions relevant to an author, definitely not the practice of attempting to link an author to some general 'meta-question' supposedly abstracted from any place in time. Instead, questions should be related to the specific context in which a given written expression was being made.

Interpretative Meaning and Evaluation

The need to separate contextual approaches to the study of the history of philosophy from unhistorical approaches, can be further clarified, here, I think, by stating that the job of a historical approach to philosophy is to be aware of the need to identify two distinct types of concern, and not to seamlessly merge the two distinct types of concern together into a hybrid conflation of the two (as difficult, as it is, at times, to put this into practice). Of the writings of any author in the past (or indeed the present), it is possible to firstly explore the notion "what did the author say and mean by this statement?" and secondly, given our exploration of the first question, the second question can then start be addressed, "given that A meant B ... in what sense can the statement be said to be true or not?" The first question addresses the genesis of an idea in context. The second question, building on the first, goes on to address the epistemological status of a proposition as it was likely held by a given philosopher. The second question does not just confine itself to the accurate representation of an idea but addresses the valuational status of an idea.[8]

The effects of the work of Wittgenstein and Austin, among others, working in the philosophy of language, has been to help focus our attention on the role of factors like

---

[8] One of the clearest statements I have read by a philosopher concerning questions of textual interpretation, one that stresses the importance of respecting this twofold distinction, was made by Alistair MacIntyre in a paper written on the interpretation of a key passage in David Hume's *Treatise on Human Nature*—"There are, of course, two distinct issues raised by this paper so far. There is the historical question of what Hume is actually asserting in the passage under discussion (Treatise Bk. III Sect. I Pt. I), and there is the philosophical question of whether what he does assert is [both] true and important." See his "Hume on Is and Ought," *Philosophical Review* 68 (1959): 451-68.

utterances, intention, and contextual linguistic background, in trying to come to terms with the possible meaning of a philosophical text. This represents something of a move towards an appreciation of the methodology seen in the hermeneutic analysis of literary texts and promises to be a useful avenue for the cross-fertilization of ideas among 'post-analytic' philosophers and literary theorists.

A salutary lesson to be learned from literary theory for the analysis of philosophical texts, acknowledged and supported, as I have said, by some leading work in ordinary language philosophy, is that the genuinely meaningful analysis of a text must place the given text of a thinker against a weave of human conventions, expectations, and practices that crucially inform the meaning of a text (or at least delimit, in a boundary setting way, the array of meanings that can be usefully inferred). Such a lesson for philosophy would, of course, be easier to absorb and put into practice if it were not for what Richard Rorty has identified as the skewing that occurs in the philosophers' perception of their own discipline as the 'queen of the sciences', exalted above all others, with its quest for the indubitable foundations of all reality. This inflated sense of the status of philosophy among the disciplines, tends to result in a kind of 'imperial myopia,' discounting the contribution that other disciplines can make to understanding the contextual development of its own subject matter. The discipline itself, if it is to open itself up to historical inquiry, based on context, must face up to the sobering thought that philosophers are all too ready to turn their "local fallible [i.e. contingent, historically conditioned] canons of argument into a set of imperishable truths."[9]

John Locke and His *Two Treatises*

As I argued in the preceding section, if the writing of the history of philosophy is to move to the terrain of non-hagiographical or non-mythological forms of writing, and wishes instead to proceed to understand the subtleties of an array of different factors that impinge on the mind of a

---

[9] Richard Rorty, *Philosophy and the Mirror of Nature* (Princeton, NJ: Princeton University Press, 1979), p. 48

philosophical thinker and his or her production of a given philosophical text, then contextualism needs to be embraced in the pursuit of scholarly research.

In order to concretize some of the interpretative problems referred to in the preceding discussion, and to illustrate why a contextualist approach to the history of philosophy is so crucial, I will now turn to an examination of a concrete case—John Locke's *Two Treatises of Government*—an example that, I think, well demonstrates why contextualism as a methodological approach (facilitated by the development of research tools facilitating good contextualist practice), is so sorely needed in this discipline.

John Locke was a 17th century philosopher and political writer. His reputation as an innovator of philosophical ideas is centered on two of his main texts—*An Essay Concerning Human Understanding*, and the *Two Treatises*. The first text is held by philosophers to secure his place in the philosophical canon as the founding father of modern empiricism. The second text is held to secure his place as the founding father of modern liberalism with his theory of the consent of the governed (the latter text being my main focus for discussion).

Let me state it plainly here that I am not concerned to argue that Locke was not a great thinker or that his works are not works of considerable intellectual merit. That would be a fool's errand. Rather, I seek to argue that many myths have grown up about this thinker (spurred on by unhistorical, acontextual practices), myths that inevitably distort our understanding of the actual thoughts of this thinker. In what follows, I seek to show how these myths can be 'debunked,' and can best be avoided by a thoroughgoing attentiveness to good contextualist practice.

Myth Number One

Date of composition and purpose behind composition. Many standard texts in the history of philosophy continue to herald the writing of Locke's Two Treatises' as a post-hoc justification for the 'Glorious Revolution' in England of 1688, a 'revolution' that saw the deposition of the catholic King James II & VII and his subsequent replacement by the protestant King William III, of Orange.[10] The main evidence for this claim, an ideological claim, attempting to show how England at the time was motivated by the desire to instantiate and apply rational principles of representative government, is based on the wording of the preface to the original edition of the text, combined with the fact that the text was first published in 1690, some two years after the events of 1688.[11]

The problem with this claim, however, is that it cannot be reconciled with other weighty evidence that the text could not have been written for that declared purpose. When judged against contrary evidence, the claim functions as something of a 'rationalization' on the part of Locke, because it directs the reader's attention away from the actual circumstances and timing of the writing of the text. The express reasons that motivated this rationalization are not discernable for there is no correspondence on this matter. On a conjectural note, however, congruent with other evidence about Locke's 'shrewd character,' perhaps this prefactory statement was written in order to capitalize on a potential market for the book, benefiting from a turn in political events (not least, Locke's own return from exile in Holland), a turn that created a niche for a well crafted text, that would, from a Whig perspective, act as an intellectual apologia for the 'logic' of the revolution.[12]

The lesson from a simple analysis of the text alone (especially prefactory material), is to be wary of overt claims as to purpose, and carefully scrutinize them, for they may be rationalizations distorting the actual context that informed the writing of a given text. Locke's main aim in writing his Two Treatises, was not to justify to the world the throne of William III and the successful revolution of 1688, but, rather, to enlist cadres in a political conflict that had gripped England some seven to nine years earlier (the 'exclusionist' controversy that

---

[10] For example, David Hamlyn, *Being a Philosopher: The History of a Practice* (London: Routledge, 1992).

[11] John Locke, Preface to his Two Treatises "... to establish the Throne of our Great Restorer, Our present King William; and to make good his Title, in the Consent of the People ... And to justify to the World, the People of England, whose love of their Just and Natural Rights, with their Resolution to preserve them, saved the Nation when it was on the very brink of Slavery and Ruine."

[12] On Locke's character, see Maurice Cranston, *Locke*. London: Longmans Green, 1961.

tried, unsuccessfully, to change the line of succession to the English throne).

Myth Number Two

The myth that Locke wrote two separate works, not one. Part of the myth behind Locke's writing of the Two Treatises, as an exercise justifying the revolution of 1688, is spurred on by the supposition that Locke really wrote two quite independent works, not one—the first work being: *The False Principles and Foundation of Sir Robert Filmer* ..., and the second work being: *An Essay Concerning the True, Original, Extent, and End of Civil Government*. If the works are essentially independent then why is it not reasonable to suppose that the second treatise, at least, was written around 1689-1690? (No one seriously argues that the first work was not written during the years 1680-1681, a time during which Filmer's absolutist text—Patriarcha—enjoyed considerable popularity and influence.)

The 'independent nature' view of the two works has been facilitated by the subsequent printing history of the Two Treatises. It is usual to publish the Essay separately and isolate it from any connectedness to a refutation of the work of Sir Robert Filmer (with the first treatise seldom being published). Yet, this turn, of effectively isolating the text away from its natural literary companion, is akin to severing a part of a work from its contextual setting within a congruent whole.

The contextual evidence paints a different picture as to the dates of writing. The language and conceptual linkages between the two texts are very close. As John Dunn argues, the interwoven ideational dependency of the two works is such as to discount, in the case of the Essay, a period of eight or nine years of delayed authorship.[13] The intimacy that exists between the two works is falsely iterated to modern eyes by a literary and publishing device of the period, namely, the labeling of the two treatises as separate books. Historically, this was often merely used as a device for splitting up a large

---

[13] John Dunn, *The Political Thought of John Locke: An Historical Account of the Argument of the 'Two Treatises of Government* (Cambridge: Cambridge University Press, 1983), p. 23.

work into different main sections, for reasons of convenience.[14]

Bowers, Gerritsen, and Laslett, analytical bibliographers, have analyzed, in detail, the printing history behind the two books.[15] They have demonstrated that the title-page of the second book, in its original printing of 1690, was a later insertion, and was not part of the original print design. They have further demonstrated that the title-page of the whole work was then altered, at a later date, so as to reflect the subsequent incorporation of a secondary title-page for the second book. The phrase "two treatises" itself was actually a post-hoc creation incorporated by the printers into a revised title-page for the two books. Bowers, Gerritsen, and Laslett effectively illustrate the point that the way in which a text is physically presented can later influence how a whole work can be severed into its constituent parts (and, presumably, also, using the same methods of analytical bibliography, how genuinely separate texts can also appear as parts of a single common work).[16]

Myth Number Three

Thomas Hobbes, the rational defender of monarchical absolutism, *par excellence*, was the principal interlocutor of the *Two Treatises*. As I have said earlier, philosophers are fond of the vision of philosophy as a continuous conversation of great minds, across the ages, engaging one another in the battlefield of ideas. Like 'fantasy football league,' they want their heroes and foes to be a part of a 'common fixture,' even if that fixture exists only in the imagination; the fixture being a battle between two great social contract theorists who reached radically different conclusions as to the ends and purpose of civil government. Yet, fiction is not fact, even if the conceptual edges (in an era of deconstruction) are blurry, and there is little evidence to suppose that Locke had Hobbes in his sight

---

[14] On the stylistic development of literary forms in print culture, see D.F. MacKenzie's *Biblioigraphy and the Sociology of Texts* (Cambridge: Cambridge University Press, 1999).

[15] Freson Bowers, Johan Gerritsen, and Peter Laslett, "Further Observations on Locke's Two Treatises," *Transactions of the Cambridge Bibliographical Society* 2(1) (1954): 20-26.

[16] Ibid.

when he wrote the *Two Treatises*. On the contrary, the warrantable evidence points to Sir Robert Filmer as the main interlocutor of John Locke. Filmer's *Patriarcha*, because it purported to show how royal authority was biblically rooted in Adam, was therefore more amenable to the sensibilities of the population in England at the time than Hobbes' logically tighter but colder analysis of the necessity for absolutist power in the form of *Leviathan*. The question of interlocutor is important because the creation of an 'artificial dialogue' between these two thinkers helps to de-contextualize Locke's thought away from the sources that helped to inform the genesis of his ideas. Reading Locke through the lens of commentary on Hobbes, colors our understanding of the relationship between Locke's work and its relationship to the interstices of political debate in 17th century English society.

Several arguments point against the 'ideal fixture' of Locke versus Hobbes. Firstly, there is only one reference to Hobbes' work directly in the *Two Treatises*. Secondly, the precise language of textual debate does not center around a close association between the two thinkers. Locke was not engaged in writing a 'polemic' against Hobbes' highly rationalistic justification for absolutism in *Leviathan*. If he were, he would surely have made more reference to it and linked his argumentation more carefully to an attempted refutation of its core arguments. (Locke was 'tight' with his analysis of ideas and would have directed his attention more fully if he had Hobbes' work in mind.) Thirdly, Hobbes' own reputation at the time was of a comparatively minor nature. The cult of appropriation of his text *Leviathan* had not yet begun in earnest. Fourthly, the first of the two books written was expressly directed against the arguments of Filmer's *Patriarcha*.[17]

Am I, therefore, seemingly against any form of comparison of the two texts produced by two very different thinkers? No. A comparison of the thoughts of both thinkers, as an exercise in philosophical dialectic, of seeing what congruencies, dis-congruencies, and different possibilities of approach may emerge from a comparison of both thinkers, is important to

---

[17] Richard Ashcraft, "John Locke's Library: Portrait of an Intellectual," *Transactions of the Cambridge Bibliographical Society* 5 (1) (1969): 47-60.

the practice of philosophy. Notice here, however, that my focus of attention has shifted from the first area of inquiry—what was meant by a given author in a given text?, to the second area of inquiry, namely—what follows from our subsequent analysis of that delimited meaning? Given that A meant B, how does A's use of the concept differ from C's use of A? Is C's use of the concept really the same concept as A? Given that A means B, is it true?—and so on.

Misrepresentations often come about by an interpreter's assumption that the problem he or she is addressing, is the same as the problem the original author was addressing, when it is not the same problem. Correction of the misrepresentation due to misunderstanding can be accomplished, very often, by adopting a less cavalier attitude to the text and by paying closer attention to its proper context. When we start to engage in philosophical speculation, it is good contextualist practice to be cautiously aware of the different kinds of appropriation of a text, for present purposes, that we can engage upon. Often, with good contextualist practice, we may be force to revise our attribution of ideas from X argued for Y, to, Y is an idea that I have, that I want to defend, inspired by or indebted to my reading of Y ....

Myth Number Four

Locke was a consistent thinker, ergo, he was consistent, minor peccadilloes aside, in everything he wrote. It is often tempting in philosophy to opt for explanations of texts that gravitate towards coherence and consistency. These are, rightly, considered to be highly desirable qualities in philosophical thinking. Interpreters, motivated by sympathy, often lean towards this tendency. Yet, I would argue against any wholesale attempt to unduly privilege consistency of interpretation by thinking of it as a purely neutral form of interpretative device, for it is often blind as to context (as is the opposite tendency, when attacking a thinker, of generating inconsistencies, often through the device of crafty word-play). We should, in short, try and appreciate that two different forms of approach stand in danger of being muddled: a shift from the interpretative—did A recognize a contradiction in his or her

thought? or was A (implicitly) operating with a contradiction?—to the appropriative—on the basis of A's work, how can
we overcome the contradiction? how can we, with additional
insights, improve upon A's thought?

Alas, in the battle for reputation, and also in philosophy's
quasi-religious reverencing of the reputation of its past greats,
conjoined with the philosophical desire to want to either save
or condemn a thinker due to charges of inconsistency, the
conditions become ripe for the creation of distortion through
partiality.

If we attempt to impose, in high German fashion, a logic
of vigorous consistency across the corpus of Locke's writing,
we will greatly distort the different and disparate influences
that informed different facets of his work. Locke was not able
to reconcile his work in epistemology (*Essay on Human Understanding*) with his foundations for political theory (*Two
Treatises*), nor is there any evidence that he attempted to do
so, for he made little attempt to create any express linkages
between these two areas of philosophical inquiry. The latter,
for Locke, was informed by a different milieu and a very different method of approach. Many grand overarching attempts to
interpret both texts as one large exercise in continuous writing, held constantly in the mind, run the risk of gravely
distorting the meaning of both texts. This, alas, is what Leo
Strauss attempted to do in his *Natural Rights and History*.
Strauss, anxious to find a justification for Locke's 'paired'
down commitment to natural law theory, compared to its
Scholastic forms, attributed this to Locke's skeptical epistemology concerning the possibility of knowing the essences of
natural kinds. A more limited capacity to know essences
equals a more limited content to the natural law. [18]

This is an erroneous interpretation, however, charged by
the desire to seek consistency across the board of Locke's
thought. It involves a major distortion of his political thought to
make the fit. In his search for consistency, Strauss represented Locke's commitment to natural law theory as a paired
down version of full-blown natural law theory, thus more able

---

[18] Leo Strauss, *Natural Rights and History* (Chicago: Chicago University
Press, 1953).

to be reconciled with Locke's skepticism concerning our ability to now the essence of natural kinds. Whilst it is accurate to say that Locke's theory of natural law theory was substantially different from Scholastic forms, it was not simply a chopped down form of the latter. His theory of a law of nature had more flesh on its bones than that. Strauss sought to minimize the content of Locke's commitment to natural law theory in order to help with the consistency objective. Yet, Strauss did not adequately familiarize himself with the religious context of Locke's Christianity and the way this functioned as a source that inspired many of his political claims.[19]

Locke the political philosopher and strategist is not merely Locke the epistemologist transplanted into a different terrain. Locke, so to speak, in the 'political arena,' claims far more for the power of human reason, and also for divine sources of knowledge, than Locke the epistemologist would permit given his defense of our limited sources of empirical knowledge (the mind being a *tabula rasa*, with no inner power via adequation to comprehend the natural essences of things). The central problem, in the first place, is to attempt to create a neat rational fit between Locke's epistemology and what he was prepared to make use of (in terms of knowledge gained and assumed) in other contexts of discourse.

Myth Number Five

The myth of the lonely creator-genius. As I have already stated, it is not my intention here to argue that the Locke of laurelled reputation was not a thinker of prodigious talent. His *Two Treatises* is a highly accomplished work. Rather, what I do seek to argue is that his creative talent, when viewed against the period of his writing, is not so startlingly original as we might think, and indeed, when viewed contextually, is much more heavily dependent on the work of 'lesser' thinkers,

---

[19] Consider, for example, Locke's religious justification for the basic equality of persons in the state of nature, prior to civil government: "Creatures of the same species and rank, promiscuously born to all the same advantages of Nature, and the use of the same faculties, should also be equal one amongst another, without Subordination or Subjection, unless the Lord and Master of them all should, by any manifest Declaration of his Will, set one above another, and confer on him, by an evident and clear appointment, an undoubted Right to Dominion and sovereignty." *2nd Treatise*, para. 4.

as well as the general political cultural air of the time, than is generally thought.

A clue to the way in which Locke's text was less original or revolutionary than we might think, looking at the work in isolation, and relating it to an idealized pantheon of great texts, is that the work was treated somewhat indifferently by his contemporaries.[20] Locke's work did not appear remarkable to his contempories because the ideas it expressed, albeit very well written and organized, were not viewed as novel. In this case, unlike the indifference accorded to the contemporary reception of other innovative philosophical works, the prevailing judgment was not a case of 'too radical, profoundly mistaken, or incomprehensible,' so much as a case of 'well written, but not very remarkable.' Analytical bibliography is able to demonstrate that Locke's work did not give rise to any detailed critical replies in print before the year 1703, and there was no systematic refutation of it at all until 1705 with the appearance of Charles Leslie's *Rehearsal and the* A*nonymous Essay Upon Government.*[21]

Part of the reason for this, surmised by Martyn Thompson, was due to the unremarkable nature of many of Locke's claims and arguments when viewed against the contextual background of English political writing during the latter part of the 17th century. (The pamphleteers of the period popularized much of the Whiggish stock of political ideas, as they fermented in the political atmosphere of the time). While the *Two Treatises* is now taken as the best articulation of classic English (and North American) liberal political theory, contemporaries saw James Tyrrell's *Patriarcha non Monarcha, or The Patriarch Un-monarch'd* (1681), James Harrington's *The Commonwealth of Oceana (*1656), Henry Neville' s *Plato Redivivus (1681)*, and George Lawson's *Politica Sacra et Civilis,* or, A *Modell of Civil and Ecclesiasticall Government* (1660), as more effective justifications for the general Whig position on constitutional affairs. All of these authors, like Locke, were concerned in the first instance to

---

[20] Martyn P. Thompson, "Reception of Locke's Two Treatises of Government, 1690-1705," *Political Studies* 24(2) (1976): 189-204.
[21] Ibid.

provide a detailed refutation of Filmer's absolutist position (due to his popular influence), and they all then branched out to analyze and assess general issues of liberal political theory—consent, social contract, limitations on power, representative government, and so on.[22]

An article written by B.A. MacLean, is particularly interesting in this regard, concerned, as it is, with the intellectual dependency of ideas, and raises a key question concerning Locke's familiarity with the work of George Lawson, an Anglican cleric. MacLean argued that if a reader were to make a detailed textual comparison between Lawson's *Politica* and Locke's *Two Treatises,* the reader would be struck by the many similarities of principles and arguments advanced by both texts. The conclusion, for MacLean, is that Locke must have read and studied Lawson, and was directly influenced by him as he drew up the structure he used for the subsequent composition of the *Two Treatises.*[23]

Challenging Professional Myths

The rarefied view that we have of Locke, as the brilliant *ex nihilo* creator of classical liberal political theory, is decidedly broadsided by MacLean's assessment of Locke. Locke created his text upon the foundation of crucial preliminary work done by another theorist of the period. There is, however, much work to be done in advancing this kind of analysis of key thinkers against the contextual background of ideas that influenced them in their philosophical writings. Apart from MacLean's article, for example, I have been unable to trace very much in the way of work done by philosophers in the Anglo-American tradition that systematically attempts to assess the creative novelty of Locke's political writing against the background of his lesser known predecessors or contemporaries.[24] The comparative lack of scholarly output, here, I think, is related to the non-generation of a sufficient critical

---

[22] James Farr and Clayton Roberts, "John Locke and the Glorious Revolution," *The Historical Journal* 28(2) (1985): 385-98.

[23] A. H. MacLean, "George Lawson and John Locke," *Cambridge Historical Journal* 9(1) (1947): 69-77.

[24] An exception that I have not been able to assess, but looks very promising, is Conal Condren's *George Lawson's 'Politica' and the English Revolution* (Cambridge: Cambridge University Press, 2002).

mass of interest in the academy, inhabited, as it is, by a professional cadre of analytical philosophers who are haunted still by the ghost of Immanuel Kant, and who still seek to replicate, in the minds of their students, their indifference towards, or even open hostility to, contextualist approaches to the study of philosophical thinkers and their concepts.

The indifference or hostility to the kind of method that I have been arguing for, has itself an historical basis in the way that philosophy as a profession has developed over the last 150 years in Anglo-American philosophical culture (though the reception of contextualist approaches to the study of philosophy has been rather more popular in continental Europe); a profession with its own mythology of inculturation passed on from one generation of professional philosopher to another as the initiated in turn become the future initiators. It entails claims of 'respectability' concerning what philosophers as professionals are essentially about and do, contra many claims associated with its messy and 'disreputable' past. An implied principle of the analytical credo is the belief that an 'us' versus 'them' gulf emerged between traditional philosophers and professional analytic philosophers such that what emerged was not simply some new set of concerns for philosophy, new variations, so to speak, on past themes, but what was virtually tantamount to a new discipline of inquiry.

Analytical philosophers looked to an idealized Kant as their model for the professional code of the philosopher, a thinker who was prepared to slash and burn away the obfuscations of the past with the two torches of logic and analytical rigor. Kant, it is held, established not just the purity of reason itself, but also the purity of philosophy as an autonomous discipline. Hegel, Schelling, Schopenhauer, Fichte, and much German philosophy of the 19th century, betrayed the legacy of their intellectual father who had rescued them from the jumble of confusing philosophy with sophistry, with pseudo-science, with metaphysics, or with religion (German philosophy, according to the folklore of Anglo-American philosophers, is still caught in this legacy of 'corruption,' by engaging in 'incautious speculation').

The belief, so it goes, that Anglo-American philosophers managed to preserve themselves against 'German' decadence, was due to their faithful adherence to Kant's sobering lessons. Philosophers adhering to this tradition were, in short, Kant's orthodox disciples. They inherited Kant's mantle. At the turn of the 20th century, commitment to orthodox Kantian rigor, with its support for logic and analytical methods, came to faithful fruition in the form of logical positivism, exemplified, for example, in the thought of Bertrand Russell and the thought of the early Wittgenstein—philosophy without a past— pure thought without the taint of historically distorting influence—in short, an infallible method for establishing incontestable, if somewhat unexciting, truths about the world.

This kind of professional myth about the calling of a profession, outlined above, still inhabits the environs of many academies, at least, the corridors inhabited by many Anglo-American philosophers. The myth still exudes a powerful ideological force, shaping professional dispositions, even though the promised land of logical positivism, the new philosophical Jerusalem, has been rejected by some of their 'wayward' children who now stand estranged.

If greater inroads are to be made in the contextualist study of philosophy, in Great Britain or the United States, then greater efforts will be need to be expended by the 'new evangelists' of the contextualist message in order to help seed the academy and produce a new crop of academic philosophers who are receptive to the validly of such an approach to philosophical inquiry.

If a gradual change in the 'historical consciousness' of the academic philosopher in the Anglo-American tradition were to occur, on a wider scale, then the first signs of this growing movement would likely be seen in a change to the curriculum for the teaching of philosophy, whereby courses in historical method would be required for the training of philosophers. Students would need to be come aware of the kinds of tools of approach needed to avoid the cavalier attitude of misrepresenting past texts for present ideological purposes, or of anachronistically imposing on a past thinker views that would not have been seriously entertained by them.

Careful attention to historical context is a powerful counter corrective to the temptation to claim the reputation of a past thinker, when it is not warranted, as an ally in present discourse. Locke did not write his *Two Treatises* to persuade Adam Smith or Robert Nozick of the supreme merits of a minimalist state, or to launch the careers of John Jacques Rousseau or Karl Marx. He wrote to those individuals, then living, who would be willing and able to read him and who, if persuaded, would help him accomplish the political (and other) ends for which he labored in the writing of the *Two Treatises*. Above all, an awareness of interpreting a text contextually would expose students to pseudo-historical-interpretations—to the past works of analytical philosophers that claim to be, on the face of it, historical accounts of the thoughts of a given thinker.

Secondly, we would also expect to see a significant increase in historically aware output as reflected in the traditional philosophical journals of Anglo-American philosophy—*Analysis, Mind, Journal of Philosophy*, etc. If the profession is to become more receptive to the goals of textual analysis, then this ought, in due course, to be reflected in the publications appearing in those professional journals, journals that have hitherto been key gate keeping sources, shoring up the mythical concept-ualization of analytical philosophy's own understanding of the philosophical past.

Thirdly, more downstream, the undergraduate literature would also start to reflect a change in method, for that subgenre of the philosophical literature, the standard student textbook on the history of philosophy, would begin to be substantially revised in order to reflect this shift in methodological allegiance. The existing array of textbooks relied upon in instruction would become less useful for pedagogical purposes. In Anglophone academic culture, introductory textbooks play a prominent role in the education of students. No philosophy professor can be assumed to have firsthand knowledge if all relevant philosophical thought. However, what really helps to differentiate a good from a bad introductory textbook, is the fact that a good textbook, paradoxically, tends to be subversive of the genre of textbook writing in general. Janet Coleman's recent two volume narrative on political philosophy, from Antiquity to the Renaissance is, I think, an excellent example of such a textbook, an 'anti-textbook,' that is subversive of the standard genre of philosophical textbooks with their worn allegiances to the ideas of the great philosophers padded out with some human interest stories.[25] Excellent examples of such textbooks may be more common place in other disciplines, but they are not, at least according to the author's experience, common place in philosophy. Colman's book is an example of the genre at its best, and demonstrates how a textbook can be non-trivial, subtle, and nuanced, while also engaging in the valuable expository task of presenting often very difficult ideas in a form appropriate to a 'fledgling' audience of readers.

Conclusion

Professional philosophers, as a breed, tend to trail behind on the coattails of other disciplines as far as their ability to appropriate useful research tools, for their own work, is concerned. This problem is exacerbated when the question becomes one of developing resources for an approach to philosophy that analytical philosophy itself has been disinterested in, or even openly hostile towards, namely, the contextual analysis of philosophical texts.

Here, I think, technological developments in the electronic storage, retrieval, manipulation, and analysis of text-based sources, offers considerable potential for advancing the goal of cultivating an historically aware approach to the treatment of philosophical texts. Scholars have long had access to and array of print editions of scholarly works of the past. Yet, these editions tend to be of the canonical works of philosophers who are already heralded as being worthy objects of study. Critical scholarly editions of the works of many past thinkers, works that contextually inform the political, social and cultural milieu of a past era, may not be available for consultation, thus creating a barrier to the kind of research for which this paper has been arguing.

Contextual based approaches place a much higher demand on the researcher for access to primary source materials than non-historical treatments. If a text is located on

---

[25] Janet Coleman, *A History of Political Thought* (Oxford: Blackwell, 2000). Vol. 1 *From ancient Greece to early Christianity*; vol. 2 *From the Middle Ages to the Renaissance.*

a bibliographical source and cannot be lent to a borrower via inter-library loan, then the classic method of approach, especially for rare or older material, has been to travel to the sites where the sources reside and to assess them *in situ*. This can be very time-consuming process and can demand considerable financial resources to undertake such programs of travel. While the development of print culture, and the development of great libraries, has lessened the need to travel as extensively and as frequently as the medieval scholars of the past were required to do, these burdens may not be inconsiderable. Travel also presupposes that permission by the institution that has custody of a text, in order to examine and hopefully copy it, will be granted in the first place (not something that can be automatically assumed).

On the basis of my own work on John Locke, my studies have been hampered by my inability to have ready access to manuscript collections and to rare book collections, mainly in England (Bodleian Library, Oxford, and the British Library, London). The development of an electronic library of resources, benefiting from the advantage of distributed access over the internet, promises to be a fruitful way of connecting scholars to the primary textual materials they need in order to advance their context-based research.

Standards have been developing in the storage and retrieval of full text documents. There has been a trend away from merely using information technology for the provision of bibliographic data about primary sources (important as this is), to the provision of access to the full text itself. While there are many organizational and institutional issues surrounding questions of who pays for the creation and the maintenance of electronic resources on the internet, it is not impossible to envisage a future in which scholar entrepreneurs in philosophy may emerge and help push forward a research agenda that includes a commitment to the development of digital library resources for scholarly research into the history of philosophy.

At present, there are a number of web sites that provide access to classic philosophical texts (often in poor translations that are outside copyright)—Plato's *Republic*, Aristotle's *Ethics*, Hobbes' *Leviathan*, Locke's *Second Treatise*, etc.

Contextualism & Philosophy

There is, however, little or no coverage of less well-known figures in philosophy (or of other disciplines) who have written works of direct interest to the research of the historically aware philosopher. In the paper above, I have mentioned several thinkers writing in 17th century political philosophy that would be excellent candidates for digitization so that scholars can have ease of access to accurate reproductions of these texts. This list, without too much difficulty, could be very considerably extended.

Digitization, as a medium of communication, offers the scholar more exiting prospects than just the accurate digital representation of a text as a surrogate for being able to look directly at the original text (important as this is). Microform, despite its comparative inconvenience of use compared to online digital library access, has been able to provide accurate reproductions of primary documents for several decades. The additional advantage afforded by the digitization of primary sources is centered on the ability of information retrieval systems to search through a large corpus of texts in order to locate the context for the relational use of many words and phrases. Many authors, can, with ease, search very rapidly through a corpus of texts using the techniques of Boolean searching, proximity searching, and incidence ranking in order to locate key terms. This is potentially a very fruitful way of locating and comparing the different contexts for the use of a particular word or phrases denoting an idea, and how its use may have been subtly adapted, changed, or augmented by different thinkers over the years.

In my own research on the historically conditioned conception of 'suicide,' for example, by making use of text based electronic searching capabilities, I have been able to make some very profitable connections revealing many anachronistic usages of the term, thereby exposing the foisting of present definitions onto past usages without regard to differences in meaning.[26]

The moral of this story may be obvious, but it is still well worth stating in bold terms: the greater the resource base at

---

[26] Dan Kolak, The Philosophy Source. *100 Classic Masterworks on CD-ROM.*

the disposal of a scholar, the greater will be the fruits of this kind of comparative analysis, reinforcing the need for a properly contextualized understanding of philosophical ideas.[27]

Pioneering interpreters, who utilize these technological opportunities, who seek to examine the contextual settings out of which past intellectual thought emerged, challenge the cozy picture of the hagiographical history of philosophy discussed in the introduction. They render an eminently useful service to philosophical inquiry. They enhance our capacity to view the world as our historically rooted thinkers viewed it, with all the social, cultural, and ideological issues that they faced, brought into sharper focus. Once we have grasped the issues that a given thinker's age confronted, and the kinds of conflicts those issues invited, then we can, with greater insight, interpret the meaning of a philosophical text that a given thinker bequeathed to posterity.

---

[27] Craig Paterson, "Suicide, Assisted Suicide, and Euthanasia," *International Philosophical Quarterly* 43(3) (2003): 351-58.

TRIANGLE CONCEPT OF UNIFICATION DEMILITARIZATION-NEUTRALISATION OF KOREA: AN OUTLINE

Darko Bekić

Abstract

The following essay is an author's proposal on how to solve the last but burning international problem from the Cold War era. Based on the comparative analysis of political crises on the Balkan and Korean Peninsula in the mid-20th century, the author concludes that the regional crises can not be solved by imposing an outside solution or by singular, unilateral arrangements that are most commonly in the interest of external factors and not of the region concerned. Consequently, the author does not see the solution in the negotiations of Pyongyang and Seoul with neighbouring countries or major world powers, but in the patient negotiation of a number of bilateral agreements among the two Korean states on the crucial questions: re-unification, de-nuclearization / de-militarisation and neutralisation of the Korean Peninsula. According to the author, neighbouring countries and the entire international community need to limit their role to the facilitation of intra-Korean talks and – after their succesful completion - to guarantee their implementation and maintenance in practice.

Only by doing so, the Korean Peninsula will be truly neutralised and exempted from any new division of interest spheres. For its part, the future, reunified Korean state must guarantee to the rest of the world that it is ready and capable to serve as a main pillar of regional security and the lasting peace. With this objective in mind, the author proposes an institutional framework, some concrete solutions as well as the road-map of the bilateral settlement. Although author has studied a great deal of literature on the Korean issue, he did not use any idea or quotes of other authors, so in this article there are no footnotes.

Law, Ethics & Society

Introduction

Let's start with some basic philosophical beliefs of mine: the true heroism is to avoid and prevent the war, not to win it. Consequently, the diplomat who is able to negotiate a reasonable peace or, better, a "win-win" solution, is ethicaly superior to the general who proudly proclaims the victory over his adversary. Annihilating the enemy is morally inferior to the survival and coexistence of both former adversaries. This was the case in the entire history as it is today.

As far as Korean Peninsula is concerned, one could make a comparative study with the Balkan Peninsula in the 40ies and 50ies of the 20th century.

The case of the Balkans

In 1949/50 the world was plagued by the *Cold War*. Everybody was speculating that the new, global war or, at least, some regional *Proxy War* was imminent. The two hot-spots of the possible outbreak were the Balkan and the Korean Peninsula.

In 1944, Churchill and Stalin have secretly divided the states of the Balkan Peninsula, according to different percentages. In the case of Yugoslavia the agreed formula was *fifty-fifty*. But, contrary to the master-plan of the Big Powers, the deciding role in the Yugoslav case was held by the independent-minded Josip Broz-Tito, leader of the National Liberation War against German and Italian occupation, who established the Communist-led Federal Republic of Yugoslavia in 1945. Three years later, in 1948, Tito managed to use the outbreak of the *Cold War* to his own interests. He reckoned that the *fifty-fifty* could be also interpreted as a *zero-zero* solution. In the folowing years, together with Nehru, Nasser, Sukarno, Haile Selasie and other leaders of the Third World, Tito developed a new foreign policy which, for different reasons, suited the interests of both the democratic West and the Communist East. It was based on *active neutrality*, *peaceful co-existence* and *non-alignment* with both confronted blocks

Ironically, Tito's enlightened concept did not survive the end of the Cold War. One-party, Communist Yugoslavia was a multinational state where the equality of different peoples could be maintained only by the charismatic Tito's personality but also, the repressive *apparatus*. Soon after his death in 1980, the disrupted national balance gave rise to secessionist movements which, in turn, provoked military intervention by the centralist forces. The bloody war in the 1990s, finally ended by the establishment of seven ethnically based nation-states, including my own, the Republic of Croatia.

The Case of the Korean Peninsula

The correlation of forces on the Korean Peninsula in the mid-20th century was utterly different: while the territory was nationally unique, it lacked charismatic leader supported by a strong army.

After the unilateral U.S. decision to accept the surrender of the Japanese south of the 38th parallel and the corresponding Soviet decision to disarm Japanese forces north of the same parallel, the Korean Peninsula was divided into two Big Powers' sattelite states. An anticommunist Korean politician Syngman Rhee was airlifted from the U.S. to be installed in the US occupied southern part of the Penninsula and establish the Republic of Korea, a presidential constitutional republic, while in the northern part of the country, the Soviets brought back the Korean Communist guerilla fighter Kim Il Sung to establish a Soviet-modelled Democratic People's Republic of Korea. And not just that! In 1950, Great Powers pushed the Korean people into a bloody war that *de facto* ended in 1953 but until today has not been *de jure* terminated.

Thus the *Cold War* division of the world, combined with ideologically sharply opposed, client leaderhips of both parts of the country sealed the division of Korea for almost 70 years. Not even the fall of the Berlin Wall in 1989, nor the dissolution of the Soviet Union in 1991, triggered the reunification process of the Korean state and people. The leaders of both parts of Korea continue to claim to be the only legitimate government of the entire Peninsula but are wary enough not to repeat their bloody experience from the 50ies or the similarily violent Vietnam reunification from the 70-ies of the last century. This historical lesson, in my opinion, proves that particular or solutions imposed from outside are never durable.

The two Korean states have yet to master these historical lessons even though they have invested a lot of effort towards possible *rapprochement* and the policies of peace, if not reunification. It is worth remembering two important initiatives from the ROC governments: one inaugurated President Roh Tae-woo, in mid 80s, known as *Nordpolitik* (mimicking the Western German *Ostpolitik* towards East Germany), and the other, called *Sunshine Policy*, inaugurated by the President Kim Dae-jung. They resulted with some concrete results, *inter alia*, the Summit meeting with the North Korean leader Kim Jong-il, which earned the South Korean President the Nobel Peace Prize in the year 2000. North Korean leader Kim Il Sung did not remain idle either: since 1960, the advanced several reunification proposals, out of which the one from 1973 entitled Five Policy Line for Independent and Peaceful Unification as well as the 1980 project of a Democratic Confederal Republic of Koryo were most elaborated. Until 2012, the regime in Pyongyang signed a series of denuclearisation agreements with Seoul, the United States and four neighbouring states, but it never stuck to those agreements.

Unfortunately, neither of these proposals and accords from both sides of the Peninsula, proved effective to move towards the reunification of the country. On the contrary, in the last decade, North Korean nuclear armament and its bellicose rhetoric additionally blocked diplomatic efforts in this direction. After the first North Korean nuclear test in 2009, the relationship between the two Korean states have worsened further. Consequently, despite its formal title of the *Korean Demilitarized Zone*, the border on the 38th parallel remains one of the most heavily militarized territories in the world.

In spite of all this, the bilateral political communication between the two parts of Korea subsided, which resulted in several major achievements: the accession of both states to the UN in 1991, the signing by North Korea a series of denuclearization agreements with Seoul the four neigbouring states and the USA etc. Also, the patient bilateral negotiations between Pyongyang and Seoul have led to increased cultural and sport exchange which culminated with the joint participation at the 2018 Winter Olympics. This breakthrough strengthened hopes for further bilateral talks between the two Korean states to be the best way to peceful reunification of the country.

Soon thereafter, this trend was confirmed by the intra-Korean Summit meeting of 27 April of 2018 and signing of the Panmunjon Declaration. Although quite unprecedented, but highly positive, this event was overshadowed by an another summit meeting: between the US President Trump and the North Korean leader Kim Jung-un, held in Singapore on 12 June 2018. This spectacular event, however, changed the geometry of the process of peaceful reunifiction: instead of continuing the bilateral negotiations of the two Korean states on all outstanding issues, from denuclearisation to reunification, the peace process has once again come back to unilateral solutions and the leading role of Big Powers. Since successful and enduring solutions never come from the outside, especially if they are manipulative and/or imposed, the summit meeting Trump-Kim, instead of stimulating, actually complicated the denuclearization process and once again delayed the highly desirable beginning of the process of reuniting the Korean Peninsula. Equally, the subsequent diplomatic activities of both Korean states are not promising: instead of resolutely turning to intra-Korean bilateral bargining, they are consulting, seeking advice or support from Peking, Moscow, Washington and, even, Tokyo.

Possible Reunification Scenario

The reunification of the Korean Peninsula is the latest unresolved but burning international problem since the end of the Cold War. Despite severe military incidents and political ups and downs, both South and North Korea have long tried to foster this process. To my opinion, the two states of the great Korean nation, instead of negotiating separately, and seeking advice or support from outside, should resolve all the outstanding issues through a series of bilateral agreements. In the medium-term, this should lead to reunification and, more important, to transformation of the Korean Peninsula into an economically and politically potent Asian-Pacific nation-state, capable to defend itself and promote international peace and security. However, it is highly questionable whether such a role of the future, reunified Korea corresponds to the interests of all those foreign capitals where Pyongyang and Seoul seek advice or support.

Let us concentrate now on the possible and desirable scenario for the Korean unification, based on the principle of self-determination. If we accept the fact that it as a gradual, painful and risky process, both politically and economically, the first analogy to come in mind is the one from neighbouring China.

One Country, Two Systems was an unortodox constitutional principle formulated during the early 1980s by Deng Xiaoping the then leader of the People's Republic of China. He suggested that there would be only one China, but the two Chinese regions: Hong Kong and Macau could retain their own economic and administrative system, while the rest of China would continue on its *"path to socialism with Chinese characteristics"*. Under the principle of *One Country, Two Systems*, these two parts of the Chinese state could continue to have its own governmental system, legal, economic and financial affairs, including foreign trade relations. This concept finally materialized in the 1990s which contributed massively to restoring economic stability and an outstanding pace of PR of China's growth in the following twenty years.

The alternative model of reunification which comes to mind is, understandably, the one of Germany in 1989/90. However, the regional balance of powers in Eastern Europe was dramatically different then it is the case today in the Korean Peninsula. The Soviet Union was collapsing as well as the East Germany. Consequently, East Germany was not reunited but was "swallowed" by the rising, prosperous West Germany. In today's East Asia, the correlation of forces is completely different: Korean states are bordering with the two super-powers: Russia and China which both traditionally tolerate a chain of "buffer-states" around them. Notwithstanding that, the German experiences with the reunification of the country, especially in the economic sphere, could represent a serious burden for South Korea. According to some analysis, in 1991, West Germans were only 2-3 times wealthier than their eastern brethren, while South Koreans are now between 12 and 40 times richer than North Koreans. Thus, German reunification - although extremely costly - proved to be bearable, which is much harder to say for the Korean Peninsula. The task of equalising the degree of economic, infrastructural and social development, i.e. the living standard between the southern and northern parts of Korea may prove to become "Mission Impossible". In addition to this, one could speculate that, politically and strategically, for the neighbouring powers, China and Russia, but also Japan and the US, the Korean unification is even less desirable than was the German unification for their suspicious Western alies as well as for Gorbachov's Russia.

There are more instructive historical lessons and one could go as far as to invoke the division between the American Union and Confederate States and the Civil War that broke in 1861. The *Gentleman's Agreement* between generals Grant and Lee reached at Appomattox in 1865 also deserves to be studied since it graciously brought to an end the bloody war that deeply frustrated and divided the American nation for five years.

"One country, two systems" – Korean Way?

Taking all this into account, the Deng Xiaoping's concept of *One Country, Two systems* seems to be the only mutually acceptable transitional solution for the Korean unification, with the duration not of fifty, but of aproximately twenty years:

- The first, preparatory step should be to formulate a mutually acceptable political platform and time-table, based on comparative analysis of the various historical lessons and experiences;
- Second step towards reunification and based on the accepted political platform should be the establishment of the High-Level Political Committee (HLPC), from both North and South Korea, which should adopt a formal bilateral, yet common 20-years transitional strategy – "The Triangle Process of Demilitarisation – Unification - Neutralisation of Korea";

- Thirdly, based on the overall strategy, the HLPC should elaborate a precise road-map, i.e. identify specific tasks which are to be tackled with, in each of the transitionary 20 years period: political & constitutional, economic, financial & monetary, social & cultural etc.
- Accomplishments should be examined at the beggining of each year: if the HLPC establish that the annual tasks are being realised swiftly, the transitional period could be shortened and if obstacles prove to be more serious, the transitional period could be modified or prolonged. In any case, HLPC should be the only authority in both parts of Korea to approve such decisions by consensus;
- The formal reunification should be proclaimed only after the succesfull completion of the agreed strategy and the mutual agreement that the time for unification was ripe and desirable.

Denuclearisation and Demilitarisation

Denuclearisation (of the North) and the demilitarisation of the South (withdrowal of USFK) should constitute the second of the three pillars of the Korean unification. However, it is my deep conviction that the unification-oriented Korea should take a two-way strategy: on one side, it should actively participate in all relevant international accords and cooperate in the process of transforming the Peninsula in the "Non-Nuclear Zone". On the other hand, Korean nation, taken as a whole, should consider its nuclear capability and technological expertise as precious as it is the classic Celadon ceramics. Both of them represent the legitimate heritage of the Korean people and serve as the highest proof of the national genius that no other has the right to deny or to take away.

Based on this ground principle, the HLPC should take account of the legitimate "security concerns" of both parts of the country as well as the long-term interest of the future, unified Korea, particularly, by taking into account the Ukraine and Ghadafi's Libya experience with the renouncement of their nuclear warfare and/or technological capabilities for the peaceful use of nuclear energy. Also, is important to note that denuclearisation and demilitarisation of the Korean Peninsula

Triangle Concept of Unification

should be processed gradually, with the vision of being fully accomplished within twenty transitional years and in accordance with the international developments in this field. To my opinion, the only realistic solution which could be reached consensually is to preserve nuclear capability of the unified Korean state, inspired by the Swiss model of "armed neutrality" or – in the Korean case - "nuclearized neutrality".

On their side, the three super-powers: Russia, China and the US, as well as India and, possibly, Japan should act as facilitators of the proposed "Triangle Concept of Unification of Korea", by signing an Agreement at the end of an International Conference on the Korean Unification, Denuclearisation and Neutralisation. However, in the absence of such international guarantees and the possible intensification of the (missile and nuclear) arms race, the only remaining solution for the two Korean states should be to preserve and transfer nuclear capability to the future unified state, inspired by the Swiss model of "armed neutrality" or - to put it bluntly – "nuclear armed neutrality".

Neutralisation

The differences between the Chinese concept of *One Country, Two Systems* and the Korean one should be mainly in the field of foreign policy and national defence. While, in the Chinese case, Hong Kong and Macau preserved their independence in all areas except for foreign affairs and defence for a period of fifty years, in the Korean case, the concept of denuclearization and demilitarization of the country as well as the neutral foreign policy should be the most important of the three pillars of the "Triangle" concept for the unification.

Alhough seemingly contradictory, it is politically more difficult and less acceptable for the international community to see attacked the neutral country than a member-state of a military alliance. In that respect, any reject of "finlandisation" proposals as well as the arguments raised against the "imposed neutrality" are unfounded. Claiming that all states are entitled to choose with whom they align is equally unbearable as it is the false belief that *"relying on its own forces"*, i.e. the

33

self-imposed isolation from the rest of the world, gives any guarantee for the national sovereignty and/or security.

Concluding Remarks

I would like to stress once again my belief that external powers should not guide nor even participate actively in the process of denuclearisation, reunification and neutralisation of the Korean Peninsula. National, economic and security interests of the Korean nation from both sides of the 38th parallel should be the guiding idea for these negotiations.

This is why these goals should be primarily the result of intra-Korean dialogue and negotiations. Neighbours and the entire international community need to restrain their role to only facilitate intra-Korean talks and - at the end of the process - ensure their implementation and maintenance in practice. Only by doing so, the Korean Peninsula will be truly neutralised, i.e. exempted from any new division of *interest spheres,* regional or global. For its part, the future, reunified Korean state must guarantee to the rest of the world that it is ready and capable to serve as a main pillar of regional security and the lasting peace.

ECONOMIC DIMENSIONS OF ARMED GROUPS AND INTRA-STATE TERRORISM: PREVENTIONS THROUGH GEOSTRATEGIC CHANGES IN THE INTERNATIONAL LAWS OF FINANCIAL SYSTEMS

Orlando Mardner

Abstract

Asymmetric terrorism and economic dimensions of armed groups are growing concern for the local and international community, especially with the increasing cases of attacks and economic conflicts. Armed groups exist in various countries; however, the disparities in their existence are based on size, population, level of attack and economic dimensions. Caribbean Community (CARICOM) is not an exception in the debate over the geostrategic measures to mitigate the threat of terrorism within geopolitical and international law standards. In this study, the primary objective was to provide insight into how the changing economic factors in CARICOM implicates the development and enhanced activities of armed groups and the potential occurrence of intra-state terrorism. Consequently, there are geostrategic measures that have been put in place to ensure that CARICOM and to a larger extent the world appreciate improved international laws on financial systems to help mitigate the increasingly diversifying and complexity in funding armed groups and intra-state terrorism. Thus, it was found that the CARICOM cannot effectively fight the challenges posed by the increased advancements in intra-state conflicts and armed groups. It is therefore important that geostrategic measures focusing on international financial support and changes in the global financial systems can all help the region fight against terrorism and thus provide human security.

Law, Ethics & Society

Background of the research

The changing dynamics in the societal values, geopolitical transformations and asymmetric threats posed by intra-state armed groups have undoubtedly gone unnoticed. The majority of the intra-state terrorism, since the end of the Cold War, have exhibited asymmetric paradigm in terms of how security apparatus and inter-governmental agencies deal with these cases.[1] In the wake of various terror groups around the globe, with various links in regions such as the Caribbean Community (CARICOM), the focus has been on the adoption of geostrategic policies and systems to help curb the menace. Various studies have focused on the economic, social and political geostrategies to fight the armed groups and intra-state terrorism (e.g Arnaud (2011)[2] and Achim (2011)[3]). Some of the outstanding findings in the studies include aspects like the impacts of globalization in causing a flare-up in the conflicts and continued struggling by the international community in redefining the rules to bring about peace. According to Karen and Nitzschke[4], intra-state terrorism undertaken by armed groups cause serious socio-political and economic problems around the world. The economic dimensions and paradigm shifts in the armed conflicts in the world has been studied and written about; however, this has not been done in the expected full complexity. Looking at any United Nations proceedings, scholarly investigations and various initiatives targeting economic dimensions of armed conflicts, there is a lot of sense in the financing and costs of the armed conflicts. However, it is difficult to appreciate tangible information on the diverse economic aspects of armed groups in the CARICOM. What is in place are projection and interpretations of studies

---

[1] Dudouet, Véronique, Katrin Planta, and Hans J. Giessmann. "The political transformation of armed and banned groups." *Lessons learned and implications for international support framework paper. Berlin: Berghof Foundation-United Nations Development Program* (2016).

[2] Blin, Arnaud. "Armed groups and intra-state conflicts: the dawn of a new era?" *International Review of the Red Cross* 93, no. 882 (2011): 287-310.

[3] Wennmann, Achim. "Economic dimensions of armed groups: profiling the financing, costs, and agendas and their implications for mediated engagements." *International Review of the Red Cross* 93, no. 882 (2011): 333-352.

[4] Ballentine, Karen, and Heiko Nitzschke. "Beyond greed and grievance: Policy lessons from studies in the political economy of armed conflict." *Security and Development: Investing in Peace and Prosperity* 164 (2003).

Economic Dimensions of Armed Groups

from other parts of the world into the context of the CARICOM. The absence of reliable sources on the economic dimensions of the armed groups in the CARICOM is a major limitation in the development of geopolitical strategies and international laws that can help curb terrorism emanating from the CARICOM.

Even though terrorism has not been a major concern in the CARICOM, this region is associated with individuals or groups that link up drug traffickers and other established terrorist groups.[5] The existence of such groups poses a serious threat to terrorist financing from the region. Economic dimensions of armed groups are particularly important in appreciating the conflict dynamics, especially in the wake of the asymmetric threats in the CARICOM. The understanding of such economic dimensions provides a platform for insightful mediation at an international level. Besides, it allows for proper structuring of the contexts under which the armed groups in other parts of the world, with a link to the CARICOM region, fights. This study, therefore, looks into the economic dimensions of the armed groups rather than the armed conflicts, where the analysis of the findings focuses on the dimensions imply for the fight against international terrorism as well as engagements of these groups through a geostrategic method such as mediation and dialogue. In that respect, the primary objective is to provide an insight into how the changing economic factors in CARICOM implicates the development and enhanced activities of armed groups and the potential occurrence of intra-state terrorism. The research also focused on investigating the implications of developing proper prevention strategies by embracing geostrategic changes in the international laws on financial systems. Overall, in the subsequent sections and analysis therein, the economic dimensions of the CARICOM's armed groups are unpacked through the analysis of the current state in the knowledge of the groups in the member countries as well as the financing strategies of the groups.

---

[5] Maguire, Edward R. "A Review of Global and Regional Trends Likely To Impact Crime In The Dutch Caribbean." (2014).

Law, Ethics & Society

Review of Literature

Overview of CARICOM

There are 20 countries that make up the CARICOM; where 15 countries are full members while five referred to as Associate Members. The geographical boundaries of the CARICOM stretch from north coast of the South American mainland (Guyana and Suriname) to the Bahamas Islands located in the north and to Barbados in the west of Central America mainland.[6] The member countries are Antigua and Barbuda, Bahamas, Barbados, Belize, Dominica, Grenada, Guyana, Haiti, Jamaica, Montserrat, Saint Lucia, St Kitts and Nevis, St Vincent and the Grenadines, Suriname, and Trinidad and Tobago. The associate members are Anguilla, Bermuda, British Virgin Islands, Cayman Islands, and Turks and Caicos Islands. Some of the characteristics of these countries include: all are classified as developing countries; they have diverse geography and population; they are small in size and in population; and they have varied levels of economic and social development. The countries have made significant transition in their economic activities including the financial services due to their proximity to South and North America, which are the major markets in the region. Considering the characteristics and locations of the CARICOM member countries, there are various socio-economic issues which can be appreciated from the countries.

Armed groups in the CARICOM

Terrorism is definitely a global phenomenal, which depicts several forms of political and social violence and domestic resistance supported by illegal armed groups in a given country.[7] There are various armed groups who have reportedly existed in some of the CARICOM countries. In Jamaica, Leslie[8] investigated the political economy and the use of small

---

[6] https://caricom.org/about-caricom/who-we-are/our-governance/members-and-associate-members/
[7] Griffith, Ivelaw L. 2004. *Caribbean security in the age of terror: challenge and change*. Kingston, Jamaica: Ian Randle Publishers.
[8] Leslie, Glaister. *Confronting the don: the political economy of gang violence in Jamaica*. Geneva, Switzerland: Small Arms Survey, 2010.

Economic Dimensions of Armed Groups

firearms by gangs involved in violence in the country. Since the days of the garrison community[9], the politicians, politicians contributed to the reservation of the scarce resources like houses, cash, land and jobs, giving room for a possible existence of small armed groups (gangs) with the primary objective of committing criminal while trying to acquire the little resources. The gangs that have been associated with homicides include Rat bat Gang, Top Greenwich Town Gang, the Sparta Gang, the Klans Gang and the Umbrella Gang among others.[10] From the study by Leslie, the typology of the gangs and levels of operations in Jamaica can appreciated from the political relationships amongst the gangs. However, there are little literature on the relationships between the political associations and the operations of the gangs, including the degree of the threats that the gangs posses to a community as well as the longevity and ability to extend their operations to the global level. Given an approximate number of gangs in Jamaica at 266 as of 2015[11] it is important to appreciate the structure and distributions of these gangs in terms of their economic dimensions of their operations and thus the potential strategies to help solve cases of insecurity in the region. Notably, in Jamaica, one of the violent nations in CARICOM has a complex criminal landscape of transnational gangs and the local groups, contributing to 40.9 homicides per 100,000 inhabitants.[12] According to Leslie, criminal gangs are superior than the community gang in terms of organization and operations; therefore, the existence of these armed gangs in Jamaica does not only pose a threat to the country but the entire CARICOM as well as the neighboring regions like North and South America mainland. Moreover, the existence of transnational armed groups in Jamaica (posses) is associated with the political conflicts that have been witnessed between the Jamaica Labor Party and People's National Party.

---

[9] Leslie (2010).
[10] http://www.jamaicaobserver.com/news/pastor-names-190-gangs-operating-across-jamaica_106423?profile=1373
[11] Saunders, Alphea. *266 Criminal gangs creating mayhem across island.* Retrieved from http://www.jamaicaobserver.com/news/266-criminal-gangs-creating-mayhem-across-island_19238301
[12] Jamaica country profile. Retrieved from < https://issat.dcaf.ch/Learn/Resource-Library/Country-Profiles/Jamaica-Country-Profile>

Law, Ethics & Society

The motivations of the people, particularly youths in join-ing armed groups in the CARICOM is motivated by the need to be associated with protective groups, financial stability (poverty), popularity of the violent culture, and widespread un-employment.[13] There are various proposals on the strategies to prevent these motivational factors from influencing the youth into joining the armed gangs. In the study by Leslie[14], a careful assessment of the anti-gang legislation, dialogue be-tween the stakeholders, governments and academics, development of crime control approaches, and adoption of dif-ferentiated response to address proliferation of firearms and ammunition, were proposed. Engagement, as a geostrategic measure to solve violence in Haiti was investigated by Schu-berth[15]. In the study, it was established that the involvement of the international agencies can help protect the vulnerable population from the urban armed groups in Haiti.[16]

The Economic dimension of armed groups and intra-state terrorism

In the analysis of the economic dimensions, various theories have been put forward to help appreciate the context and dy-namics of the subject. The broader systems of the armed violence requires the understanding of the state, actors, dy-namics and motivations, the economy and the available natural resources.[17] In that regard, the foundational state fea-tures of the CARICO member states predispose the individual countries to possible transnational homicides, based on the close proximity of the violent armed groups in the community. A security dilemma in the CARICOM centers on the weak fi-nancial and political nature of the majority countries

---

[13] Mogensen, Michael. *Corner and area gangs of inner-city Jamaica*. COAV, 2004.

[14] Leslie, Glaister. *Confronting the don: the political economy of gang vio-lence in Jamaica*. Geneva, Switzerland: Small Arms Survey, 2010.

[15] Schuberth, Moritz. "To engage or not to engage Haiti's urban armed groups? Safe access in disaster-stricken and conflict-affected cities." *Envi-ronment and Urbanization* 29, no. 2 (2017): 425-442.

[16] Ibid.

[17] Cone, Cornelia. "An analysis of the economic dimension of the conflict in the Democratic Republic of Congo with recommendations for track one di-plomacy." PhD diss., University of Pretoria, 2007.

Economic Dimensions of Armed Groups

predisposes the community to violence; thus, there is a possibility in the flow of the small arms and gangs over the boarders. The risk of conflicts or terrorism in countries is associated with a close spatial proximity with countries which may be embroiled in conflict.[18] However, in the case of the CARICOM, there has not been a major concern on terrorism in the recent past. Nevertheless, with the increased dimorphism in terror activities, where allies of the developed countries are target, it is no doubt that any country is at threat of terrorism. Thus, using the knowledge of transitional political linkages and the underlying foreign interventions, a region like the CARICOM must ensure that all member states and associate members surround each other with reputable political and security credentials. For example, in the case of Democratic Republic of Congo, the transnational political linkages is not conducive, where the surrounding countries were either dependent on foreign economic and political interventions or constant conflicts; it is not possible to obtain adequate help or sustainable support to end violence.[19]

The economic dimension of the armed groups, with a possibility of addressing conflicts, the concept of conflict economy provides the basis in which linkages between the global level and local level security measures can help provide human security. According to Guaqueta[20], the economic activities that are linked to armed conflicts and to larger extent terrorism are characterized by militarized production, criminalized transactions and anarchic exploitations. The integrated global criminal economy can allow for the insurgence in the transformation of illegally exploited natural resources in the CARICO countries to fund the armed groups. However, reversing a criminally active and well rooted transnational gang is complex[21] [22]; thus, it is imperative that economically viable

---

[18] Ibid.

[19] Cone, Cornelia. "An analysis of the economic dimension of the conflict in the Democratic Republic of Congo with recommendations for track one diplomacy." PhD diss., University of Pretoria, 2007.

[20] Guaqueta, Alexandra. *Economic Agendas in Armed Conflict: Defining and Developing the Role of the UN*. International Peace Academy, 2002.

[21] Mandel, Robert. *Dark logic: Transnational criminal tactics and global security*. Stanford University Press, 2011.

[22] White, Rob. "Gangs and transnationalisation." *Youth in crisis* (2011): 198-214.

preventive measures are put in place, within the international laws and geostrategic political austerity.

Overall, the literature provides insight into how understanding the economic dimensions and the proliferations of economic interests of various stakeholders in human security are important. With a possibility of various actors in the terrorism diversifying their activities in terrorism with no country entirely safe, it is imperative that the existing natural resources and laws governing financial systems are put in place. Notably, in order to ensure that the existing armed groups and proliferation of small arms into the CARICOM countries is mitigated, then the economic dimension of terrorism must be appreciated. Moreover, the contemporary conflict theories such as the "self-financing nature of conflicts"[23] have brought about the understanding of how the retraction of the global superpower financing contributes to potential increase in the prominence of conflict in terms of the economic factors. For example, the civil war economies or countries with higher homicide cases like Jamaica, there is possible expansion of targets and purposes of violence, where capturing of natural resources and ideas is gaining prominence. As a result, a conventional geostrategic measures should are proposed in this research, with the view of enhancing geopolitical and practice of international laws.

Methodology

The study design employed a suitable data collection technique a qualitative data, where both primary and secondary data were collected. Reports from the relevant government authorities and international security agencies were also reviewed. The bulk of information in this study comes from the primary data, which involved personal experience and observations made as an ex-military.

---

[23] Ibid 13.

Results and Discussion: The financing of local armed groups and transnational terrorism

The greatest concern is where the armed groups and terrorist organization get their funds. There are conventional methods that have been proved effective to help the armed groups obtain funds. They include charities, illegal activities and front companies. Charities involve getting donations from charities and other wealthy individuals. Cases of donations have been reported from charities and individuals based in Saudi Arabia for the then Al-Qaeda.[24] In terms of funds obtained from illegal activities, one of the security experts indicated that:

> *Largest sources of funds that are channeled to initiate and sustain their criminal activities are illegal drug trade, illegal commerce like money laundering, and counterfeiting goods and brands.*

Similar case of illegal activities and funding of terror activities was witnessed in 2004 bombing of train in Madrid, where the perpetrators of the attack sold counterfeited CDs as well as trafficking of drugs to fund their operations. There are other cases of front companies, where several terrorist groups have strived to operate legitimate businesses and the profits used as front in the quest for money laundering. Further, the United Nations Office on Drugs and Crime (UNODC)[25] pointed out a new form of money laundering, which includes unverified correspondences circulated through mail or internet, claiming association with the UNODC or the officials. The scams seek to collect money from the recipients, charging fee for recruitment, requesting personal details such as bank accounts, offering prizes, scholarships, certificates or lotteries. Such cases are indications of the money laundering activities, which is a serious problem in the CARICOM.

---

[24] https://www.crisisgroup.org/latin-america-caribbean/haiti/keeping-haiti-safe-police-reform
[25] https://www.unodc.org/unodc/en/fraud-alert.html

Law, Ethics & Society

Cryptocurrencies and terrorism funding

The asymmetric threats and the possible funding strategies are currently taking a new shape, particularly in the manner in which money is transferred from the charities, individuals or front businesses to the armed groups or terror organizations. The development and spread of the cryptocurrencies such as bitcoins have indeed opened new avenues in which terror funding can be achieved. In the recent studies, the focus of the academicians has been in the investigation of the threats of cryptocurrencies to the fight against terrorism as well as the geostrategic initiatives to help mitigate such threats. The results confirmed that the cryptocurrencies create a new economic dimension in which terror groups and other armed gangs can successfully finance their activities. For example, the anonymity in the identity of the transactions enhanced by the transfer of the cryptocurrencies can enable the armed groups' exchange funds or receive funds from the financiers.

It is no doubt that the security of the cryptocurrencies and the transactions involved pose a great threat to the majority of the international law enforcers on money laundering and terrorism funding. It was important acknowledging the threats that weak financial laws in the CARICOM mean in the fight against terrorism in the region with respect to cryptocurrencies. Inasmuch as the region has put well-structured policies in the fight against illegal economic activities, the complexity in the transactions presented by the virtual currencies cannot be regulated by the existing regional regulations. Therefore, it is only imperative that the international laws, geopolitical players and the financial regulators consider the vulnerability of the CARICOM to terror funding using the cryptocurrencies.

Summarily, the CARICOM countries have weak rule of law, and coupled with the porous borders, the region remain susceptible to various economic crimes such as drug trafficking and smuggling among others. The urban dwellings have overcrowded urban slums, which are characteristically fragile for cases of violent crime, poverty, weakened government institutions and limited economic opportunities. This is a typical case of Haiti's porous land as well as the boarders in the sea.[26] Therefore, having an internationally viable geostrategic approach can help in the fights against funding the armed groups or terror organizations that may exist in the CARICOM or other neighboring countries.

Funding of Jamaican Criminal Gangs through fake lottery

There is increase in the number of gangs terrorizing people in Jamaica. The rise in the gang numbers and expanded activities are linked to the news funding sources, fake lottery[27] with unrealistic lotto winning schemes such as the case where Americans sent over $30 million in a fake Jamaican lottery.[28] The criminals pose as lotto officials, where they end up convincing foreigners of their winning of big payouts through MoneyGram, Western Union or Green Dot prepaid card. However, for the winners to retrieve their winnings, the criminals demand modest "processing fee". People who run online businesses, tourists and gamblers from the US and other developed countries have been victims of the lottery scams, especially where they can access personal details of the victims from hotels and call centers.[29] Moreover, some gangs ('dons') collect funds from local businesses (in what is referred to as "taxes") while others (lottery scammers) have transnational support in the US and in Jamaica.[30] Besides, Jamaica is now known as the international lottery scheme, where scam artist create new networks that aids in networking of the violent gangs.[31] The funds obtained from the fake lottery schemes are used to finance the illegal purchase of more small arms from neighboring countries through fishing boats

---

[26] Keeping Haiti Safe: Police Reform. Retrieved from <https://www.crisis-group.org/latin-america-caribbean/haiti/keeping-haiti-safe-police-reform>

[27] Bourne, P.A., Chambers, C., Blake, D.K., Sharpe-Pryce, C. and Solan, I., 2013. Lottery Scam in a Third-World Nation: The Economics of a Financial Crime and its Breadth. *Asian Journal of Business Management*, 5(1), pp.19-51.

[28] http://www.fraudaid.com/in_the_news/foxnewsmobile.htm

[29] http://www.jamaicaobserver.com/latest-news/US_researcher_outlines_link_between_scamming_and_gang_wars_in_Jamaica?profile=1228

[30] https://assets.publishing.service.gov.uk/government/uploads/system/uploads/attachment_data/file/598136/Jamaica_-_Org_Crim_Gangs_-_CPIN_-_Feb_2017_-v.2.pdf

[31] http://www.fraudaid.com/in_the_news/foxnewsmobile.htm

and across the sea locally, the armed groups pose great negative impact on the investment climate in the CARICOM as well as erosion in the development of human capital in the region.[32]

There are other scamming issues that have been associated with Jamaican gangs and their funding, especially since 2006 where lottery has been considered a lucrative source of revenue. In Montego Bay area, lottery scams are associated with homicides and weapons dealing, the activities which resulted into a 14-day state of emergency aimed at flushing out the gangs and recovery of the ammunition[33]. The fraudsters obviously need protection from other criminals. Since most of the lotto fraudsters are rich and powerful in the society, they purchase manpower and weapons, where they end up forming criminal gangs to provide security, as well as fight to gain control of the Montego Bay area. Such cases only threaten the human security in the neighboring areas and to large extent the region. Moreover, lotto scamming which is now a thriving business in the country has become a global threat, which is similar to the transnational gangs such as MS-13. As a result, it is imperative that the local and international community help the CARICOM prevent a future intra-state violence or criminality, especially in targeting a geostrategic approach in curbing the international network of money laundering through the lottery schemes to fund the criminal gangs in Jamaica.

The changing economic factors in CARICOM: implications on the development and enhanced activities of armed groups

The region suffers from diverse economic and social issues, which make the member countries vulnerable to victimization and crime. Economic instability makes it difficult for the youths to achieve their full potential in education or secure

---

[32] Harriott, Anthony, ed. *Understanding crime in Jamaica: New challenges for public policy.* University of West Indies Press, 2003.
[33] http://www.jamaicaobserver.com/latest-news/US_researcher_outlines_link_between_scamming_and_gang_wars_in_Jamaica?profile=1228

employment that leads to emigration to developed countries. The overall result is a disjointed social structure. Terror organizations and armed gangs are all different in terms of their purpose and nature. The intra-state conflicts, which are characterized by sustained political violence between groups representing a non-state and the other representing the state, have increasingly become common in the today's conflicts. A case where the intra-state conflicts occurred in CARICOM was the case of Haiti. However, one key underlying factor is that they all require resources to facilitate, self-maintain and fund their conflicts (political, violence or cultural). The financing of armed groups[34] encompasses complex structures, especially when the intentions involve transnational attacks.[35] From the security experts, it was found that groups that are supported by any political or governments, there are higher chances that such groups can engage in financially motivated violence such as kidnapping, killing of civilians and extortion. Thus, in this section, the objective was to analyze the current economic state of the CARICOM in the wake of possible implementation of the Caricom Single Market and Economy (CASME) vis a vis the changing dynamics in crime and intra-state conflicts.

There few concerns on the implementation of the CASME, which is the free movement of goods and services across the member and associate countries. Since the CARICOM has been identified as a safe haven for criminals; where, the countries "serve as offshore financial centers, which also attract both legitimate and illegitimate clients"[36]. The availability of the offshore financial centers in these countries offers opportunities for money laundering, terrorist funding and other illegal transactions. Moreover, geographic layout and gambling enterprises only contribute to the vulnerability that region is exposed, which is money laundering. The elimination of the existing barriers to the intra-regional movement of goods and services as well as the harmonization of

---

[34] In this study, this term is used interchangeably with terror organizations
[35] Ryder, Nicholas. *The financial war on terrorism: A review of counter-terrorist financing strategies since 2001*. Routledge, 2015.
[36] Maguire, Edward R. "A Review of Global and Regional Trends Likely To Impact Crime In The Dutch Caribbean." (2014).

the standards will definitely ensure that CARICOM improves economically and increased illicit transactions.

It is imperative that economic integration strategies that are to be implemented in the region include the right to establish a business (through a permit), a common external tariff, free circulation of goods and services, free movement of capital, common trade policy and free movement of labour.[37] Another notable step towards the integration of the CARICOM economic policies involves the harmonization of laws such as the intellectual property and the harmonization of the company. Another aspect that required the analyses of the possible implications revolved around the Caribbean Community Strategic Plan for 2015-2019[38], where the strategies involved: deepening of the initiatives and programs on crime prevention; strengthening of the boarders within the CARICOM; pursuing of the cooperative security agencies and measures to tackle and mitigate shared threats; and strengthening of the security systems within the region.

Inasmuch as the implementation of the CASME will benefit the region, there are concerns on the applicability of the joint CARICOM laws and how war on armed groups and intra-state conflicts can be mitigated. Further, the integration of the economic activities and harmonization of the laws on economic progress have more negative implications in the region in terms of the war on asymmetric threats than the benefits. It is no doubt that the economic benefits of the integration will be experienced in terms of the improved capabilities of the region in the fight against terrorism and armed groups. The security agencies will be better equipped once the finances are consolidated and channeled to a single, more powerful agency that can fight against for the region. However, this argument is only valid when the region gets financial support from the international community such as the European Union or the US to help them ensure smooth implementation of the harmonized laws and the Caribbean Community Strategic Plan for 2015-2019 on social justice and human rights.

---

[37] https://caricom.org/our-work/the-caricom-single-market-and-economy-csme/
[38] https://caricom.org/our-work/crime-and-security/

Economic Dimensions of Armed Groups

However, with the development of the cryptocurrencies and continued various in the economic dimensions of the sources of funding and funding strategies by the terror groups, it is quite a risky affair to integrate such a community without taking into account the geopolitical aspects of the region, political and economic risks with the armed groups and possible proliferation of the boarders to other intra- and international terror groups.

Geostrategic changes in the international laws on financial systems

The threat of terrorism is based on the flexibility and transnational structure in terms of the network and contemporary sophisticated technologies. Besides, there is a characteristically loose connectivity between the terror groups and the security agencies. As a result, most modern terrorism has found the financial support of their activities at the global stage easier; especially with the advancements in the sharing of intelligence as well as the funding, logistics and execution of the attacks. The creation of avenues that can help the terror groups improve on the funding strategies or operations on the transnational terrorism should, therefore, be mitigated and proper geostrategic strategies put in place to help ensure human security in all countries. The availability of weapons such as the small firearms from north to south and specifically from the US[39], pose a direct and serious threat to both the CARICOM countries and their international neighbors such as the US, Colombia and Brazil among others. This study, therefore, established that the fight against armed groups and the transnational terrorism can be achieved through geostrategic and well-executed measures though finance, leadership, control, material support, and communication. All these strategies are important; however, for this study, the emphasis was on the financial initiatives that can help mitigate proliferation of armed groups into transnational conflicts, especially with the changing dynamics in the war global terrorism and financial

---

[39] Maguire, Edward R. "A Review of Global and Regional Trends Likely To Impact Crime In The Dutch Caribbean." (2014).

transactions. The international laws and geopolitical players should focus on achieving the following strategy:

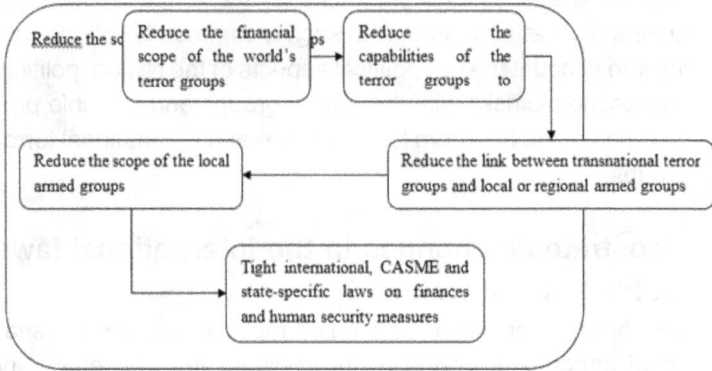

The fights against terrorism should be the world's primary and immediate priority. Human security in part of the world ensures sustained economic development, as well as social and political stability. From the geostrategic approach above (in figure 1), the international laws on any financial transfer must be conducted with the international standards as this will significantly curtail the activities of the transnational terror organizations. Depriving the terror organizations of the platform to fund their activities at the global stage will ensure that the organizations can only operate at a regional or country level. Once the capabilities of the transnational terror organizations to finance their allies in various countries is reduced, then the armed groups that exist within CARICOM will be significantly affected in terms of lack of firearms to undertake their activities and funds to support their internal operations. Further, this strategy will enable weak states and regional communities such as CARICOM effectively mitigate threats and risks posed by armed groups within the community member countries such as the Jamaican and Haitian armed groups. Lastly, the CARICOM countries will deal with the armed groups within the region through the newly formed CASME and strategic policies on human rights and criminal activities. Otherwise, of the greatest importance is for the international community to finance the CARICOM's security agencies in their fight against crime recent changes in the financial transaction complicated by the introduction of cryptocurrencies and advanced technologies.

Conclusion

Intra-state violence and political conflicts are endemic to humanity; however, the world cannot continue tolerating the activities of terrorist and other armed groups. Inasmuch as the modern technology seem to favour the economic dimensions of terror financing, the geopolitical and international laws must be modified to ensure that asymmetric threats do not overwhelm the existing security agencies in weak and developing countries such as the CARICOM countries. It is a fact that the CARICOM cannot face the security challenges from armed groups and transnational terrorism in a similar fashion like their counterparts with more multidimensional compelling and more organized bodies and equipment to face terrorism. Therefore, it is through the development of stringent international financial systems and laws on money (both virtual and real currencies) that can help the CARICOM fight against transnational terrorism and mitigate the existing regional armed groups from committing criminal activities in the region.

References

Ballentine, Karen, and Heiko Nitzschke. "Beyond greed and grievance: Policy lessons from studies in the political economy of armed conflict." *Security and Development: Investing in Peace and Prosperity* 164 (2003).

Blin, Arnaud. "Armed groups and intra-state conflicts: the dawn of a new era?" *International Review of the Red Cross*93, no. 882 (2011): 287-310.

Bourne, P.A., Chambers, C., Blake, D.K., Sharpe-Pryce, C. and Solan, I., 2013. Lottery Scam in a Third-World Nation: The Economics of a Financial Crime and its Breadth. *Asian Journal of Business Management*, 5(1), pp.19-51.

Cone, Cornelia. "An analysis of the economic dimension of the conflict in the Democratic Republic of Congo with recommendations for track one diplomacy." PhD diss., University of Pretoria, 2007.

Law, Ethics & Society

Dudouet, Véronique, Katrin Planta, and Hans J. Giessmann. "The political transformation of armed and banned groups." *Lessons learned and implications for international support framework paper. Berlín: Berghof Foundation-United Nations Development Program* (2016).

Griffith, Ivelaw L. 2004. *Caribbean security in the age of terror: challenge and change*. Kingston, Jamaica: Ian Randle Publishers.

Guaqueta, Alexandra. *Economic Agendas in Armed Conflict: Defining and Developing the Role of the UN*. International Peace Academy, 2002.

Harriott, Anthony, ed. *Understanding crime in Jamaica: New challenges for public policy*. University of West Indies Press, 2003.

http://www.fraudaid.com/in_the_news/foxnewsmobile.htm

http://www.jamaicaobserver.com/latest-news/US_researcher_outlines_link_between_scamming_and_gang_wars_in_Jamaica?profile=1228

http://www.jamaicaobserver.com/news/pastor-names-190-gangs-operating-across-jamaica_106423?profile=1373

https://assets.publishing.service.gov.uk/government/up-loads/system/uploads/attachment_data/file/598136/Jamaica_-_Org_Crim_Gangs_-_CPIN_-_Feb_2017_-v.2.pdf

https://caricom.org/about-caricom/who-we-are/our-govern-ance/members-and-associate-members/

https://caricom.org/our-work/crime-and-security/

https://caricom.org/our-work/the-caricom-single-market-and-economy-csme/

https://www.crisisgroup.org/latin-america-carib-bean/haiti/keeping-haiti-safe-police-reform

https://www.unodc.org/unodc/en/fraud-alert.html

Jamaica country profile. Retrieved from < https://is-sat.dcaf.ch/Learn/Resource-Library/Country-Profiles/Jamaica-Country-Profile>

Keeping Haiti Safe: Police Reform. Retrieved from < https://www.crisisgroup.org/latin-america-carib-bean/haiti/keeping-haiti-safe-police-reform>

Leslie, Glaister. *Confronting the don: the political economy of gang violence in Jamaica*. Geneva, Switzerland: Small Arms Survey, 2010.

Economic Dimensions of Armed Groups

Maguire, Edward R. "A Review of Global And Regional Trends Likely To Impact Crime In The Dutch Caribbean." (2014).

Mandel, Robert. *Dark logic: Transnational criminal tactics and global security*. Stanford University Press, 2011.

Mogensen, Michael. *Corner and area gangs of inner-city Jamaica*. COAV, 2004.

Ryder, Nicholas. *The financial war on terrorism: A review of counter-terrorist financing strategies since 2001*. Routledge, 2015.

Saunders, Alphea. *266 Criminal gangs creating mayhem across island*. Retrieved from http://www.jamaicaobserver.com/news/266-criminal-gangs-creating-mayhem-across-island_19238301

Schuberth, Moritz. "To engage or not to engage Haiti's urban armed groups? Safe access in disaster-stricken and conflict-affected cities." *Environment and Urbanization* 29, no. 2 (2017): 425-442.

Wennmann, Achim. "Economic dimensions of armed groups: profiling the financing, costs, and agendas and their implications for mediated engagements." *International Review of the Red Cross* 93, no. 882 (2011): 333-352.

White, Rob. "Gangs and transnationalisation." *Youth in crisis* (2011): 198-214.

THE CHALLENGE OF EDUCATING REFUGEE CHILDREN TO AVOID CREATING TOMORROW´S EXTREMISTS[*]

Stephan U. Breu

Abstract

An estimated 65 million people have been forced to flee their homelands in the last few years. Average length of displacement for a refugee is now estimated at 17 years. A whole generation of young people are forced to spend their whole youth in refugee camps and can only be educated there. On the other side the international community is strongly underfinancing any education efforts by aid agencies and international organizations. So, it is common that classes have as many as 100 children and teachers must deal with inevitable language barriers. We also have to remember that most children are traumatized by their experiences of fleeing their homes. Whereas the focus of most efforts is aimed at primary education it should not be forgotten that it is also necessary to support older children even up to higher education. A lot of the refugee adolescents have to support their families through activities that make education impossible.

According to the UNHCR, more than 3.5 million refugee children do not have the chance to attend an appropriate school education. The inclusion of refugees in the national education systems of their host countries is a promising way of softening the challenges but the financial burden is too heavy to be carried without substantial support from the international community. Unfortunately, this is still dramatically lacking. Seeing these challenges in the world's toughest classrooms we need to be aware that missing this opportunity to help and educate these traumatized children will fuel the feelings of

---

[*] First presented at 6th International Conference "Ohrid-Vodici 2018" "Diaspora, Transnationalism, Transculturalism and Inter-Cultural communications as new forms of social capital".

being disadvantaged and forgotten by the rest of the world. Such feelings are smoothening the way for disaffection and they may become lured to be part of religious extremist organizations if not sufficiently addressed by providing enough infrastructure and finances for proper primary and secondary education.

Introduction

According to the UNHCR, The UN Refugee Agency, by the end of 2016 a total of 65.6 million individuals were forcibly displaced worldwide because of persecution, conflict, violence or human rights violations. Out of this number approximately 22.5 million individuals are registered as refugees. About half of these individuals are below 18 years of age and are in a strong need for primary and secondary education. These numbers do not include displaced individuals who are leaving their homes due to severe situations such as lack of food, water, education or health care. From the school-aged children under the mandate of UNHCR about 50 % do not have a school to go to. Some 1.75 million refugee children are not in primary school and another 1.95 million refugee adolescents are not in secondary school. Young refugees are five times more likely not to be in school than the global average.

One has to understand that we do not just neglect the education of these children, but we also loose the opportunity to transform and build a new generation of adults that can take responsibilities for their lives and families. It will be this generation that gives their experience of having to leave their homes and how they have been treated by the societies hosting them to their children. The way these young individuals are treated and what opportunities they will find to improve their lives will have a sustainable impact on social and political shifts in the coming years.

Feeling the positive support of the international community and having opportunities to learn and being educated will minimize tendencies to extremism strongly. Missing this opportunity to address this generation of refugees will lead to feelings of being forgotten and discriminated and open doors for religious and fundamental extremists to recruit new extremists for their organizations.

Under this aspect it is difficult to understand that the UNHCR refugee camps are constantly underfinanced by the international community and that there is no more earnest approach to address the education needs of these individuals. Especially taking in account that the traumas, size of classes and various languages are asking for highly skilled and flexible education staff and teachers and a lot of the young adolescent refugees are forced to contribute to the survival of their families what gives them a lot of pressure not to attend secondary school but to find ways to generate money through any possible means.

Given this situation, we have to fear that we will generate a lost generation of displaced young people that are suffering minimal education and are not capable to integrate in the society and business life of their host countries and have no other option that rely on social support or any illegal means to finance their lives and families.

The Refugee Crisis

The world remains on a record height of a population of approximately 65.6 million forcibly displaced people. Out of this number a total of approximately 22.5 million individuals are registered as refugees. More than half of all refugees worldwide are coming from just three countries – Syria, Afghanistan and South Sudan. Especially the group from South Sudan is fast-growing and the majority of new refugees are children.

The host countries for the refugees are mainly Turkey (up to 3 Mio. individuals), Pakistan (approx. 1,4 Mio. individuals) and Lebanon (approx. 1 Mio. Individuals). The next host countries with many refugees are Islamic Republic of Iran, Uganda and Ethiopia which are not famous for having a strong economic growth rate and strong economy internally. One can easily understand that these countries will not be in a position to solve the inherent problems of hosting such large number of refugees and meet their special needs.

For years we hear the warnings of the UNHCR that the nutrition and medical situation is dramatically limited in the refugee camps but the international community and the political responsible leaders are not willing to sustainably invest into the well-being and future of these displaced individuals. Today's geopolitical situation does not give a lot of hope that the interests of the leading world powers are allowing the original countries of most refugees to find peace and stability. On the contrary one has to fear more displaced individuals from Yemen, South-Sudan, Democratic Republic of Kongo and possibly Zimbabwe in the future.

The idea of "regime change" by supporting political opposition in unstable countries in Africa and the Near East has not proven to be effective but is still applied today by the leading world powers forgetting that ethical and democratic values are not only empty phrases but are also asking for respectful acting of the elite emphasizing such.

Situation in Refugee Camps

As we have learnt the big refugee camps are located in countries that do not have a largely developed economy. The only exception might be Turkey. Pakistan and Lebanon can be considered middle-income countries at best and Iran, Uganda and Ethiopia have a lot of own problems to solve either from former sanctions or from a generally struggling economy. It is obvious that the international community has to bear a sustainable share of the burdens coming from hosting such large numbers of refugees as otherwise the social stability of the hosting countries is in danger.

Before we start speaking about the educational situation we have to remind us that it is a nearly impossible task for the UNHCR to finance nutrition of the refugees under their mandate and the necessary funds are provided slowly and unreliably by the donor countries. Insufficient nutrition is one of the major reasons that made refugees leaving the camps in 2016 going on their way to Europe but still politicians in Europe are discussing about fighting against causes of migration and flight but are not keeping their basic promises regarding finances.

But even with this problem solved we have the situation that schools open for refugee children are most often at their organizational limits. It is common to have classes with over 100 students with various mother tongues. Such situation asks for more teaching staff which should be trained on a high standard to address the inevitable language barriers and the traumas of the children. Approximately 79 % of the refugee children have experienced death in their families and a lot of them show symptoms of posttraumatic stress disorder. These children need psychological and emotional support before they can go back to learn mathematics and writing.

Today most focus lies on primary education in refugee camps. But as the average length of displacement for a refugee adds up to 17 years now we have the situation that most refugee children are spending their whole school careers in camps. If we shift our attention to secondary and tertiary education, we have another obstacle there. Most families are forced to organize additional funds as it is nearly not possible to survive with the minimum support by the international community. So adolescent refugees are pushed to help organizing money for the survival of their families and so do miss opportunities to attend secondary or even tertiary education. They abandon their studies to provide for their families.

One has also to take into consideration that a heavy burden is placed on the education system of the hosting countries and the new problems are also jeopardizing the quality of education for existing students. The educational budgets of these countries are already stretched beyond capacities.

Education as a Fundamental Human Right

The right to education has been recognized as a Human Right by Article 26 of the Universal Declaration of Human Rights and Article 13 and 14 of the International Covenant of Economic, Social and Cultural Rights. Article 26 states, "Everyone has the right to education. Education shall be free, at least in the elementary and fundamental stages. Elementary education shall be compulsory." Included is also an obligation to develop secondary education accessible to all without discrimination.

Law, Ethics & Society

If our developed regions of the world are not taking care of the needs of the refugee children and adolescents to be able to access appropriate education, we are neglecting their claims according to the Universal Declaration of Human Rights. As our economic system is - nicely said - not helping their home countries to develop a sustainable economy for themselves and our political leaders deem it appropriate to get involved in the internal political affairs even using them for global strategic goals by arguing with our high ethical standards reflected in the Universal Declaration of Human Rights such behavior seems not very honest. We have a duty to care at least for the education of these displaced and traumatized refugee children.

As mentioned, the educational system of the host countries of most refugees is already stretched to the limits and only sustainable and reliable international support can help to provide necessary resources. It would be easy to grant this fundamental human right to refugee children if the international community would cooperate and take its responsibility seriously.

A pro-active approach by allocating a small percentage of the military budget to education of refugee children and adolescent would possibly generate a much more successful option for several crisis regions in the world to stabilize in the future and become pacificated. As it is agreed on the international level that education is the key for a successful and peaceful future of mankind, we should not only talk but accept our responsibilities today in this refugee crisis.

A lost Generation?

We have to be aware that we should educate the generation that hopefully will return one day to their home country and rebuild and re-shape the future of these countries. It is a unique opportunity to interact with the future generation of these unstable countries and to get appreciation for our values and ethics. Missing this opportunity will make us pay a high price in the future.

We should not deny a whole generation their right to education and leave them to religious extremists group that offer them basic education at the cost of religious indoctrination. It is human nature that most children are eager to learn and make experiences. By providing secular education we have an unseen opportunity to explain some of our core values and ethical standards to milieus we could never reach before. Being careful not to harm the social and religious manners of their origin we could build new bridges between the cultures to exchange views and idea. We could educate a new generation of leaders for these countries that will remember our support and understanding for their situation and hopefully will be more tolerant and open minded for the benefit of all mankind. The best thing you can offer a child or even an adolescent is empathy and understanding so to help him learn and develop.

On the other side the worst thing that can happen to a child or adolescent is, that he has to leave his home forcibly and the society offering him shelter is making him feel unwelcome, let him starve, deny him education and does not give him any positive perspective for his future. Every young individual will one-day start thinking why he and his family had been forced to leave their home. It is understandable that in most cases there will be a feeling that the leading powers of the world did not play a neutral or innocent role in the events leading to the displacement.

Having complete uncertainty about the future and lack of education will make it easy for religious and other extremists to interact with these young individuals and give them an easy explanation about what is good and bad. Supporting the feeling of being unworthy and forgotten the role model as a victim of international conspiracy against its own culture and society will be emphasized quickly. If such feelings are mixed with religious fundamentalism we are urging these young people directly to organizations that will use them against us. The generation of refugee children growing up in camps would become a great pond for the extremist groups to fish for new victims they can indoctrinate easily with their completely mad concept of an extremist society.

Law, Ethics & Society

(Re-)Integration into Society

Of course, the forcibly displaced individuals put a heavy burden on their host countries. Mostly they are not really welcomed by the societies that should take responsibilities for them. This is understandable and it should be the first aim to prepare conditions that these individuals can return to their home countries as soon as possible. It is the general expectation that forcibly displaced individuals will move back to their home country if it is possible to do so without high risk. Based on this assumption are the regulations in international law defining the rights of a refugee.

As far as it concerns the generation of refugee children growing up in refugee camps there are two options how they will have to integrate into an existing society. After spending the whole youth in a refugee camp this generation of young people would have to bring an enormous effort to integrate into the society at home - if they hopefully return one day. The society they will find will be unstable and people will be traumatized and without clear perspectives. They have to get accustomed to the manners and behavior of the people that stayed home during these hard times. This is the moment where we could benefit most from this generation that could return educated and open-minded with a perspective in their lives to accept responsibilities for their home countries.

In the past, more often than not, it was never possible for refugees to return to their home countries. In this second scenario all these young people will have to integrate into foreign cultures and societies. It is without saying that education and an open mind are the most crucial precondition for a successful integration. Being able to become a part of the local work force and take responsibility for its own life makes a big difference than to depending on social security and support of the host country. Also, the social tension in the host countries will be less intensive if this generation of young refugees are in the position to show a contribution to the society they are asked to become part of.

If we are not successful with granting these children their right to education, we will generate a minefield of problems in the already stretched societies that are offering a more or less safe place to survive for these forcibly displaced individuals. In both scenarios mankind would benefit largely if these young children would get an appropriate secular education. It is the decision of the developed world how we are going to handle the situation.

Climate Refugees

Today, most registered refugees by the UNHCR are fleeing their country because of wars and terrorist activities. Looking some years into the future we have to expect completely new waves of refugees. According to new studies published in November 2017 tens of millions of people will be forced from their homes by climate change in the next decade. For all these climate refugees it will most probably never be possible to return to their homes.

We have to anticipate that the host societies that have to take responsibilities for these refugees will not be easily ready to take such. We will encounter social and political tension and maybe even violence against refugees. This development could easily become an existential threat to our civilization in the longer term. As the developed countries will have no other option as to integrate these refugees as returning home will be no option education for these expected group of refugee children and adolescent will become most crucial.

As I explained before a successful integration is asking for a positive contribution of the new member to the society to reduce tension and open perspectives. So today's crisis in education of refugee children can be seen as a test for the coming challenges for our civilization to survive the coming tensions by mass migration caused by climate change and economic disaster.

Conclusion

The international community has a strong obligation to grant refugee children and adolescent their right to education as declared in the Universal Declaration of Human Rights. We have to offer appropriate education that supports the development of the individuals to build bridges between cultures and find solutions to help this generation to re-build and re-shape their home countries if they can return one day.

If we miss this opportunity to accept part of the burden of the refugee crisis we will see social problems evolving in the host countries. By neglect and non-action we will de facto be offering a whole generation to the religious extremists that can use the uncertainty of the future and the feeling of inferiority in these young people as a promising source for recruiting extremist fighters successfully.

It is an unseen opportunity to successfully master this challenge if the international community puts aside political and geo-strategic short-term thinking and bundles resources to establish a new understanding between cultures and societies and grants these refugee children and adolescent their right to education.

References

Al Hroub H. (2016). By failing to educate child refugees, we are creating the extremists of the future – *Independent.co.uk*, [online] Available at: http://www.independent.co.uk/voices/child-refugees-syria-lebanon-terrorism-education-creating-the-extremists-of-the-future-a7148901.html [Accessed 08. Dec. 2017].

Fallon K. (2017). How our refugee school in Greece is preparing children for a life in Europe – *The Telegraph*, [online] Available at: http://www.telegraph.co.uk/education/2017/01/09/refugee-school-greece-preparing-children-life-europe/ [Accessed 08. Dec. 2017].

Gordts E. and Alfred C. (2016). 10 Experts to Watch on Refugee Education – *newsdeeply.com*, [online] Available at: https://www.newsdeeply.com/refugees/articles/2016/11/22/10-experts-to-watch-on-refugee-education [Accessed 08. Dec. 2017].

hrw.org, (2016). Growing Up Without an Education [online] Available at: https://www.hrw.org/ report/2016/07/19/growing-without-education/barriers-education-syrian-refugee-children-lebanon [Accessed 09. Dec. 2017].

Educating Refugee Children

Kubwalo K. (2015). In a refugee camp, education is the only hope – *UNICEF.org*, [online] Available at: https://www.unicef.org/infobycountry/jordan_82551.html [Accessed 08. Dec. 2017].

Larpent F. (2017). Education is a way out: teacher training in refugee camps – *International Baccalaureate*, [online] Available at: http://blogs.ibo.org/blog/2017/11/04/education-is-a-way-out/ [Accessed 10. Dec. 2017].

Pinna M. (2017). Targeting education for refugee children in Kenya – *euronews.com*, [online] Available at: http://www.euronews.com/2017/01/19/targeting-education-for-refugee-children-in-the-kakuma-refugee-camp-in-kenya [Accessed 08. Dec. 2017].

Ridge H. (2016). How Are Refugee Children Being Educated In Camps? – *Education week*, [online] Available at: http://blogs.edweek.org/edweek/global_learning/2016/06/how_are_refugee_children_being_educated_in_camps.html [Accessed 08. Dec. 2017].

savethechildren.net, (2017). Refugee Education Crisis Looming In Uganda [online] Available at: https://www.savethechildren.net/article/refugee-education-crisis-looming-uganda [Accessed 09. Dec. 2017].

Schmidt C. (2013). Education in the Second Largest Refugee Camp in the World. *Wise – Global Partnership for Education*, [online] Available at: https://www.globalpartnership.org/blog/education-second-largest-refugee-camp-world [Accessed 08. Dec. 2017].

Taylor M. (2017). Climate change "will create world's biggest refugee crisis". – *The Guardian*, [online] Available at: https://www.theguardian.com/environment/2017/nov/02/climate-change-will-create-worlds-biggest-refugee-crisishttp://www.wise-qatar.org/best-practices-running-schools-refugee-camps [Accessed 10. Dec. 2017].

Tookey M. (2015). Inside a Syrian refugee camp: "Education is the only hope for children" – *theguardian.com*, [online] Available at: https://www.theguardian.com/teacher-network/2015/apr/14/inside-a-syrian-refugee-camp-education-is-the-only-hope-for-children [Accessed 09. Dec. 2017].

Tutunji S. (2016). Best Pracitices for Running Schools in Refugee Camps. *Wise – Quatar Foundation*, [online] Available at: http://www.wise-qatar.org/best-practices-running-schools-refugee-camps [Accessed 08. Dec. 2017].

unesdoc.unesco.org, (2017). Protecting the rights to education for refugees [online] Available at: http://unesdoc.unesco.org/im-ages/0025/002510/251076E.pdf [Accessed 09. Dec. 2017].

unhcr.org, (2017). Missing Out: Refugee education in crisis [online] Available at: http://www.unhcr.org/57beb5144 [Accessed 12. Dec. 2017].

unhcr.org, (2017). Global Trends – Forced Displacement in 2016 [online] Available at: http://www.unhcr.org/statis-tics/unhcrstats/5943e8a34/global-trends-forced-displacement-2016.html [Accessed 09. Dec. 2017].

unhcr.org, (2017). UNHCR report highlights education crisis for refugee children [online] Available at: http://www.un-hcr.org/news/press/2017/9/59b6a3ec4/unhcr-report-highlights-education-crisis-refugee-children.html [Accessed 09. Dec. 2017].

unhcr.org, (2017). UNHCR What We Do - Education [online] Available at: http://www.unhcr.org/education.html [Accessed 09. Dec. 2017].

weforum.org, (2017). Why refugee education is a problem – and six solutions [online] Available at: https://www.weforum.org/agenda/2016/05/why-refugee-education-is-a-problem-and-six-solutions/ [Accessed 08. Dec. 2017].

HISTORICAL CONTEXT OF MILITARY INTERVENTIONISM

Hatidža Beriša

Summary

This paper deals with the historical context of military interventionism. The author has tried to answer several questions like: "Where are the roots of military interventionism?", "What was in the past, and what is it today?" The historical context of military interventionism has been analyzed in three characteristic periods: until World War II, in the period from World War II to the end of the Cold War and in the post-Cold War period. The historical perspective is important for considering the continuity of the holders of military interventionism and making valid conclusions. Historical analysis points to the ever-present practice of military interventionism as an instrument of great powers in international relations in order to realize its interests.

The aim of the paper is to identify as many relevant facts as that unambiguously indicate that military interventionism in the post-Cold War period poses a threat to the state of global security and international relations. The space on which we live, not so long ago, was the object of a brutal military intervention by the West, and it can still be said, the object of interventionism of the same West. The consequences of the mentioned military intervention are visible and they are felt today, and it is certain that the future will only show its true face. Therefore, it can not be said with certainty that the disintegration processes in this area have been completed and that military intervention in the future can be completely excluded as an instrument of imposing the will of the mighty.

Introduction

"Curiosity pulls us to explore the past, find out what happened, who did what and why; and it exalts us and hopes that we will understand the present and will be able to recognize the way in which our time, experience and hope will shape the future."[1]

In analyzing the historical context of military intervention, or interfering with the internal affairs of another state, if it wants to start from the very root, it would be logical to begin in 1648 and the Westphalian Agreement when a sovereign state was promoted.

The Westphalian agreement was preceded by a Thirty Years War, in which, in the name of ideology, at that time of religious orthodoxy, thirty percent of the population of Central Europe was killed. The essence of the treaty was the doctrine of sovereignty, which implied that state institutions and internal relations were beyond the reach of other states. It could be said that the agreement provided a peaceful period in international relations until Napoleon's wars. Hence the subject of analysis of the historical context of military interventionism includes the period from 1815 and the creation of the Holy Alliance, to the present day.

Analysis of the historical context of military interventionism has been considered in three periods, which in some way reflect the evolution of this method of specific use of military force in international relations. The first period is from 1815 to the beginning of the Second World War, the second period is the period of the Cold War, and the third period is the period after the Cold War to date. In each of these periods, the focus is on characteristic military interventions, which in some way marked the time in which they occurred, or it is better to say that those (interventions) were precisely the product of socio-political relations and the world order of that time. On the other hand, attention is focused primarily on the great powers or their coalitions, which in the mentioned period of time, from 1815 until today, were the bearers of military interventions, which are primarily the United States and Russia (the Soviet Union).

---

[1] Jasper Griffin (Jasper Griffin), Oxford classicist in: Arne Westad, *Global Cold War, Intervention in the Third World and the Making of our Age* (Belgrade, Arpihelag, 2008), p. 9.

Historical Context of Military Interventionism

Military intervention until the Second World War

In the history of European relations, armed intervention was considered a legitimate means, especially after 1815, when the Holy Alliance was created by the power of the victors over Napoleon. Russia, Prussia[2] and Austro-Hungarian, as members of the Holy Alliance, intervened in the armed forces in Spain, Hungary and Piedmont[3] in order to preserve the feudal order, and against the bourgeois revolutions that occurred in these countries. Interestingly, Russia will be the subject of an intervention with the same sign one hundred years later after the October Revolution, only this time the capitalist forces tried to suppress the socialist revolution. The motive in both cases is to maintain existing socio-economic relations of that time.[4]

After interventions at the beginning of the 19th century, undertaken by the Holy Alliance, military interventions preceded the Berlin Congress. Of special importance was the intervention of Russia to Turkey in 1877, which was completed by San Stefano Peace in 1878 and forcing Turkey to recognize the independence of Bulgaria, Serbia and Greece. The Berlin Congress overturned the decisions of the San Stefano Treaty, somewhat appreciating the demands of the Balkan peoples (Great Bulgaria) on the one hand, and on the other hand did not appreciate all the results of the liberation wars of Serbia and Montenegro. Also, the demands of the Serbs on the other side of the Drina (Nevesinje Uprising) were not respected. The Berlin Congress has redefined the Balkans map by matching the interests of the European powers of that time, even at the cost of returning part of the territory of Turkey.

The end of the 19th and early 20th centuries marked the relative balance of forces that ruled in Europe between Great

---

[2] Prussia was a strong state at that time, and later (1870) would play a key role in the unification and creation of Germany, after the Austro-Hungarian-Prussian and French-Prussian Wars from which it emerged as a winner.
[3] Piedmont was, at the time the Sardinian Kingdom, which unite the Papal States, Lombardy, Sicily and Naples in 1870 and finaly in 1870 the whole Italy.
[4] R. Stojanović, Ibid, p. 161.

Law, Ethics & Society

Britain, France and Russia and a group of dissatisfied countries led by Germany with Austro-Hungary and Italy and preparing for the war. Events that followed in the relations of great powers inevitably led to the First World War.

At the beginning of the 19th century, on the other side of the Atlantic, the United States went through great force. The then President James Monroe (James Monroe 1751-1831) sets out the basic guidelines of his country's foreign policy, which was only thirty years before (1776) ceased to be a colony, promoting the famous "Monroe doctrine." The essence of this idea is "America Americans" and represents an open refusal of any political influence of Europe on the American continent. After the settling of new territories to newcomers from Europe, any conflict with the local population or European countries, who still had colonies on the North American soil, was used as justification for the use of military force.

The American-Spanish War, in 1898, forced Spain to abandon all of its overseas colonies - Cuba, Puerto Rico, and the Philippines, along with some smaller territories. The United States will soon afterwards intervene in Cuba twice for the first time in 1906 and for the second time in 1911-1912. year-old, preparing to extend his domination beyond the American continent. By entering the First World War in 1917, the United States began its intense presence in the rest of the world, which continues to this day.

The First World War, the Socialist Revolution in Russia (1917), the rise and development of the United States, the independence of India, the Chinese Revolution, the revolt of colonial countries against imperialism and the creation of the League of Nations are important factors influencing the development of socio-economic relations in the world in the period between two world wars.[5] The Versailles Peace Agreement concluded between the Allies and the Central Powers and the creation of the League of Nations failed to build a stable and lasting security order in Europe. The powerlessness of the League of Nations and the world economic crisis in 1929 led to the expansionism of Germany,

---

[5] M. Kovač, B.Forca: Same, p. 13.

Historical Context of Military Interventionism

Italy and Japan that led to the Second World War.

In the period between the two world wars, the most important military intervention was undertaken by Japan, Germany and Italy, by practically creating new states (the creation of Manchuria by Japan in the intervention in China), the occupation (Austria by Germany and Albania by Italy) and disintegration (Czechoslovakia by Germany). These interventions were a practical introduction to the Second World War, which had the most horrific consequences that have been recorded in history to date.

Military interventions from the Second World War to the end Cold War

The end of the Second World War marked the division of the world into the areas of interest of the winners, between the United States and its Western allies on the one hand and the Soviet Union on the other. In the security sense, the most significant event since the Second World War was the creation of the United Nations, which took care of maintaining international peace and security in the world. The Security Council, as a UN body, should have been concerned about issues of the use of force in international relations. Permanent members of the council (Great Britain, USA, France, China and the USSR) had veto power, which in practice meant that the decisions must be made by consensus.

The deterioration of international relations and the emergence of the Cold War[6] came after the collapse of the anti-Hitler coalition and the conflict between the former allies - the great powers, and above all between the two supersiliaries after the war-the US and the Soviet Union. The hope of humanity that the war will cease to be a means of politics and that all political and international problems will be

---

[6] The notion of Cold War links to British Prime Minister Winston Churchill, who coined the wing of the "Iron Curtain", which the Communists dropped between their "free world". In March 1946, he called for a "crusade against communism" in Fulton, USA, recalling the commitment of the defense of the Atlantic community and the military rapprochement of vulnerable states. These appearances were a sign that the world entered the so-called Cold War.

resolved peacefully, has begun to disappear. The United Nations has not succeeded in fully securing permanent and solid peace and always preventing the use of force in international relations.

Unfortunately, the ideological difference and socio-economic order that ruled between Western allies and the USSR on the other hand inevitably led the division of the world into two poles who fought to spread its influence, primarily towards its disobedient allies and countries third world. In the world, the bipolar division of the world dominated, marked by a collision in weapons and a constant threat that the force could be used in a general conflict. Nuclear weapons were a brake and an argument for deterrence, because a nuclear war between former allies would practically endanger the physical survival of the world.

The Cold War period represented the implementation of a policy from a position of power by large states to achieve political goals, without the general wartime conflict. Cold war was marked by mutual distrust, suspicion and misunderstandings. The United States accuses the Soviet Union of spreading communism around the world, and the Soviet Union accuses the United States of imperialism. The post-World War II period marked an increase in the number of US-led or Western-led interventions and the Soviet Union.

Table 1—shows military interventions in the period from 1945 to 1989[7]

The country against which interventions have been taken	The carrier of intervention	Year of performance
Vietnam	France, Great Britain and China	1945.
Indonesia	Great Britain and Netherland	1945.
Kuwait	Great Britain	1953.

---

[7] Ibid, p. 341-343.

Historical Context of Military Interventionism

Guatemala	USA	1954.
Vietnam	USA	1954.
Costa Rica	USA	1955.
Hunagary	Soviet Union	1956.
Vietnam	USA	1956.
Libanon	USA	1958.
Jordan	UK	1958.
Congo	Belgium	1960.
Cuba	USA	1961.
Tunis	France	1961.
Panama	USA	1964.
Gabon	France	1964.
Dominic Republic	USA	1965.
Vietnam	USA	1966.
Syria	Israel	1966.
Syria	UK, USA	1967.
Czechoslovakia	Warsaw contract (SSSR)	1968.
Equatorial Guinea	Spain	1969.
Jordan	Israel	1969.
Republic Irland	UK	1969.
Cambodia	USA	1970.
Republic of Guinea	Portugal	1970.
Cyprus	Turkay	1974.
Angola	South African Republic	1975.

Zair	France/Morocco	1977.
Chad	France	1978.
Uganda	Tansania	1978.
Vietnam	China	1979.
Libanon	Israel	1982.
Grenada	USA	1983.
Lybia	USA	1986.

After World War II, despite legal prohibition, military interventions were a tool in the hands of the great powers, above all the United States and the Soviet Union, who were at the head of the major military alliances of the North Atlantic Treaty Organization and the Warsaw Treaty. The Cold War period marks the period during which the global conflict between the US and the Soviet Union dominated international events.

In the Cold War period, the United States participated in the Korean War from 1950 to 1953. It is interesting that the US support of the United States for the participation in the Korean War was also given by the SFRY. The Korean conflict continues to this day. After the Korean War, US military interventions followed the Vietnam intervention in Guatemala in 1954, Egypt in 1956, Lebanon in 1958, and Cuba in 1961[8]

Historically, during the Cold War period, the Vietnam War is also important. Similar to the conflict between the two Koreas, the US supports South Vietnam in the struggle against the Communist North, which is supported by the Soviet Union, China and North Korea. The use of the most modern and most brutal weapons used and against the civilian population did not secure the victory of the United States. Defeated on the home ground by their own public opinion and with thousands of victims (around 55,000), they definitely retire from Vietnam in 1973, after almost thirteen

---

[8] An unsuccessful attempt by about 1500 Cuban emigrants organized by the CIA to overthrow the Communist regime of Fidel Castro by landing in the Bay of Pigs. American intervention ends with complete failure (16-30.04.1961).

Historical Context of Military Interventionism

years. In the meantime, the intervention of the Dominican Republic in 1965 against the legally elected president (Juan Bosch) was made, with the explanation that the United States will not suffer the new Cuba in the Caribbean. Military interventions to Iran followed in 1980, Lebanon in 1983, Grenada[9] in 1983, Libya in 1986, and Panama[10] in 1989.

On the other hand, the Soviet Union demonstrated its domination by performing military interventions in Hungary in 1956, in Czechoslovakia in 1968, and in Afghanistan in 1979. After eight years, the Soviet Union withdrew from Afghanistan, and Afghanistan became a symbol of the failure of Moscow's policy. Soviet communists not only failed to maintain the communist regime in Afghanistan - the neighboring country has already lost support to its politics at home due to the war.

According to Prof. Arne Westard, in the Cold War period, there were never two superpowers - one was much superior (USA) from the other, although its power was never boundless. The United States simply had more than everything: power, development, ideas and wisdom ... defeated its enemies, Germany, Japan, the Soviet Union, dictating the conditions of democratic revolutions that transformed their policies and societies. She inspired fundamental changes in European allies, helping the process of transnational integration directed towards the creation of the European Union. It established the Third World, its need for raw materials and, above all, its vision of development.[11]

From the perspective of the Third World, the results of US interventions are truly devastating. Instead of being a force good - which, undoubtedly, and intended to be - US invasions have devastated many societies and made them much more susceptible to further disasters. For now, the combination of stable development and stable democracies, which the United States allegedly desires, is striking in only two semi-states (in South Korea and Taiwan), but it has been

[9] In Grenada, Americans intervened on the basis of the Organization of the Caribbean countries, but with the same objective as in the Dominican Republic 18 years ago.
[10] The Panama Invasion was made to replace Manuel Antonio Noriega, an American man in the zone. He was charged with drug trafficking, removed from power, and arrested.
[11] A. Vestad, Ibid., p. 536.

absent in thirty other states in which the United States has intervened, directly or indirectly, since 1945. Human tragedies - among allies and opponents - behind the results are incalculable.[12]

Military interventions after the Cold War

In relation to the period until the Second World War, the number of military interventions in the Cold War period increased significantly, so this growth would be even more intense in the years of US domination after the Cold War. Table 2 shows military interventions from the end of the Cold War (1989) to the present day.

Table 2—Overview of US military interventions in the period from 1989 to 2011[13]

The country against which interventions have been taken	The carrier of intervention	Year of performance
Panama	USA	1989.
Iraq	USA, UK, France	1991.
Somalia	USA	1992.
Iraq	USA	1993.
Haiti	USA	1994.
Iraq	USA	1996.
Somalia	USA	1998.
Afghanistan	USA	1998.
Iraq	USA, UK	1998.
Iraq	USA, UK	1999.
SR Jugoslavia	NATO (USA)	1999.

[12] Ibid, p.537.
[13] Sources: M. Simic "Contemporary International Relations", Military Case No.4-5 / 91, 3/95; B. Forca, "Force in International Relations", Army of 19 March 1998; S. Radisic, "Iraqi crisis", Army of March 26, 1988; Military Balance 2005/2006. in: S. Stojanović, Ibid, p. 197.

Historical Context of Military Interventionism

Afghanistan	USA	2001.
Iraq	USA, UK	2003.
Georgia	Russia	2008.
Libia	NATO (UK, France, USA)	2011.

The end of the Cold War marked the end of the balance in terms of the world power that ruled between the two military blocs. The United States as the leading force of the Western bloc has emerged as the absolute winner and the only real superpower.

The US's superiority and its leadership position in international relations after the end of the Cold War is indicated by most American theorists of international relations, emphasizing the necessity and inevitability of the "American global leadership" as a condition that the world does not sink into disarray and chaos.[14] "The United States after the Cold War were the country that had the greatest power to cause global disorders. More than any other country, the United States had the power and responsibility to encourage and maintain policies and institutions. US military forces maintained security in Europe, but also military stability in eastern Asia and served as a guarantor that nuclear nations would have access to the Persian Gulf oil. The United States also behaved as the chief of police on the watchdog against the development of nuclear weapons in countries that will abuse it."[15]

The post-Cold War period marked two types of military interventions: humanitarian and preventive. Examples of humanitarian military interventions include those carried out in Haiti 1994, Republika Srpska 1995, Somalia 1998, and FRY in 1999. After September 11, 2001, the day when the greatest terrorist act in the history of humanity was committed, the United States took a military intervention against

---

[14] D. Simic, Order of the world, 362, in S. Stojnović, Isto, p. 57
[15] M. Mandelbaum, Ideas conquered by the world, p. 15

Afghanistan in 2001 and a preventive intervention against Iraq in 2003, and on the basis of a UN resolution in 2010, they participated in the NATO mission against dictatorial regime in Libya.

In the post-Cold War period, Russia was burdened with its internal problems, especially in the first decade. However, it did not give up the use of force in international relations, especially when it considers that its vital interests are endangered. The Caspian Basin is a region of special importance for Russia. That is why military intervention on Georgia was undertaken in order to make the West aware that the spread of their influence has a limit.

The historical analysis of military interventions carried out from 1815 to the present indicates that the great powers have never denied the use of force as a way of solving problems in international relations in order to protect their interests and impose their will on the disobedient. The efforts of international organizations to ensure that the military's large-scale military intervention was under control was largely unsuccessful. If we conduct an analysis of the number of interventions, the USA were, however, the bearers of the greatest number of interventions, from 1815 to the present, in relation to all other countries, even during the Cold War, when the apparent balance of power prevailed.

Conclusion

An analysis of the historical context of military interventions from the Westphalian Agreement to the present clearly indicates that the use of force in international relations has always been present. All military interventions, starting from the first military intervention of the Holy Alliance in 1815 to the last of the 21st century, undertaken by NATO and the United States with their Western allies and Russia, confirm the continuity of the application of military force in international relations as a means of imposing will and protecting their interests.[16] According to the number of military interventions,

---

[16] Milenko Dželetović, Hatidža Beriša: Holders of power in international relations as actors of military interventionism, Culture of politics, No. 35, Belgrade, 2018.

Historical Context of Military Interventionism

it can be concluded that military interventionism had its own continuous growth, which was particularly intense in the post-Cold War period.

The global security system, based on the UN Charter, is very slow and outdated and is not able to fully respond to any new security risks that arose as a result of global changes in the modern world. On the other hand, the most powerful force in the modern world, the United States, in the post-Cold War period has often ignored the low global security guaranteed by the UN Charter by promoting unilateral action by military interventionism without the consent of the UN Security Council or despite its opposition. If the most powerful force of the world at work shows that this system does not work, then it clearly indicates that it is time to reform it and to find ways, means, methods and institutional forms that will empower the system to innovate and revitalize.

References

1. Maldembaun, Michael. *Ideas that have conquered the world*. Belgrade: Filip Visnjic, 2004.
2. Maldembaun, Michael. *Should the world be gay*. Belgrade: Filip Višnjić, 2006.
3. Kovač, Mitar and Forca, Božidar. *History of war skills. Period 1920 - 2000*. Belgrade: Vojnoizdavački zavod, 2000.
4. Milenko Dželetović, Hatidža Beriša: *Holders of power in international relations as actors of military interventionism, Culture of politics*, No. 35, Belgrade, 2018
5. Stojanovic, Radoslav. *Power and power in international relations*. Belgrade: NIRO "Randiciska štampa", Editorial Board, 1982.
6. Stojanovic, Stanislav. *Globalization and security perspectives of the world*. Belgrade: Directorate for Publishing and Library-Information Services, 2009.
7. Simić, Dragan. *Security Security: Contemporary Security Access*, Belgrade, FRY Official Gazette and Faculty of Political Science, 2002.

THE FUTURE OF GLOBALIZATION: HELP OR HURT THE WORLD'S POOR[1]

Parvis Hanson

Overview

Globalization pro and cons have been focusing over the past years on the concerns about poverty and inequality of discussion in a way that few other topics, except for international terrorism or global warming, have. Most people have a strong opinion on globalization, and most of them express an interest in the well-being of the world's poor. The financial press and influential international officials confidently assert that global free markets expand the horizons for the poor, whereas activist-protesters hold the opposite belief with equal intensity. Yet the strength of people's conviction is often in inverse proportion to the amount of robust factual evidence they have.

As is common in contentious public debates, different people mean different things by the same word. Some interpret globalization to mean the global reach of communications technology and capital movements, some think of the outsourcing by domestic companies in rich countries, and others see globalization as a byword for corporate capitalism or American cultural and economic hegemony. So it is best to be clear at the outset of this article that I shall primarily refer to economic globalization—the expansion of foreign trade and investment. How does this process affect the wages, incomes and access to resources for the poorest people in the world? This question is one of the most important in social science today.

For a quarter century after World War II, most developing countries in Africa, Asia and Latin America insulated their economies from the rest of the world. Since then, though, most have opened their markets. For instance, between1980

---

[1] First published in E-Journal, *Global Processes* Vol. 1/2018 p. 313. Published with consent of GPJ.

and 2017, trade in goods and services expanded from 23 to 72 percent of gross domestic product (GDP) in China and from 19 to 59 percent in India.

Such changes have caused many hardships for the poor in developing countries but have also created opportunities that some nations utilize, and others do not, largely depending on their domestic political and economic institutions. (The same is true for low-wage workers in the U.S., although the effects of globalization on rich countries are beyond the scope of this article.)

The net outcome is often quite complex and almost always context dependent belying the glib pronouncements for or against globalization made in the opposing camps. Understanding the complexities is essential to taking effective action.

Free Trade Case

The case for free trade rests on the age-old principle of comparative advantage, the idea that countries are better off when they export the things they are best at producing, and import the rest. Most mainstream economists accept the principle, but even they have serious differences of opinion on the balance of potential benefits and actual costs from trade and on the importance of social protection for the poor. Free traders believe that the rising tide of international specialization and investment lifts all boats. Others point out that many poor people lack the capacity to adjust, retool and relocate with changing market conditions. These scholars argue that the benefits of specialization materialize in the long run, over which people and resources are assumed to be fully mobile, whereas the adjustments can cause pain in the short run.

The debate among economists is a paragon of civility compared with the one taking place in the streets. Antiglobalizers' central claim is that globalization is making the rich, richer and the poor, poorer; proglobalizers assert that it actually helps the poor. But if one looks at the factual evidence, the matter is rather more complicated. On the basis of household survey data collected by different agencies, the World Bank estimates the fraction of the population in developing countries that falls below the 1-a-day poverty line (at 1993 prices) an admittedly crude but internationally comparable level. By this measure, extreme poverty is declining.

The trend is particularly pronounced in East, South and Southeast Asia. Poverty has declined sharply in China, India and Indonesia - countries that have long been characterized by massive rural poverty and that together account for about half the total population of developing countries. Between 1981 and 2016 the percentage of rural people living on less than 1 a day decreased from 79 to 15 percent in China, 63 to 34 percent in India, and 55 to 6 percent in Indonesia.

But although the poorest are not, on the whole, getting poorer, no one has yet convincingly demonstrated that improvements in their condition are mainly the result of globalization. In China the poverty trend could instead be attributed to internal factors such as the expansion of infrastructure, the massive 1978 land reforms (in which the Mao-era communes were disbanded), changes in grain procurement prices, and the relaxation of restrictions on rural-to-urban migration. In fact, a substantial part of the decline in poverty had already happened by the mid-1980s, before the big strides in foreign trade or investment. Of the more than 600 million Chinese lifted above the international poverty line between 1981 and 2015, three fourths got there by 1987.

Similarly, rural poverty reduction in India may be attributable to the spread of the Green Revolution in agriculture, government antipoverty programs and social movements - not the trade liberalization of the 1990s.

In Indonesia the Green Revolution, macroeconomic policies, stabilization of rice prices and massive investment in rural infrastructure played a substantial role in the large reduction of rural poverty. Of course, globalization, by expanding employment in labor-intensive manufacturing, has helped to pull many Chinese and Indonesians out of poverty since the mid-1980s (though not yet as much in India, for various domestic institutional and policy reasons). But it is only one factor among many accounting for the economic advances of the past 25 years.

Those who are dubious of the benefits of globalization point out that poverty have remained stubbornly high in sub-

Law, Ethics & Society

Saharan Africa. Between 1981 and 2016 the fraction of Africans living below the international poverty line increased from 42 to 52 percent. But this deterioration appears to have less to do with globalization than with unstable or failed political regimes. If anything, such instability reduced their extent of globalization, as it scared off many foreign investors and traders. Volatile politics amplifies longer-term factors such as geographic isolation, disease, overdependence on a small number of export products, and the slow spread of the Green Revolution.

Global Market competition in general rewards people with initiative, skills, information and entrepreneurship in all countries. Poor people everywhere are handicapped by their lack of access to capital and opportunities to learn new skills. Workers in some developing countries - say, Mexico - are losing their jobs in labor-intensive manufacturing to their counterparts in Asia. At the same time, foreign investment has also brought new jobs. Overall, the effect appears to be a net improvement. In Mexico, low wage poverty is declining in the regions that are more involved in the international economy than others—even controlling for the fact that skilled and enterprising people migrate to those regions, improving incomes there independently of what globalization accomplishes. A recent study by the University of California, San Diego, which took into account only people born in a particular region (thus leaving out migrants), found that during the 1990s average incomes in the Mexican states most affected by globalization increased 10 percent more than those least affected.

In poor Asian economies, such as Bangladesh, Vietnam and Cambodia, large numbers of women now have work in garment export factories. Their wages are low by world standards but much higher than they would earn in alternative occupations. Advocates who worry about exploitative sweatshops have to appreciate the relative improvement in these women's conditions and status. An Oxfam report quoted Rahana Chaudhuri, a 23-year-old mother working in the garment industry in Bangladesh:

This job is hard—and we are not treated fairly. The managers do not respect us women. But life is much harder for those working outside. Back in my village, I would have less money. Outside of the factories, people selling things in the street or carrying bricks on building sites earn less than we do. There are few other options. Of course, I want better conditions. But for me this job means that my children will have enough to eat and that their lives can improve.

In 2015 Naila Kabeer of the University of Sussex in England and Simeen Mahmud of the Bangladesh Institute of Development Studies did a survey of 2,380 women workers in Dhaka. They discovered that the average monthly income of workers in garment-export factories was 92 percent above that of other wage workers living in the same slum neighborhoods.

Another indication of this relative improvement can be gauged by what happens when such opportunities disappear. In 2014, anticipating a more restrictive U.S. ban on imports of products made using child labor, the garment industry in Bangladesh dismissed an estimated 30,000 children. UNICEF and local aid groups investigated what happened to them. About 10,000 children went back to school, but the rest ended up in much inferior occupations, including stone breaking and child prostitution. That does not excuse the appalling working conditions in the sweatshops, let alone the cases of forced or unsafe labor, but advocates must recognize the severely limited existing opportunities for the poor and the possible unintended consequences of fair trade policies.

The Local Roots of Poverty

Integration into the international economy brings not only opportunities but also problems. Even when new jobs are better than the old ones, the transition can be wrenching. Most poor countries provide very little effective social protection to help people who have lost their jobs and not yet found new ones. Moreover, vast numbers of the poor work on their own small farms or for household enterprises. The major constraints they usually face are domestic, such as lack of access to credit, poor infrastructure, venal government officials and insecure land rights. Weak states, unaccountable regimes, lopsided wealth distribution, and inept or corrupt politicians and bureaucrats often combine to block out the opportunities for the poor. Opening markets without relieving these domestic constraints forces people to compete with one hand tied behind their back. The result can be deepened poverty.

Conversely, opening the economy to trade and long-term capital flows need not make the poor worse off if appropriate domestic policies and institutions are in place - particularly to help shift production to more marketable goods and help workers enter new jobs.

Contrasting case studies of countries make this quite apparent. Although the island economies of Mauritius and Jamaica had similar per capita incomes in the early 1980s, their economic performance since then has diverged dramatically, with the former having better participatory institutions and rule of law and the latter mired in crime and violence.

South Korea and the Philippines had similar per capita incomes in the early 1960s, but the Philippines languished in terms of political and economic institutions (especially because power and wealth were concentrated in a few hands), so it remains a developing country, while South Korea has joined the ranks of the developed. Botswana and Angola are two diamond-exporting countries in southern Africa, the former democratic and fast-growing, the latter ravaged by civil war and plunder.

The experiences of these and other countries demonstrate that antipoverty programs need not be blocked by the forces of globalization. There is no race to the bottom in which countries must abandon social programs to keep up economically; in fact, social and economic goals can be mutually supportive. Land reform, expansion of credit and services for small producers, retraining and income support for displaced workers, public-works programs for the unemployed, and provision of basic education and health can enhance the productivity of workers and farmers and thereby contribute to a country's global competitiveness. Such programs may require a rethinking of budget priorities in those nations and a more accountable political and administrative framework, but the obstacles are largely domestic. Conversely, closing the economy to international trade does not reduce the power of the relevant vested interests: landlords, politicians and bureaucrats, and the rich who enjoy government subsidies.

The Future of Globalization

Thus, globalization is not the main cause of developing countries' problems, contrary to the claim of critics of globalization - just as globalization is often not the main solution to these problems, contrary to the claim of overenthusiastic free traders.

What about the environment? Many conservationists argue that international integration encourages the over-exploitation of fragile natural resources, such as forests and fisheries, damaging the livelihoods of the poor. A common charge against transnational companies is that they flock to poor countries with lax environmental standards. Anecdotes abound, but researchers have done very few statistical studies. One of the few, published in 2003 by World Bank and University of California, Berkeley, considered Mexico, Morocco, Venezuela and Ivory Coast. It found very little evidence that companies chose to invest in these countries to shirk pollution-abatement costs in rich countries; the single most important factor in determining the amount of investment was the size of the local market. Within a given industry, foreign plants tended to pollute less than their local peers.

Like persistent poverty, lax environmental standards are ultimately a domestic policy or institutional failure. A lack of well-defined or well-enforced property rights or regulation of common property resources often leads to their overuse.

Responding to pressure from powerful political lobbies, governments have deliberately kept down the prices of precious environmental resources: irrigation water in India, energy in Russia, timber concessions in Indonesia and the Philippines. The result, unsurprisingly, is resource depletion. To be sure, if a country opens its markets without dealing with these distortions, it can worsen the environmental problems.

When Talk Gives Way to Action

Fortunately, the two sides of the globalization debate are - slowly - developing some measure of agreement. In many areas, advocates in both camps see the potential for coordination among transnational companies, multilateral organizations, developing country governments and local aid groups on programs to help the poor. Going beyond the contentious debates and building on the areas of emerging consensus and cooperation, international partnerships may be able to make a dent in the poverty that continues to oppress the lives of billions of people in the world. Here are some measures under discussion.

Capital controls. The flow of international investment consists both of long term capital (such as equipment) and of speculative short-term capital (such as shares, bonds and currency). The latter, shifted at the click of a mouse, can stampede around the globe in herd like movements, causing massive damage to fragile economies. The Asian financial crisis of 1997 was an example. Following speculators' run on the Thai currency, the baht, the poverty rate in rural Thailand jumped 50 percent in just one year. In Indonesia, a mass withdrawal of short-term capital caused real wages in manufacturing to drop 44 percent. Many economists (including those who otherwise support free trade) now see a need for some form of control over short-term capital flows, particularly if domestic financial institutions and banking standards are weak. It is widely believed that China, India and Malaysia escaped the brunt of the Asian financial crisis because of their stringent controls on capital flight. Economists still disagree, though, on what form such control should take and what effect it has on the cost of capital.

Reduced protectionism. The major hurdle many poor countries face is not too much globalization but too little. It is hard for the poor of the world to climb out of poverty when rich countries (as well as the poor ones themselves) restrict imports and subsidize their own farmers and manufacturers. The annual loss to developing countries as a group from agricultural tariffs and subsidies in rich countries is estimated to be 45 billion; their annual loss from trade barriers on textile and clothing is estimated to be 24 billion. The toll exceeds rich countries' foreign aid to poor countries. Of course, the loss is not equally distributed among poor countries. Some would benefit more than others if these import restrictions and subsidies were lifted.

The Future of Globalization

Trust-busting. Small exporters in poor nations often lack the marketing networks and brand names to make inroads into rich-country markets. Although transnational retail companies can help them, the margins and fees they charge are often very high. Restrictive business practices by these international middlemen are difficult to prove, but a great deal of circumstantial evidence exists. The international coffee market, for example, is dominated by four companies. In the early 1990s the coffee earnings of exporting countries were about 12 billion, and retail sales were 30 billion. By 2015 retail sales had more than tripled, yet coffee-producing countries received about half their earnings of a decade earlier. The problem is not global markets but impeded access to those markets or depressed prices received by producers, as a result of the near-monopoly power enjoyed by a few retail firms. In certain industries, companies may actively collude to fix prices. Some economists have proposed an international antitrust investigation agency. Even if such an agency did not have much enforcement power, it could mobilize public opinion and strengthen the hands of antitrust agencies in developing countries.

In addition, internationally approved quality-certification programs can help poor-country products gain acceptance in global markets.

Social programs. Many economists argue that for trade to make a country better off, the government of that country may have to redistribute wealth and income to some extent, so that the winners from the policy of opening the economy share their gains with the losers. Of course, the phrase to some extent still leaves room for plenty of disagreement.

Nevertheless, certain programs stir fairly little controversy, such as assistance programs to help workers cope with job losses and get retrained and redeployed. Scholarships allowing poor parents to send their children to school have proved to be more effective at reducing child labor than banning imports of products.

Research. The Green Revolution played a major role in reducing poverty in Asia. New international private-public partnerships could help develop other products suitable for the poor (such as medicines, vaccines and crops). Under the current international patent regime, global pharmaceutical companies do not have much incentive to do costly research on diseases such as malaria and tuberculosis that kill millions of people in poor countries every year. But research collaborations are emerging among donor agencies, the World Health Organization, groups such as Doctors Without Borders and private foundations such as the Bill & Melinda Gates Foundation.

Immigration reform in rich countries. A program to permit larger numbers of unskilled workers into rich countries as guest workers would do more to reduce world poverty than other forms of international integration, such as trade liberalization, can. The current climate, however, is not very hospitable to this idea.

Simplistic antiglobalization slogans or sermons on the unqualified benefits of free trade do not serve the cause of alleviating world poverty. An appreciation of the complexity of the issues and an active interweaving of domestic and international policies would be decidedly more fruitful.

COMMON LAW AND CIVILIAN LEGAL CULTURES: FINDING A LANGUAGE OF LAW FOR THE GLOBAL AGE[1]

Joseph P. Garske

Law and Language

The project of globalization is often thought of in terms of technology, commerce, communication, and travel, but it has an important legal aspect as well. In fact, all of the great advances in technology—the ability to transmit sound and image, the ability to transfer and store information, to trade and travel across great distance—take place within an atmosphere defined by law, and against standards of legal oversight and regulation. More than that, every one of the technical advances has emerged from a process of research, patent, copyright, finance, and incorporation. Each of these steps shaped their eventual use and impact on the world, and each of these steps was legal in nature.

Moreover, governing structures that are being assembled to tie all localities and peoples together into a single seamless unity around the world are constructed on foundations of law. Whether this involves the merging of nation-states, treaty agreements, international organizations, or multi-national corporations, all of these entities and initiatives are fundamentally legal creations. Their methods of oversight, governance, and regulation are done by instruments of law. Even those incidents of crime, terror, subterfuge, and warfare that may occur outside the boundary of legal constraint are defined as being prohibited and are investigated and suppressed by means of legal authority.[2]

However, in this proliferation of legal instruments and institutions there are many challenges concerning how a global regimen of law should be constructed. For one thing, many national governments are involved, each of which has its own legal system. There is continuous debate not only over

---

[1] First published in E-Journal, *Global Processes* Vol. 1/2018 p. 31. Published with the consent of GPJ.
[2] Slaughter, 2004, p. 166.

methods to solve immediate and practical problems, but there are also questions about how a global regimen should be framed, according to what standard, and decided by which body. It goes without saying that such questions and problems can become extremely divisive, because they can involve matters of national interest, or sometimes national survival. But even more than these practical problems, there are deep questions about what kind of legal regimen should be constructed, and for what ultimate purpose.

The central axis around which this discussion revolves is between the two great legal systems that developed out of the Western tradition. These are usually referred to as the Continental, or Civil law on one side, and the English Common law, or Anglophone law on the other. Outwardly these two legal traditions seem to have much in common; however, there are stark differences that divide them. Obviously, they both have courts presided over by judges. Lawyers or advocates represent clients and present arguments in both systems. A continuous production of legislation shapes the internal content of the work in both legal methods.[3]

But on a deeper, less obvious level, they have very different conceptions of what the law is, or should be. They employ very different methods in their work. They have markedly different views on what underlying purpose should guide the work of legislatures and courts. As traditions of law with these important differences, they also take part in the project of globalization in different ways. Moreover, when being employed to assemble what amounts to the legal basis for a future world order, each has certain advantages in its approach just as each has certain disadvantages.

There are many ways to contrast approaches to a global regimen under these two legal traditions, Civilian and Anglophone. But there is perhaps no more useful way than to examine them from the perspective of language.

That is, the matter of using which language or languages to construct this enveloping mechanism of governance. In fact, the proliferation of English as a global language in the late twentieth century has a great deal to do with the legal

---

[3] Habermas, 2008, p. 115.

method coming to predominate within this new transnational realm of authority. The Anglophone legal approach also has a great deal to do with how and why a global regimen of governance is being constructed in a particular manner. Perhaps the key to understanding, within this context, the purely legal significance of language in both traditions, Continental and English, is to begin with a fundamental difference that separates them. Examining this difference can provide an important way to understand the importance of language in the project of globalization.[4]

Principle and Consensus

The two legal traditions were born, almost simultaneously, in the eleventh century, and they continued to develop in parallel isolation from one another into modern times. Although they have inevitably borrowed from and influenced each other, their limited contact over the centuries was infrequent and usually unfriendly. To understand their different approaches, it is useful to return to the medieval period to examine their nascent forms and to identify what was basic to the nature of each. Although their origins were very different and quite separate, their beginnings were actually both part of a great turning point in Western history usually called the Gregorian, or Cluniac Reform.

This seminal event began to unfold with the rise of Gregory VII as Bishop of Rome in 1073. Although generally viewed in religious terms, it also marked the onset of a legal transformation that would take place across all of Latin Christendom.

The beginning of the Civil tradition is usually marked from the founding of the University at Bologna in 1088. That institution was, from its inception, a place for the study and teaching of law. The great scholars Accursius and Irnerius attempted to adapt the rediscovered Roman Code of Justinian to a rather backward and agrarian medieval world. The result was a legal regime that combined the two elements of jurisprudence and theology; it was known as the jus commune, or common law of all Christendom. Following on these origins the study of law came to be integral to the scholarly tradition

---

[4] Benton, 2016.

of the Latin world. Over time the University at Bologna, and those universities that followed it, included in their course of study not only legal matter but also other disciplines. These included literary, philosophical and artistic elements that comprised the whole of a Western tradition extending back to the ancient Greeks and Romans. Law came to be considered one part of a great continuum of knowledge that comprised a single unified whole.[5]

At Bologna, the language of instruction had been, of course, Latin, the universal language of scholarship. But the students who gathered there were often from many parts of Christendom, each a native speaker of the vernacular from his own region. Most of these dialects were variations of the Latinic, French, Germanic, and Slavic linguistic groups. It was also quite natural for the students to house themselves together in lodges as a natio, or nation, in which they spoke their common language while living together at the university. When the students completed their training and returned to their home regions, the bond of fellowship made in each natio continued, and over generations came to be more formalized into a kind of permanent regional fraternity. A rudimentary national law began to develop in each separate locale of Europe. Yet, because the concepts and principles of the Roman law were abstract in nature, its methods could be adapted to each of the languages.

Thus, all the kingdoms, principalities, and cities of Christendom were still united under a broad panoply of legal principle that was expressed in Latin and was universally intelligible among them.[6]

Although this realm of law included England, there were other separate and peculiar aspects to legal development in that kingdom that did not exist on the Continent. Historians mark the origin of its unique tradition of English law from the time of the Norman Conquest, in 1066. In that catastrophic invasion, one of the turning points of history, tens of thousands of innocent victims died. Entire regions were depopulated as virtually all the arable land was seized by an

---

[5] Radding, 1998, p. 158.
[6] Bellomo, 1991, p. 55.

imposed nobility of foreign invaders. William II established a highly centralized form of rule over what came to be the servile population of an inescapable island domain. Norman rule was extremely harsh, often imposed under the auspices of an absentee king. Included in this new regime were three Royal Courts of Justice centered in London. The main function of these courts was to resolve disputes between the nobility over questions of possession and title to land. Land was extremely important, because during the medieval period it was virtually the only form of wealth and the main source of revenue for the king.[7]

Originally, the three Royal Courts were presided over by judges who had been trained at Bologna. But, following a dispute in 1166, King Henry II banished the learned jurists and took control of legal matters himself. Attached to the courts was a retinue of recorders, messengers, servants, scribes, and guards—functionaries who, in the practice of the time, had organized themselves into guilds of trade. In place of the jurists, the king granted a monopoly to the guildsmen, who would thereafter administer legal affairs. The arrangement worked well for the king, because the courts now worked at no expense to him. Instead, the guildsmen were self-supporting from the fees and gratuities they extracted from the litigants, and the royal treasury benefitted from a continuous flow of fines, bails, and forfeitures.[8]

From that time forward, the guildsmen operated their courts as a commerce in litigation. Like all such fraternities of trade, theirs was an organic fellowship based on oath of membership and an enforced discipline. Being only semiliterate during an age when most persons could not read and books were scarce and precious, they developed their own peculiar terminology that eventually became secreted among themselves as the basis of their trade. They employed only a few inscribed writs and forms inherited from the learned jurists. As a collegial body, they operated on the basis of internal consensus, their method of applying those writs and forms developed by increments over generations to match ever-

[7] Lesaffer, 2010, p. 207.
[8] Potter, 2015.

Law, Ethics & Society

changing circumstance. Because their internal procedures worked mostly by the fluid means of argumentation, continuous adjustments in scope and practice were not difficult to make.[9]

The method and learning of the guildsmen had almost nothing to do with legal scholars or the university, including Oxford and Cambridge. Within the workings of English Common law, the judge, like the king in Norman Kingship, acted as an oracle of law; his pronouncement was quite literally law, because he had spoken it and could enforce it. The judge derived his coercive power from the monarchy, but he received his authority as judge from the fellowship of trade in which he was embedded and in which he was presiding authority.

To him, the Civilian professor of law, was part of an alien community, its scholars, the central figure in a Romanist law, were viewed as dangerous rivals. From the twelfth century onward university Doctors of Law and their philosophical teachings were shunned as anathema by the Royal Court guildsmen.

The Modern Age

A profound change began to overcome the medieval world around the year 1500, a change made possible by a dramatic advance in technology. Although many engineering and scientific advances came during that period, none were more important in their effects than what came to be called the Three Great Inventions: maritime compass, gunpowder weapons, and the printing press. Their impact was both immediate and profound. The compass brought improved navigation, an increase of foreign trade, and the rise of fabulously wealthy cities. The new weapons brought mass armies and a kind of total war that had never been seen before. The printing press brought an ease of publication and widespread literacy. Moreover, with the innovation of moveable type, books could easily be published, not merely in Latin, but also in the vernacular languages spoken in the various parts of Christendom.[10]

---

[9] Baker, 2002, p. 30.
[10] Misa, 2011, p. 19.

Common Law & Civilian Legal Cultures

There were many other factors giving rise to what became a dramatic turning point, but two were especially important. On one side was the increasing influence of the newly ascendant merchant townsmen, a class that was impatient under rule by the old landed nobility. They also resented the strict regulation of commercial affairs under provisions of the jus commune. The second factor, and allied with the merchant class, was an increasingly powerful stratum of judges and advocates in each region. They resisted close oversight by the Universal Church, which at that time, in its combined religious and secular aspects, represented the single great unifying body of authority in the Latin world. The Church, after all, was not only a religious institution, it was equally, a legal one. Its continuing predominance through the centuries was not only sustained by its doctrinal teachings, but also had much to do with the acumen of its judicial bishops and the inventiveness of its canon lawyers.[11]

The result of these converging factors, old and new, ecclesiastical and secular, manorial and mercantile, was a period of civil and religious upheaval that engulfed Europe and England throughout the sixteenth and seventeenth centuries. It would finally resolve itself only after an unprecedented catastrophe of bloodshed and destruction. Out of an accommodation between the old nobility and the merchant townsmen, the old Church and the national religions, Christendom was broken into a pattern of nation-states, each with its own language, its own religious teachings, and its own law. It would not be an exaggeration to say that the Three Great Inventions had been the catalyst that made these changes, not only possible, but almost inevitable.

From a legal perspective, this was especially true in the case of the printing press. Moveable type had made printing in the various languages possible. With only a change in the order of characters, books could now be published in any language. They could be produced inexpensively, distributed widely, and literacy became common. With a code of law, a Bible, and a reading public in each national language, a world of nation-states became practical. Moreover, because the

---

[11] Bellomo 1991, p. 65.

Law, Ethics & Society

Civil law was based on abstract principles, that law could be adapted to the use of each of those polities. The triumph of the nation-state, symbolized by the Peace of Westphalia in 1648, was based on the principle of sovereign nationality, and would be the crowning achievement of the Civil law tradition.[12]

In England, the period of chaos and bloodshed which occurred during the sixteenth and seventeenth centuries resolved itself somewhat differently. But events there were also shaped by the confluence of a rising merchant class and the impact of the great technical innovations. One most critical change was that the Royal Court lawyers, under the great jurist Edward Coke, worked to restate their law into standard English, and began to adjust its methods so they could now litigate matters of monetary as well as landed interests. Once again, in this new phase of development, the Royal Courts would establish themselves at the crucial juncture where knowledge of the law coincided with the power of wealth. Although their importance within the monarchy had already increased over the centuries, their alliance with the merchant class gave them infinitely more autonomy. Instead of being merely a kind of bureau within the monarchy, serving at the pleasure of the king, they had now come to dominate both the Criminal Courts and Parliament as well. Eventually, combined with a newly empowered monetary class, they were actually able to overthrow the Monarchy itself.[13]

In its place, they established a theocratic Puritan Commonwealth in England. But after its failure and a brief restoration of the old monarchy, real and permanent change came in 1689 with the Glorious Revolution. It was the English counterpart to that which had occurred on the Continent at Westphalia in 1648. England now had a Parliamentary Monarchy which was founded on three elements. First was a new king invited from Holland, William III. Along with that was a reconstituted House of Lords, no longer comprised of men-atarms, but instead, men who combined enormous land holdings with monetary wealth. Finally, the House of Commons was reconstituted in such a way that the guild lawyers were

---

[12] Bellomo 1991, p. 108.
[13] Lesaffer, 2010, p. 336.

integral to the foundation of government itself. With the infu-sion of Dutch financial and naval resources, London would soon become the capital city of a vast imperial system.

The new Constitution of 1689—famously unwritten—was organic in its makeup and operation. Unlike the Civilian nation-state, the English method of rule was inexplicit in its construction and amorphous in its procedure, unconstrained by rigid principle or doctrine. Its departments and functions were highly personal in nature, not clearly defined as institu-tions. The entire hierarchy of rule—from the hereditary and ennobled at the top, and the professed and fraternal in the middle, to the great mass of individuated subjects at the bot-tom—moved by small increments to match changing conditions domestically and around the world. Its malleable technique, still proudly insular, was even able to absorb ele-ments of both Civil law and the Law Merchant from Europe. But the unifying element holding the entire edifice together, including its heredity peerage, and its professed fellowship of law, was its mono-phone reliance on the English language. That language, highly cultivated and effectual in its use, be-came the primary, and illocutionary, instrument of rule.

Geopolitics and Crisis

For more than eight hundred years, the two traditions of law, Anglophone and Civilian, operated and developed in relative isolation from one another-that is, until a second technological revolution brought dramatic change during the nineteenth century. Many mechanical and scientific advances appeared at that time, but they can be symbolized by three: the steam-ship, railroad, and telegraph. Their impact was not as profound as those of the fifteenth century; but they were equally important in that they had the effect of spreading the Western modes of commerce and governance to all parts of the world. With new abilities of trade and transport, conquest and control, a new form of modern empire began to arise. England, which had become the undisputed arbiter of world order, now had competitors from among the Continental na-tions. Various countries had moved quickly to acquire or annex any remaining unclaimed territory around the world.

Among them were Italy, Belgium, Russia, and especially the recently unified Germany.[14]

The world came to be defined in terms of geopolitics and now existed under threat of a possible worldwide war. Not only were the Continental nations able to employ the new means of communication, commerce, and warfare, they also had one important advantage over the British. Until that time, Britain and its Empire comprised a rather haphazard collection—a Mother Country and an assortment of colonies, outposts, and dependencies. Administered by treaty, client kingship, and military compulsion, it was not really an empire in the sense of a uniformly governed realm. One reason for this deficiency was that Britain had no adequate system of law for such organization. The old Common law was an anachronism, quaint and often crude in its application, suited only for the topography and people of the island kingdom where it had originated. This legal weakness in the imperial structure had shown itself most dramatically with the loss of the American Colonies, beginning in 1776. But, during the nineteenth century, that weakness had an even greater potential importance: it might now imperil the very existence of the Empire itself.[15]

By contrast, the Continental Empires were able to not only administer from afar, they were able to explicate and adapt their method of law to various populations in distant regions, and in the local language. As this competition of empires grew more alarming, Britain sought a legal answer to the geopolitical problem. Ironically, it did so in Germany which had become pre-eminent and widely emulated for its legal studies—even in America. English jurists, including John Austin and Henry Maine were among the first who travelled to the University of Berlin, which had become famous around the world for the study of law. They and others launched a program within England to surpass the old forms and writs of guild law by creating entirely new legal instruments—especially of contract and incorporation.[16]

---

[14] Lesaffer, 2010, p. 431.
[15] Karsten, 2002.
[16] Rumble, 1985.

However, they did not adopt the principles and concepts that guided the jurisprudence of the Continent, not precisely. Nor did they adopt an enveloping external framework of universal ideals and assumptions by which English law could be guided, in the manner of Civil law practice. Instead, they inverted the Germanic approach, constructing principles and concepts to be employed as internal instruments of legal rule.

English law, once known as a law without books, came to be developed as a complex science, with the law library as a central feature. By adapting, through inversion, the Continental methods of complex legal reasoning, a medieval fellowship of law was able to engage the modern imperial world in a way that came to be called Abstractionism, or Formalism—while still retaining its fundamental basis as a fellowship of trade. To these legal methods were added a geopolitical strategy as well. Britain, quite naturally, sought to win back the United States as a permanent ally, to balance against both its potential European rivals and against Russia.

This new Atlantic Alliance would be based on historicism, racialism, commercialism, intellectualism, and especially legalism. American law, which in the nineteenth century had become highly influenced by German scholarship, began late in that century to re-align itself with the Anglo-Saxon tradition.

A Great World War effectively ended German legal influence in America and around the world. Within a generation the English-speaking peoples had come to be united as a predominant force in world affairs, with a Special Relationship between Britain and America. It was a relationship founded on the authority of law.[17]

A Technological Turn

One factor contributing to the scale, ferocity, and destructiveness of the second worldwide war in the mid-twentieth century was the advent of new types of communication technology, particularly radio and cinema. For the first time, using these devices, it was possible to mobilize entire national populations for purposes of production and warfare.

---

[17] Churchill, 1983.

Law, Ethics & Society

This was also an important factor in the nation-state reaching its highest level of consolidation during the early twentieth century. Political leaders in each country, each national enclave, each with its own language, were able to unify their people against foreign rivals. One result of this ability to create and orchestrate atmospheres of thought was a scene of unparalleled carnage, with the assembling of mass armies and the advent of Total War, with the people of one nation bitterly united against the people of an enemy nation.

One outcome in the aftermath of the second worldwide war was the ascent of the English-speaking alliance, with its military power at its peak and its industrial capacity almost unscathed. Having such advantages, it was not surprising that the Anglophone nations came to dominate trade and finance around the world.

One incidental aspect of this rise was the proliferation of English as an international language of commerce, of broadcast, and even diplomacy-especially among those of the affluent and educated classes on all continents. Moreover, those countries that had once been either colonies or possessions of the British Empire—including not only Britain and America, of course, but also Canada, Australia, New Zealand, and, on a jurisprudential level, Hong Kong, Singapore, and Israel—amounted to the skeletal basis of an alternative world system based in a fellowship of law and a common language.[18]

But the first half of the twentieth century and its great war was only a prelude to much more dramatic technological developments to come. The latter part of the century brought even more phenomenal devices, especially television and the computer. Initially, their effect on systems of government and methods of law seemed to be contradictory, both potentially strengthening and weakening. The computer was an unqualified positive for the multinational corporation, with its calculative and data storage capacities, and the ability to direct information and its uses. This made international finance and trade matters of instantaneous transaction, while it brought new potentials for corporate management over long

---

[18] Northrop, 2013, p. 75.

distance. However, although large business enterprises benefited, those same technical advances began to undermine the protective borders of each individual nation-state. For territorial governments they created difficulties of economic oversight, regulation, and taxation.

At the same time, television expanded the reach of commerce with an ability to create large audiences of viewers across each nation. Marketing campaigns could now reach entire populations. But television was also able to instantly broadcast graphic stories, especially from distant countries around the world, countries that had long existed almost beyond public awareness in the world centers of power. Unregulated journalistic influence contributed to discontent and upheaval, which sometimes erupted into demonstration and revolt, not merely in the third world, but in Europe, England, and America as well. However, once again, television and computer were merely the second wave of advance and would be followed by a third wave with the arrival of the twenty-first century. The new age of technology brought not only change; instead, it brought change as the basis of a way of life, and it did so around the entire globe.[19]

By the beginning of the twenty-first century, the new computer and communication networks had made it possible to penetrate any domicile on the face of the earth with a constant flow of electronically transmitted sound and image. Any amount of information could be transmitted from any one location on earth to any other. Capital, resources, and labor could be assembled, and military invasion carried out on any continent, regardless of distance or topography. Enormous networks of communication had come to encircle the earth, leaving a world of nation-states in disruption. Moreover, because of their strategic advantage, the English-speaking nations led in these developments as well. Now, English was not only an international language among a high stratum of finance and trade. It was also becoming a global language, spoken at least on a rudimentary level by nearly the entire rising generation in every region of the world.

---

[19] Misa, 2011.

Law, Ethics & Society

Universal or Transcendent

Both traditions of law, Anglophone and Civilian, are extremely important and both are extremely influential in the project of building a seamless atmosphere of oversight and governance across all lands and peoples. But they approach the task by different means, with different ultimate purposes in mind. These differences are basic to the nature of each, and can be traced in their nascent forms, back to the simultaneous beginning of both laws in the eleventh century. In that these traditions represent two different foundations upon which governance is based, they have different ways of ordering human life and shaping human thought. They approach the project of globalization in different ways.[20]

These differences between the two legal approaches to shaping a global order become apparent in the way each has certain advantages and each has certain disadvantages. In particular, their varying aptitudes can be understood in the way the Continental is universal in outlook and the Anglophone law is transcendent in its operation. Universality carries with it the implication that a law can apply equally in all regions, to all people of every rank and status, rich or poor, male or female. Its encompassing philosophical principles are thought to be everywhere valid as well as an assumed capacity of reason naturally inherent to all humans. It is not based on a premise of superiority and inferiority of persons, on a distinction between privilege and right, knowledge and ignorance, or ethics and norms.

In that sense, it produces a legal culture built as much from the ground upward as from the top downward. The workings of law and government must conform closely to its underlying principles, or the basic premise will be discredited. Such a view of human capacity also presupposes the importance of culture in the sense of cultivation of all persons in thought, word, and deed. It assumes that where persons are able to govern themselves, and conduct their own affairs—the Common Sense, or *Sensus Communis* of Kant—they will have less need to be ruled over by the coercive force of law; all of which will conduce to a happier and more prosperous

---

[20] Habermas, 2008, p. 115.

way of life. Because of these assumptions, the first concern of a Civilian legal culture in the modern secular age was that all persons within its realm were educated in its egalitarian premise, that they were unified on its principle of philosophical, ideological, or scientific understanding.

By contrast, the Anglophone tradition has from its inception been transcendent; it wields a collegial authority superior in its workings, above all persons and things. By this elevated independence, it administers the affairs of human thought and action—and does so impartially, by the application of concepts and doctrines. In fact, the English tradition operates on a strict division of knowledge between those who rule by the instruments of law, and those who are ruled over. In effect, jurists and practitioners of law occupy an entirely different realm of knowledge than does the public generally. That realm of legal knowledge and authority is assumed to operate beyond the reach of public understanding. In Anglophone tradition, the basis of stability does not rest with an assumed faculty of reason shared by both legal authorities and the public at large. Instead, the basis of stability rests with the unity and discipline that exists within the fellowship of law. A public attitude of inviolable sanctity toward judicial oversight is essential to its ordered and continuing rule. Thus, the first concern of Anglophone law is always to maintain the unquestioned authority of its institutions, with its unchallenged hierarchy of enforcement in place.[21]

Nonetheless, this transcendent law offers the public two great benefits: one is an unusual degree of freedom—even though it is freedom within particular limits. In other words, individual persons are provided great latitude to think and act any way they desire, as long as they do not exceed the boundaries set by judicial authority. The second marked advantage of the Anglophone tradition is that of flexibility and adaptability. Its authority is vested in a unified fellowship of jurists and practitioners, answerable to no outside authority. Unconstrained by strict principle, their methods and techniques can be readily adjusted by consensus to meet changing circumstance.

---

[21] Kennedy, 2016, p. 218.

Moreover, there is very little required in the sense of a complicated ideology or philosophy, topics that require laborious and expensive measures to instill among a global public. There is no urgent need for transcending beliefs or attitudes toward this type of legal rule extending across all regions and peoples. However, it is essential that those who rule speak the same language among themselves, as a basis of collegiality, and that those ruled over, at least on a rudimentary level, are able to understand the language in which that authority expresses itself. In other words, unlike the principled basis of Civil law, which must rely on the medium of thought, Anglophone law must rely on the medium of language.[22]

Language and Global Law

As the twenty-first century began and the seismic impact of technology spread across the earth, the two necessary linguistic elements of an Anglophone global law were also being completed. Those were, first of all, a transnational fellowship of legal transaction and adjudication that could wield a common legal authority around the world. Its members were united by commonalities of training, interest, purpose, and by a common language. Equally important, the second essential element of Anglophone legal rule was being added: an understanding of its language of authority by the global public. In fact, an entire rising generation around the world was coming to be conversant in English. But even the miracles of technology and the proliferation of a common language, still preserved the absolute division of knowledge, the always unbridgeable chasm separating those above from those below in an Anglophone legal realm. In fact, the combination of linguistic penetration and immersive dissemination had now made this division possible in a different way and on a global scale.[23]

In this new regimen, much of the transcendent ruling strata would operate as it had before. It would still work on the principle of face to face collegiality acting upon the fixed printed text. The unity of such an organic tradition had always

---

[22] Giddens, 1991.
[23] Misa, 2011.

lay in strong personal commitments to a strictly imposed ethos, along with a shared collective purpose—as well as the financial opportunity it represented. It had begun centuries before as a guild of trade, with induction to membership and investiture to office; it had grown into a bond of cohesion by close familiarity and mutuality. Its members were not precisely joined together by institutions, doctrines and principles, or religious beliefs—even though all of these may have been accoutrements of their legal rule. Instead, fundamentally, it was a fellowship joined by voice. That is, by the oath of membership, the argumentation of their procedures, the oracular pronouncements of their judges, and the constant deliberation by which they maintained a workable consensus among themselves.

For purposes of legal rule on a global scale, the many national publics of the world would be comprised of dispersed families and individuated persons. Communication among them would be formatted primarily through mediated channels. Their understanding of the world would not be according to a deeply instilled ideals as in the past; instead, they would inhabit a reality shaped by the continuous flow of electronically transmitted sound and image. Rather than principles formally instructed, they would be guided by the immersive ephemera of information. The level of culture and learning of the global public would be less important than their access to the electronic sources of information. By this immersive atmosphere of sound and image the global population would have a mediated understanding of the world adequate to the purposes of global governance. The internal consensus within the legal fellowship could be matched with an attitude of compliance among the global public over which its rule of law extended. Within such a regimen, however, it was necessary that the whole be done in a single language.

The great advantage of this combination of fellowship and technology was that it could be pragmatically adaptable to changing circumstance. Unlike the Civilian approach, it was not bound by impinging principle and inhibiting doctrine. Nor was it forced to undertake the prohibitively expensive task of educating an entire global population—through an array of innumerable languages—in complicated structures of

Law, Ethics & Society

knowledge. Instead, peoples of the world could remain individuated, separated by identities of culture, ethnicity, gender, and degree of wealth, but united by a common language of law. Its only real requirements were internal consensus within the fellowship and external compliance among the public. By this means, it may be able to provide, for the first time in human history, a stable and cohesive, overarching and seamless legal authority—an Anglophone Rule of Law in the age of globalization.[24]

References

Alston, William 2000: *Illocutionary Acts and Sentence Meaning*, Cornell University.

Austin, J.L. 1962: *How to Do Things with Words*, Oxford University.

Baker, J.H. 2002: *English Legal History*, Butterworths.

Bellomo, Manlio 1991: *The Common Legal Past of Europe 1000-1800*, CUA Press.

Benton, Lauren 2016: *Rage for Order: The British Empire and the origins of international law 1800-1850*, Harvard University Press.

Breyer, Stephen 2015: *The Court and the World: Americn law and the new global realities*, Knopf.

Churchill, Winston 1983: *History of the English-Speaking Peoples*, Greenwich House.

Giddens, Anthony 1991: *Modernity and Self-Identity*, Stanford University.

Habermas, Jurgen 2008: *The Divided West*, Polity Press.

Habermas, Jurgen 1981: *The Theory of Communicative Action: Reason and the rationalization of society*, Heinemann.

Habermas, Jurgen 1979: *Communication and the Evolution of Society*, Beacon Press.

Kallendorf, Craig 2002: *Humanist Educational Treatises*, Harvard University.

Kennedy, David 2016: *World of Struggle: How power, law, and expertise shape global political economy*, Princeton University.

---

[24] Breyer, 2015, p. 167.

Common Law & Civilian Legal Cultures

Kennedy, George 1999: *Classical Rhetoric: Christian and secular tradition*, North Carolina.

Karsten, Peter 2002: *Between Law and Custom: The British diaspora 1600-1900*, Cambridge University Press.

Lambropoulos, Vassilis 1993: *The Rise of Eurocentrism, Princeton University Lesaffer, European Legal History: A cultural and political perspective*, Cambridge University Press.

Luhmann, Niklas 2000: T*he Reality of Mass Media*, Stanford University.

Misa, Thomas 2011: *Leonardo to the Internet: Technology & culture from the Renaissance to the present*, Johns Hopkins University.

Northrop, David 2013: *How English Became the Global Language*, Palgrave.

Ong, Walter 2002: *Orality and Literacy*, Routledge.

Potter, Harry 2015: *Law, Liberty, and the Constitution: A brief history of the Common law*, Boydell Press.

Radding, Charles 1998: *The Origins of Medieval Jurisprudence*, Yale University.

Rumble, Wilfred 1985: *The Thought of John Austin: Jurisprudence, colonial reform, and the British Constitution*, Althone Press.

Searle, John 1969: *Speech Acts: An essay in the philosophy of language*, Cambridge University.

Slaughter, Anne-Marie 2004*: A New World Order*, Princeton University.

Wendt, Alexander 2007: *Social theory of International Politics*, Cambridge University.

THE *SOCIETAS CIVILITAS*, HATE SPEECH AND STATE IMPOSED RESTRICTIONS

Craig Paterson

Introduction

In my paper, I seek to discuss the desirability of laws re ulating the content and availability of what is commonly known as "hate speech" in the United States of America. The method of my approach will be to spell out the two main opposing argumentative positions concerning the imposition of content based restrictions on hate speech—the first I will call the "Absolutist position"[1] and the second I will call the "Criticalist position."[2] Obviously, in a paper of limited length, I will not be able to develop many subtleties or nuances in expounding these respective positions. They are best regarded as "ideal types" in the Weberian sense—constructs for the propose of setting into higher relief basic differences of approach. Having spelled out the main lines of debate on both sides, I then turn to the work of J. S. Mill, especially his seminal essay *On Liberty*, a source respected on both sides of the political and legal debate, as inspiration for a set of ideas that suggests something of a *via media* for approaching the question of tolerating or not tolerating hate inspired speech in civil society. Along Millsian inspired lines, I will argue for a more nuanced understanding of liberty that has both negative and positive dimensions, of "negative liberty" and of "positive liberty." The remainder of the paper will be tied to working out some of the implications of this *via media* between the respective demands of the Absolutists and the Criticalists. I argue that Absolutism is too insensitive and blunt in its inability to accommodate and respond towards the nature and significance of

---

[1] By "Absolutist," I do not mean to infer that no exceptions whatsoever are recognised concerning the First Amendment Free Speech clause. The phrase Absolutist is being used here for convenience. It should be read to mean "Near Absolutist."

[2] Used in this paper as a shorthand for Critical Race Theory/Critical Legal Studies.

certain "harms" that hate speech may engender in civil society. Its account of liberty is insufficiently ameliorated, I think, by the requirements of "positive liberty." On the other hand, I find Criticalists too ambitious in what they can expect, in the name of government action, to deal with all facets of hate speech. We do not, in the name of advancing equal respect for persons, seek to cure the disease but at the expense of generating other consequential evils that may become too constraining on other basic needs of civil society. Opening up our understanding of the conceptualization of liberty, I argue, is a positive step to take in looking at the current First Amendment debate.

What I Mean by Hate Speech

The topic of what the phrase "hate speech" actually refers to is problematic. Let me be openly clear about that.[3] Equally, I do not want this paper to turn into a textual analysis of the phrase "hate speech." Time not space will permit such an investigation. I need enough guidance only to propel the paper forward. There have been several ordinances and speech codes that have merged in the United States in recent years,[4] enough, I think, to generate a basis so that I can offer the following description of what I mean to encapsulate by the phrase hate speech in the context of this paper. Hate speech is not just the mere saying offensive words. It is more than hurling epithets or uttering profanity out of frustration. Hate speech is constituted by aggressive language that targets people with a harmful intent. By hate speech, then, I mean oral, verbal, or symbolic communication that intends to vilify individuals or groups on the basis of such characteristics as race or ethnicity, and can, I think, be broken down into two broad classes: (1) face-to-face vilification; (2) the creation of a hostile or intimidating (uncivil) environment.[5]

---

[3] See for example, Charles Fried, "The New First Amendment Jurisprudence: A Threat to Liberty?" 59 *University of Chicago Law Review* 225 (1992), 244-50.

[4] For example, *R.A.V. v. City of St. Paul*, 505 US (1992), 377; and *Corry v. Stanford*, no 740309, California Superior Court, Feb. 27, 1995, unpublished, but available on Westlaw.

[5] My approach here is heavily influenced by the approach taken by Thomas C. Grey, the architect of Stanford University's hate speech code in his "How

The *Societas Civilitas* & Hate Speech

The Absolutist Position

Much has been written in recent years on hate speech, focusing mainly on, whether or not, in the context of United States constitutional law, hate speech ought to be tolerated or prohibited. Many analysts, whether for toleration or restriction, believe that the problem of hate speech is, among other things, one of privileging or subordinating the principle of liberty, on the one hand, or the principle of equality, on the other.[6] The First Amendment is commonly regarded as being a liberty enhancing principle, most fully encapsulated in the emerging value of freedom of expression.[7] The Fourteenth Amendment is often seen, by virtue of its equal protection clause, as an equality enhancing principle.[8] It would, of course, be a horrible distortion to state that Absolutists only care about liberty and Criticalists only care about equality. Such understanding is suitable only for the school yard playground. But, I think, a more accurate analysis would be to suggest that Absolutist and Criticalist positions, when centred on the nature and scope of rights concerning free speech, whenever they perceive a clash between liberty and equality (when critical interests are at stake), seek to privilege or grant a "trump card" to one value over the other.[9]

Absolutists generally seek to privilege liberty centred free speech considerations from governmental regulation or

---

to Write a Speech Code without really Trying: Reflections on the Stanford experience," *University of California at Davis Law Review* 29 (1996), 917-23.

[6] See for example, Edward Cleary, *Beyond the Burning Cross* (New York: Random House, 1994), 172-90.

[7] *US Constitution, First Amendment*, "Congress shall make no law respecting an establishment of religion or prohibiting the free exercise thereof; or *abridging the freedom of speech*, or of the press; or of the right of the people peaceably to assemble, and to petition the Government for a redress of grievances." (My emphasis)

[8] *US Constitution, Fourteenth Amendment*, "No State shall make or enforce any law which shall abridge the privileges or immunities of citizens of the United States; nor shall any State deprive any person of life, liberty, or property, without due process of law; *nor deny to any person within its jurisdiction the equal protection of the laws*." (My emphasis).

[9] See for example, Thomas C. Grey, "Discriminatory Harassment and Free Speech," *Harvard Journal of Law and Public* Policy 14 (1991), 157-64; Edward J. Eberle, "Hate Speech, Offensive Speech, and Public Discourse in America," *Wake Forest Law Review* 29 (1994), 1135-48. The phrase "trump card" is borrowed from Ronald Dworkin's seminal text, *Taking Rights Seriously* (London: Duckworth, 1977).

censorship. They can be said to take a hard line with respect to content-based or viewpoint restrictions on the exercise of free speech rights whether oral, written, or symbolic.[10]

Both the ACLU and the ALA can be said to advocate for near Absolutist positions with respect to their collective understanding of the nature and scope of the First Amendment of the United States Constitution.[11] The First Amendment, the Absolutist claims, grants extensive blanket protection to all manner of speech, savoury or unsavoury. Except for speech used in the furtherance of crime, for example, of speech that presents a "clear and present danger" to the life or bodily integrity or another, few restraints on its rightful exercise are considered acceptable in a liberal democratic society. If university councils or school boards, for example, wish to censor racist slogans or graffiti vilifying students on the basis of colour, censoring speech cannot be thought of as an appropriate remedy to deal with this vexed situation.[12]

Absolutists maintain that the way speech functions in a free society is to permit those who are aggrieved or slighted to organise and counter the speech of their vilifiers through the effective exercise of speech on their own behalf. Offensive speech should be sidestepped by counter-speech or boycott. Both authorities and students, for example, are free to condemn the views of those they oppose. Crucially, however, they cannot be allowed to silence the content-based viewpoints of their opponents. Arguments based on equality of treatment and respect for persons are indeed worthy of cultivation in civil society, but, and this is a crucial but, only insofar

---

[10] See John D.H. Downing, "Hate speech and First Amendment absolutism discourses in the US," *Discourse & Society* 10 (1999), 175-189.

[11] See Office of Intellectual Freedom. *Intellectual Freedom Manual.* 6th ed. (Chicago: American Library Association, 2002), *passim.* On the ACLU's position see Samuel Walker, *In Defense of American Liberties: A History of the ACLU* (New York: Oxford University Press, 1990); Walker, *Hate Speech: The History of an American Controversy* (Lincoln: University of Nebraska Press, 1994), and official policy statements, for example, "Policy Statement: Free Speech and Bias on College Campuses," on their Web Site at www.aclu.org.

[12] David Cole, "Racist Speech Should be Protected by the Constitution," in *Hate Crimes*, P. A. Winters ed. (San Diego, CA: Greenhaven Press, 1996), 89-96; and Calvert, Clay and Robert D. Richards, "Free Speech and the Right to Offend: Old Wars, New Battles, Different Media," *Georgia State University Law Review* 18 (2002), 671-719.

as they do not limit the free speech rights of others as guaranteed by the First Amendment.[13] The right of "negative liberty" then trumps equality based considerations centred on controlling or framing the content of the public forum, whether in be a park, a university, or a library. To quote Justice Black, something of a revered figure in Absolutist circles,—"I read 'no law abridging' to mean no law abridging ..." means that no censorial gloss may be created around the free speech clause of the First Amendment.[14] Again, as stated by Justice Black, "the First Amendments unequivocal command that there shall be no abridgment of the rights of free speech ... shows the men who drafted the Bill of Rights did all the balancing that was to be done."[15]

This is not to say that free speech is entirely without a framework of exercise. There may be need for some content-neutral restrictions on the manner, timing, and circumstances in which free speech is exercised (for example, Justice Holmes' famous dictum concerning the right to shout fire in a crowded theatre),[16] but this cannot extend to the selection and evaluation, by government, of the worthiness or unworthiness of ideas and thoughts in themselves. Any censorship of speech based on content must therefore be viewed as unconstitutional, a free speech abridgment. Under this approach, therefore, the only real question is whether the action that is being scrutinised is truly "speech" (and therefore protected) or "conduct" (and therefore subject to some reasonable forms of governmental regulation, an example of the latter being the use of "fighting words.") Speech *qua* speech cannot be prohibited. Governments cannot seek to control messages on the basis of any content it finds pernicious, offensive, or hateful (*contra bona mores*). Hate speech is constitutionally protected speech and therefore cannot be repressed by means of censorship laws.[17]

---

[13] James Kelley, "Restricting Speech Does Not Fight Racism on Campuses," in *Hate Crimes*, 97-9.

[14] In *Smith v. California*, 361 US (1959), 147, 157.

[15] *Konigsberg v. State Bar of California*, 366 US (1961), 36, 61.

[16] *Schenck v. United States*, 249 US (1919), 47, 52.

[17] See Burton Caine, "The Trouble with Fighting Words: Chaplinsky v. New Hampshire is a Threat to First Amendment Values and Should be Overruled," *Marquette Law Review* 88 (2004), 441-533. See also, Nat Hentoff,

Law, Ethics & Society

Both the ACLU and the ALA believe that their position on hate speech is constitutionally very strong. They rely on arguments centred on the foundational value of negative liberty itself to underpin the lexical priority of free speech over other competing considerations that may otherwise call for content-based restrictions on speech.

Underlining the Absolutist understanding of the right of free speech are a number of core beliefs that serve to shore up fidelity to that value. They believe that the surest way to undermine the liberty of the individual in society is to transfer to the government the power to determine what ideas can and cannot be heard in public fora.[18]

Secondly, government censorship of ideas is usually regarded as the first step on the "slippery slope" to advancing the tyranny of the state over the individual. Governments may seize the opportunity of censorship to insulate themselves from public scrutiny or criticism, the very foundation of democratic society.[19]

Thirdly, they point to the importance of a "marketplace of ideas" to the creation of new and exciting trends in thought. As Justice Holmes noted, in terms paralleling the earlier thought of John Milton, "the ultimate good is better reached by free trade in ideas and ... the best test of truth is the power of thought to get itself accepted in the marketplace of ideas."[20]

Fourthly, the "chilling" consequences of censorship of content are such that it stifles creative thought in society. The ripple effects of censorship are enormous. No one can be confident that they possess the "royal road to truth." The

Free Speech for Me—But Not for Thee: How the American Left and Right Relentlessly Censor Each Other (New York: Harper Perennial, 1993).

[18] See, for example, Robert C. Post, "Racist Speech, Democracy, and the First Amendment," *William & Mary Law Review* 32 (1991), 267-325; David A.J. Richards, "Free Speech and Obscenity Law: Toward a Moral Theory of the First Amendment," *University of Pennsylvania Law Review* 123 (1974), 45-91.

[19] Eugene Volokh, "The Mechanisms of the Slippery Slope," *Harvard Law Review* 116 (2003), 1026-1136.

[20] *Abrams v.United States*, 250 US (1919), 616, 630. As Milton states in the Aeropagitica, as early as 1644, "And though all the windes of doctrin were let loose to play upon the earth, so Truth be in the field, we do injuriously by licencing and prohibiting to misdoubt her strength. Let her and Falshood grapple; who ever knew Truth put to the wors, in a free and open encounter."

spectrum of diversity of opinion in society must therefore be vigorously defended and supported.[21]

A combination of these arguments has been advocated for by the ACLU and the ALA in briefs and policy papers they have submitted to the Supreme Court over the years.[22]

Criticalist Position

Critical Race Theory emerged in the United States in the 1970's in response to a perceived lack of critical analysis in existing "liberal" dominated civil rights scholarship and was fuelled by frustration with the relatively slow progress of racial reform following the belief that United States was now a citadel for the protection and promotion of civil rights.[23]

The Criticalists started to ask: whose protection? whose civil rights? Critical Race Theory emerged as an intellectual and political movement that placed the whole notion of race at the centre of critical analysis. The Criticalist movement, in general, was underpinned by two very broad conceptual commitments. Firstly, as a critical intervention into the traditional rhetoric of civil rights scholarship, Criticalism sought to describe and expose the relationship between seemingly race neutral ideas, like "the rule of law," "merit" and "equal protection," and to examine them in the light of interrogating dominant power structures. Secondly, as a race-conscious form of assessing and analysing legal scholarship and policies, Criticalism sought to develop ways of analysing the relationship between law and racial power in order to call for a radical change in the way we understand and evaluate the functioning of law in civil society.[24]

---

[21] Richards, "Free Speech and Obscenity Law," 54-91. See also Rodney Smolla, *Free Speech in an Open Society* (New York: Vintage, 1993), 14-25.
[22] See earlier footnote 11.
[23] Richard Delgado and Jean Stefancic, *Critical Race Theory: An Introduction* (New York: New York University Press, 2001), 1-26. See also Dinesh D'Souza, *The End of Racism: Principles for a Multiracial Society* (New York: The Free Press, 1995).
[24] Katheryn K. Russell, "Critical Race Theory and Social Justice," in *Social Justice/Criminal Justice: The Maturation of Critical Theory in Law, Crime, and Deviance*, Bruce A. Arrigo, ed. (Belmont: Wadsworth, 1999), 176-88; H.L. Gates, "War of words: Critical Race Theory and the First Amendment." in *Speaking of Race, Speaking of Sex*, Gates *et al.* eds. (New York: New York University Press, 1994), 17-58.

Law, Ethics & Society

A seminal text in advancing the position of Criticalism is Mari Matsuda et al. *Words That Wound*, first published in 1993.[25] My understanding of the main thrust of the collection is that racism is an endemic fact of American life and that attempts to improve society, our peaceful and respectful coexistence with one another, cannot be realised until the structural and deeper aspects of this problem are faced up to and addressed. It is through the lens of marginalisation, domination, and suppression that Criticalists approach the assessment of the functioning of the law in society. Laws are not neutral. The are shaped by politics and can legitimise structures that may serve to shroud and conceal the true fabric of the reality of racism in contemporary America.[26]

If laws are shaped by power structures, laws are also the manifestations of ideology. Criticalists propose the examination of laws by looking to the interests and outcomes served by them. They are especially attuned to the impact of laws on outcomes of equality of opportunity and treatment. It is through this lens that Criticalists examine the framework of the way that the First Amendment has emerged and been interpreted in the United States polity. As the title of Matsuda *et al.* book states, words, like sticks and stones, can assault, they can injure, and they can exclude. The text draws on the experience of injury from racist hate speech in the United States to call for the development of First Amendment interpretation that recognises the realities of such injuries and the impact they have on marginalised and underprivileged groups in society. In this text it is argued that only a history of institutionalised racism that ignores the impact of ostensively neutral policy on critical outcomes, can really explain why it is that certain defamations, invasions of privacy, and frauds to deceive, are exempted from the constitutional guarantees of free speech, as interpreted by the Supreme Court, but the invective of racists, vitriolic words that assault and create a hostile environment for minorities to live and work, are not

---

[25] Man J. Matsuda, Charles R. Lawrence, Richard Delgado, and Kimberle Crenshaw, *Words That Wound: Critical Race Theory, Assaultive Speech, and the First Amendment* (Boulder, Colo.: Westview Press, 1993).
[26] *Ibid.*, 1-17.

exempted from guarantees to free speech.[27] The authors maintain that an Absolutist approach to First Amendment jurisprudence does not adequately reflect the reality that certain words and actions wound minorities and contribute to their continuing subordination.

Lu-in Wang, for example, in her "The Transforming Power of Hate: Social Cognition Theory and the Harms of Bias-Related Crime," and Steven H. Shiffrin, in his "Racist Speech, Outsider Jurisprudence, and the Meaning of America," both discuss in detail the range of many diffuse harms caused by hate speech, specifying why these harms are different from those caused by other crimes due to targeting and the social background of disempowerment that frames the context.[28]

The Criticalists focus on the corrosive and destructive consequences of hate speech to call for its criminalisation in society. In his book, *Destructive Messages: How Hate Speech Paves the Way for Harmful Social Movements*, for example, Alexander Tsesis sets forth a thesis about the relationship between "hate speech" and action that follows from it. His broad claim about the relationship is simple and straightforward: when systematically developed over long periods of time, hate speech lays the foundation for harmful social movements and discrimination that results in the continuing oppression and persecution of marginalised and subordinated groups.[29]

Tsesis relies on historical analysis to critique current Supreme Court doctrine. For Tsesis, Supreme Court hate speech doctrine fails to take into account the long-term social dangers of hate speech. From this perspective, Tsesis argues that United States Supreme Court ought to abandon the rule that advocacy or incitement must be put up with in the name of free speech and that legislatures should move to criminalise hate speech. Only a policy of non-toleration can tackle the

---

[27] *Ibid.*, 17-49, 59-87.

[28] Wang, *Southern California Law Review* 71 (1977), 47-120; Shiffrin, *Cornell Law Review* 80 (1994), 43-87.

[29] Alexander Tsesis, *Destructive Messages: How Hate Speech Paves the Way for Harmful Social Movements* (New York: New York University Press, 2002), 14-31.

significance of the problem. He then explains that much of the rest of the world criminalises hate speech in some form, recognising its particular corrosiveness, concluding that the United States should do the same. The need for equality and the welfare of the community requires that censorship in this case must temper liberal freedom. Censorship here is simply the imposition of a set of standards on freedom of expression for the protection of others from the invidious and evil effects of racism.[30] As Matsuda *et al.* state "tolerance of hate speech is not tolerance borne by the community at large. Rather it is a psychic tax imposed on those least able to pay."[31]

The Criticalists are especially hostile to the Supreme Court case of *R.A.V. v. City of Saint Paul*, as a paradigm case for misunderstanding the nature and significance of harms generated by hate speech directed towards minorities, misunderstanding the power of racist cultural messages.[32] In that case the majority of the bench found that a statute prohibiting the " ... placing on public or private property a symbol, object, appellation, characterization or graffiti, including, but not limited to, a burning cross or Nazi swastika, which one knows or has reasonable grounds to know arouses anger, alarm or resentment in others on the basis of race, color, creed, religion or gender," was unconstitutional because it was a content-based restriction on free speech.[33]

Criticalists reject this content neutral approach to First Amendment interpretation and call for an understanding of speech as a socially mediated form of power. Criticalists call for a way to understand speech that is flexible, policy-sensitive, and mindful of communication theory, politics, and setting. The idea that victims of hatred can counter the consequences of hate speech with powerful rhetoric of their own, for example, is treated with dismay and yet another sign of the

---

[30] *Ibid.*, 143-89. See also Tsesis's "Empirical Shortcomings of First Amendment Jurisprudence: A Historical Perspective on the Power of Hate Speech," Santa Clara Law Review 40 (2000), 729-65.

[31] Mari J. Matsuda, "Public Response to Racist Speech," in *Words That Wound*, 18.

[32] See for example, Charles R. Lawrence, "Crossburning and the Sound of Silence: Antisubordination Theory and the First Amendment," *Villanova Law Review* 37 (1992), 787-823. He is very critical of the Supreme Court Judgement.

[33] See footnote 4.

liberal inability to understand the systemic nature of the problem. Most especially there is a failure to realise that the inability of disempowered minorities to counter derogatory images with more constructive images, arises in large part from racial disparities in wealth. For the Criticalists, the Supreme Court failed to recognise that racial insults are in no way comparable to statements such as "X is a God damned liar." Racial insults whether verbal or symbolic are qualitatively different because they conjure up an entire history of racial discrimination and subordination. The patterns of speech must be understood and judged against that background, and not by a misplaced fidelity to any form of ahistorical abstract absolutism.[34]

The conclusion for the Criticalists is clear, extensive laws must be enacted to regulate content-based speech that currently permits hate speech in the name of protecting free speech, a price bourn by the minorities who suffer by it.

Turning to the *Via Media*

Freedom of expression is celebrated as one of the glories of the American legal system. But does all speech deserve immunity? In particular, should speech designed to vilify or degrade on the basis of race be protected? Opinions on racist speech are complicated because they must accommodate two fundamental democratic principles that operate at cross purposes: freedom of expression, which implies support for racist speech, and racial equality, which implies the opposite.[35] In the preceding explication and analysis of the two opposing strands of thought, we have sought to show how one strand emphasises freedom of speech, notwithstanding the possible effects of that speech on minority sections of society. On the other, we saw the emphasis being placed on racial equality and equal protection as privileged forms of intervention and restriction on free speech, at least as far as racially motivated hate speech is concerned.

---

[34] Gates, "War of words," in *Speaking of Race*, 17-58.
[35] Cass R. Sunstein, *Democracy and the Problem of Free Speech* (New York: Free Press, 1995), 167-208.

Law, Ethics & Society

Here I wish to argue that John Stuart Mill's classic, *On Liberty* is an important text for us to consider as we seek to explore the minefield of ideas that has now been unleashed. I especially want to consider his work because it a great text defending the value of liberty, and secondly, because it has, I think, been overly distorted as a text placing it firmly within the rhetoric of the Absolutist camp, while he actually offers arguments that may act as something of a limit on liberty, arguments that may act as something of a bridge between the seemingly insoluble gap between free speech, on the one hand, and concerns about equality and respect, on the other.

In 1859 Mill published his small treatise *On Liberty*. It is the best known of his many writings concerning freedom of speech. The central thrust of Mill's argument appears deceptively straightforward, but it is easily misunderstood. His aim, as he tells us right away, is to make the case that, as much as possible we should permit individuals to say and do what they want, subject to only one limitation, namely, that they should inflict no harm on other people. In all other cases, individuals should be left free to say and to do what they want, with no legal penalties.[36]

Without such a principle, Mill believes, society is in danger of stagnating. In other words, maximising the freedom of all is in the best interests of every one in society. Unlike the paternalists of the past, Mill believes that people will not threaten the stability of society if they are granted more freedom. Mill's position then is that extensions to the frontiers of negative liberty will provide direct practical benefits to everyone, for freedom of thought and expression are vital to the continuing social progress of society.

The basis of Mill's faith in such progress comes from a central claim that, in the tradition first established by the Greeks, liberty will breed competition and variety and these, in turn, will better foster excellence. Only by competing with each other in the realm of ideas and practical experiments for living and in trade will our society improve. For example, in the realm of ideas, free speech is essential for a number of

---

[36] J. S. Mill *On Liberty*, Stefan Collini, ed. (Cambridge: Cambridge University Press, 1989), 15-29.

reasons. Without it we may stifle some ideas which may be true, or we will collectively lose the opportunity to have our ideas challenged and to think through how we can better defend them.[37]

Mill's case here is not a simple plea for tolerance, for the permissive society which lets anything go, nor is it moral relativism, which thinks that all ideas are equally valid. Mill firmly believes that tolerance is not enough, for tolerance is essentially a negative attitude. Mill sees free speech as a much more proactive element in social interaction. It is a matter of constant debate: we must allow opinions a public hearing so that we can engage with them, debate them, sharpen ourselves in a constant testing and refinement (and improvement in) our beliefs.

So far, one might be forgiven in thinking that Mill's text is practically a charter for the Absolutist position concerning the interpretation of the First Amendment. Mill is the intellectual father of many of the arguments used to support the case of opposition against content-based or viewpoint-based restrictions on freedom of speech. How then can Mill's text possibly be thought of as offering us a *via media* by which to engage the concerns of the Criticalists? The essay seems, does it not, distinctly libertarian in its central arguments?

On further reflection, however, Mill's case for placing no restrictions on speech is actually decidedly more qualified that it would appear. Mill does not endorse a blanket prohibition on all forms of the censorship of thought and discussion for he endorses what has subsequently been called the "Harm Principle." According to the Harm Principle, roughly stated, the state may coerce a person by legal penalty only if it can thereby prevent harm to others (not "harm to self" however). Mill contends that it is obvious that the government must be able to legislate concerning actions which do cause harm to others in order to maintain the existence of a civil society, but that it is certainly not necessary for the survival of civil society to pass laws regarding actions which do not involve harm to others. As Mill states,

---

[37] *Ibid.*, 50-63.

"... the sole end for which mankind [humankind] are warranted, individually or collectively, in interfering with the liberty of action of any of their number is self-protection. That the only purpose for which power can be rightfully exercised over any member of a civilised community, against his [or her] will, is to prevent harm to others. His [or her] own good, either physical or moral, is not a sufficient warrant."[38]

Nowhere in *On Liberty* is it stated that speech, *qua* speech is incapable of harming others in term of its impact. Mill, moreover, asserted that "Whenever, in short, there is a definite damage or a definite risk of damage, either to an individual or to the public, the case is taken out of the province of liberty, and placed in that of morality and law."[39] Moreover, Mill also stated the following, that "... even opinions lose their immunity when the circumstances in which they are expressed are such as to constitute in their expression a positive instigation to some mischievous act."[40]

When these kinds of qualifications are focused upon, especially the nature and significance of certain kinds of harms or offences that may be generated by speech in civil society, the case for regarding Mill purely as a friend of First Amendment Absolutism, starts to look decidedly more qualified and less robust than it would first appear. Judgments about harm are often controversial (think, for example, of recent debates about the harmful effects of mind-altering drugs). Does "harm" designate damage only to a person or property, or is there a class of moral harms, or harms to character, which may legitimately circumscribe liberty? What of indirect harms?

To be sure, I am not saying that the extent of the range and scope of action demanded by Criticalists, will ultimately be found to be compatible with the plausible frontiers of Mill's restrictions on free speech. I am not a miracle worker. What I do believe is possible, however, is that taking Mill's "Harm

---

[38] *Ibid.*, 13.
[39] *Ibid.*, 82.
[40] *Ibid.*, 56.

Principle" somewhat further may offer grounds for extending protections against certain forms of hate speech beyond those permitted by present constitutional interpretation of the First Amendment. Those steps, in the name of advancing the civil rights of minorities, can be justified by a kind of "Millsian inspired" balancing act, notwithstanding the consequences that those very restrictions may have on the exercise of some kinds of speech in civil society.

At this point it is also worth mentioning another aspect of Mill's thought conducive, in some degree, to the concerns of the Criticalists—the question of equality in the light of power structures, another concern of Mill. Mill was a critique of orthodox laissez-faire economics. Pedro Schwartz's *The New Political Economy of J. S. Mill,* is, I think, a useful text to mention here because he amply demonstrates how Mill was acutely aware of how the distribution of wealth in society could affect the ability to promote free speech in civil society, especially the speech of the poor, marginalised, and subjugated.[41] The major targets of Mill's critique were property systems of inheritance and oppressive systems of industrial organisation. Large fortunes accumulated in the hands of a few, for Mill, are actually an enemy to free speech since they tended to seek to stifle the input of others (think here how business monopolies act!) and act for their own selfish interests.

If the marginalised are to be effective partners in the free speech stakes, it is not incompatible with Mill's social thought, therefore, to argue that positive social conditions need be created to make such fora much more accessible and engaging to the interests of minorities.

Mill's Harm Principle

In an excellent essay on the interpretation of the Mill's Harm Principle, J. C. Rees's "A Re-reading of Mill on Liberty," Rees distinguishes between actions that merely affect others and actions that affect others' interests, especially critical interests, and gives textual support for the claim that Mill's working conception of harm in *On Liberty* is that of "harm to

---

[41] London: Weidenfeld & Nicolson, 1972.

Law, Ethics & Society

interests."[42] According to Rees, an interpretation I support, Mill emphasises that interests depend for their existence on social recognition and are closely connected with prevailing standards about the sort of behaviour a person can legitimately expect from others. It is precisely in order to distinguish human interests from arbitrary wishes, fleeting fancies, or capricious demands that Rees stresses Mill's assessment of interest in terms of their dependence on the norms and values which enjoy social recognition.[43]

In the context of the United States, and debate over the recognition of civil liberties, I think that the phrase "others' interests" may be translated into the enumeration and protection of basic civil liberties, among them the positive right not be the object of hate and vilification in civil society. By expanding on the notion of the Harm Principle in terms of the identification of critical interests, I would think that a plausible Millsian inspired line of development here would be along the conceptualisation of liberty or autonomy as having positive and negative interests at stake that need to be protected, constituting critical interests than may be harmed by the unfettered non-regulation of content-based free speech concerning racial hatred.

Autonomy—a very rich notion, one based on the rights and responsibilities of personhood and respect for their dignity—is a value that, I think, ought to invoked and comprehended more fully in order to underpin the Supreme Court's jurisprudence in this field, a key value that, I think, can provide a coherent and principled base upon which to develop a better articulation of policy in this field, helping to reconcile freedom of speech with the demands of freedom from vilification or living in a hostile and inhospitable environment.[44]

In openly recognising that the actions of autonomous individuals operating in a society can clash, it is necessary, out of an articulation of critical interest to assert that the state can bring its coercive power to bear against its citizens and

---

[42] John C. Rees, "A Re-Reading of Mill on Liberty," *Political Studies* 8 (1960), 113-29.
[43] *Ibid.*, 113-29.
[44] Filimon Peonidis, "Freedom of Expression, Autonomy, Defamation," *Law & Philosophy* 17 (1998), 1-17.

The *Societas Civilitas* & Hate Speech

thereby limit their freedom, when some actions unduly fetter the positive autonomy conditions needed to preserve *the very autonomy of others*. Such coercive action by the state is necessary in order to protect the dignity of its citizens by ensuring that people act in a civil manner that respects the critical autonomy interests of others. Importantly, an adequately framed notion of autonomy demands that our very capacity for autonomy imposes an obligation, enforceable by the state, to act such as to respect the autonomy of other persons.

The debate over liberty/autonomy that has emerged in First Amendment jurisprudence, in recent years, both generally and in specific contexts such as hate speech, broadcast regulation, and obscenity, is I think, often badly framed. Often, in attempting to frame the debate over the question of prohibiting the regulation of speech content, we view liberty only negatively as personified by self-interested individuals acting with little regard for the community or for the welfare of others. We fail to grasp that negative autonomy is also circumscribed by the rightful positive autonomy interests of others. Liberty, as negative liberty, the right to be let alone to do what the individual wills, is then all too readily but falsely juxtaposed with "paternalism"—government regulation nefarious to the liberty of individuals.[45]

To me, one of the most misunderstood aspects of the current debate between the Absolutists and the Criticalists, is the one-sided conception of liberty that all to often prevails. It seems as if liberty and equality are opposites instead of understanding them as two facets of the same underlying reality. Liberty is always too readily equated with negative liberty. Liberty is then juxtaposed in opposition to balancing equality concerns. Instead, I would argue that a better-founded notion of liberty, one conducive to accepting some criticism of free speech jurisprudence that has predominated, is the idea that a rounded notion of liberty is not incompatible with some

---

[45] On this important topic, of positive liberty as well as negative liberty, see the very influential essay by Isaiah Berlin, "Two Concepts of Liberty," in his *Liberty* (Oxford: Oxford University Press, 1969), 166-217. In fact, the basic distinction, though not the terminology, can be traced back to Aristotle in his *Nicomachean Ethics*.

significant regulation of speech content.[46] Autonomy, of "negative liberty" is too readily translated into freedom from government interference. Autonomy thus becomes equated with negative liberty, and is thus conceived of as "freedom from," that is, the absence of constraints on the agent imposed by other people. Once conceived of as only a negative liberty, autonomy then all to readily becomes equated with the freedom to say whatever we want. Alas, it is this characterisation of autonomy, in my view, that makes the debate over hate speech, more distorted, driving out any middle ground, than it ought to be.[47]

It is often stated that the purpose of free speech is to protect the weak from the tyranny of opinion of the strong. But what about protection of speech aimed not at the powerful but at the weak, speech whose purpose is to disparage and vilify, to undermine the autonomy of the marginalised and weak in society? When we turn to the notion of harm as others' interests, especially critical interests, and frame our understanding more in terms of positive as well as negative autonomy, it is possible to see how major harms can be envisaged and described when we turn again to the context of hate speech. If, for example, one has been socialised, in large part as a result of others' speech, to expect very little of oneself, or to defer to others, one is hardly in a position to make fully autonomous choices. Likewise, if one has very few genuine options to choose from, one's very capacity to make choices is diminished. Can these not be classified as harms to critical interests that the government many have a legitimate mandate to balance against the interests of free and unfettered hate speech? It would seem to me that the above can yield a strong positive liberty-based argument for restricting hate speech if one grants the empirical claim that failure to restrict such speech

---

[46] Kimberly Gross and Donald R. Kinder, "A Collision of Principles? Free Expression, Racial Equality and the Prohibition of Racist Speech," *British Journal of Political Science* 28 (1998), 445-71.
[47] Joseph Raz, *The Morality of Freedom* (Oxford: Clarendon Press, 1988), 400-29. See also Jeffrie Murphy and Jules Coleman, *Philosophy of Law* (Boulder, Colo.: Westview, 1990), 74-93.

can significantly impair the ability of individuals in targeted groups to act autonomously.[48]

Another argument that I wish to make a few remarks on here is the distinction often made between speech and conduct. Speech, it is often said, cannot be regulated, but conduct can, for speech is not conduct. Words do not really "harm" anyone. This is, to my mind, decidedly superficial and unconvincing. Absolutists concerning freedom of speech far too readily assume the "sticks and stones" principle, that words can only ever cause offence, never harm, and so freedom of speech is near absolute. As the philosopher, John L. Austin, has astutely pointed out, however, we do not just communicate thoughts and ideas with words, we can actually do things with them. A vicar, for example, can instigate a state of marriage between two people by saying "I now pronounce you man and wife."[49] (If gays and lesbians wish to marry, but regard equal civil rights as non-equivalent to marriage, they surely have a point!). Words can change a great deal. Words can incite hatred, inspire violence and create an intolerable climate of fear. Thus, when people use words in this way, it is quite incorrect to protest that people are merely "expressing opinions."[50] Their words can be seen to cause tangible harm to the critical interests of others—the rights of "positive liberty" to be left in peace.

The *Via Media* & Constitutional Interpretation

First a caveat on application. It is not my intention to suggest that the *via media* position that I am advocating is a position that is likely to be adopted in future United States constitutional analysis (at least for the foreseeable future!). It is a humble conceptual work composed of largely theoretical thoughts and reflections on my part. I am after all, at heart, an

---

[48] For an excellent extended discussion of harm and critical interests, see Gerald F. Gaus, *Social Philosophy* (Armonk, NY: Sharp, 1999), 136-59.
[49] J. L Austin, *How to Do Things with Words* (Oxford: Clarendon Press, 1962). See further Marilyn Frye, "Force and Meaning," *Journal of Philosophy* LXX (1973), 281-94.
[50] Claudia Lacour, "Doing Things with Words: Racism as Speech Act and the Undoing of Justice," in *Race-ing Justice, En-gendering Power: Essays on Anita Hill, Clarence Thomas, and the Construction of Social Reality*, Toni Morrison, ed. (New York: Pantheon Books, 1992), 127-58.

armchair philosopher! Perhaps that is too strong. Some facets may already be in play in ways that I have not the training or time to analyse or properly assess. What I do however hope to achieve here is to offer sufficient "food for thought" that points to a course of constructively moving the lines of debate forward beyond the ready rhetoric of opposing and somewhat entrenched viewpoints—an endeavour, in itself, surely worth-while pursuing—towards a structure that takes on board some important concerns of both camps.

As briefly state earlier in the paper, restrictions on speech are held under strict scrutiny standards. First Amendment jurisprudence distinguishes between content-neutral restrictions on speech that restrict the time, manner, and place of speech but not its content, and content-specific restrictions that restrict forms of speech on account of the viewpoint expressed in the speech.

The first ground that I have for arguing for greater constitutional recognition of the regulation of hate speech in society is that the present standard for strict scrutiny is currently too heavily weighted in terms of categorising speech in term of negative liberty without adequately taking on board the damage to positive critical interests posed by hate speech invective. It is possible, as other countries have succeeded in doing, for example, Great Britain, Canada, and Germany, to draft a statute sufficiently targeted and directed in scope to be neither vague nor overly broad in its framing, thus not unjustly impinging on other vital free speech interests. Such statutes can target the use of verbal, written, or symbolic language intended to cause fear or emotional distress to a racial or ethnic minority.[51]

Take the Canadian case of *R. v. Keegstra* (1990). In that case, the Supreme Court of Canada perceptively argued that hate propaganda caused two sorts of injury. First, there is harm done to members of the target group. The emotional damage caused by words may be of grave psychological and social consequence. Second, the effect of hate speech on

---

[51] See Michel Rosenfeld, "Hate Speech in Constitutional Jurisprudence: A Comparative Analysis," *Cardozo Law Review* 24 (2003), 1523-66.

society at large is to create a more hostile environment in which minorities are able to exercise their civil rights.[52]

As I understand the framing of the United States Constitution, the Fourteenth Amendment was passed to include the equal protection clause. This clause should be given greater significance in the effective balancing of the First Amendment with other considerations of dignity and respect for persons. If there truly are rights to equal concern and respect, then these rights cannot simply be trumped by the appeal to a negative freedom of W to do X without the recognition that W's right to do X affects Y's ability to do Z. Such rights cannot be turned into absolutes, denying the qualification of X in the light of Y and *vice versa*.[53]

Questions of balancing or weighting here, of finding a reasonable accommodation, are surely where gains in one of the values would be outweighed by greater losses in the other. Freedom of speech would be better protected were there are no legal constraints whatever on the circulation of hate speech, while the security of minorities would be more effectively safeguarded by statutes that could be decidedly authoritarian in scope and coverage. Somewhere between the two extremes we must seek a balanced point at which the greater protection for minorities afforded by stronger protection would be outweighed by the damaging impact on speech, while the greater protection for expression afforded by weaker protection would be outweighed by the increase in racial hatred.

It is, of course, often objected that such a statute would not be constitutional because it would unduly grant privileges to classes of person not readily available to all. In response to this, in agreement with Criticalists, I would state that these hate crimes must be set in the context of the balance of power in society and the relative ability to find other channels for redress. There is no good reason why the Supreme Court may

---

[52] *Regina v. Keegstra* SCR 3 (1990), 697. In this case, James Keegstra, a public high school teacher, viciously propagated Holocaust denial and anti-Semitic propaganda to high school students, despite warnings to cease. See discussion in Steven J. Heyman, "Spheres of Autonomy: Reforming the Content Neutrality Doctrine in First Amendment Jurisprudence," *William and Mary Bill of Rights Journal* 10 (2002), 666-98.

[53] Heyman, "Spheres of Autonomy," 688-714.

Law, Ethics & Society

not take into account particular evils and remedies that call for special treatment where historical and cultural factors have an important conditioning role to play. The state need not be neutral where the very ground rules tend to disproportionably impact and prejudice the critical interests of minorities.

So framed, I think that the greater recognition of the government's interest in preventing harm to certain critical interests, namely, the autonomy right of minorities, may justify the criminal punishment of patterns of communication that are specifically intended to incite or promote the kinds of harms described.

Contrary to the demands of the Criticalists, however, I do not believe that the serving of critical interests could ban all forms of discussion of race-based content. I am particularly thinking here of the university or the academy. Here, I believe, that the open exchange of ideas in academic fora do need to be protected from the chilling consequences of hate speech restrictions as outlined above. I do not think that hate speech statutes can be used as a basis for suppressing, for example, research on the comparative performance of minorities in schools or colleges, or the reporting of crime statistics, or the discussion of sensitive social and political issues (providing that *the intent* is not to incite the very kinds of harms outlined above).

Bias and distortion will always be with us and a certain amount of toleration for research or analysis that we judge profoundly mistaken or ignorant cannot be expunged from any relatively open and discursive community of ideas. I think that this kind of distinction is compatible with the kind of Millsian analysis that I have been discussing. An assessment of the prevailing values and standards needs to take account of hate speech while not seeking to remove valid and important academic discussions on issues of fact and value, providing their intent is not to promote the deliberate autonomy undermining of minorities.

The second string to my bow, so to speak, would be the use of the distinction recognised in First Amendment jurisprudence between low-value and high-value speech. The negative liberty to engage in low-value speech is not a fundamental liberty. Thus, content-specific regulation of low-value speech, as a result, need not satisfy strict scrutiny but be reasonably directed to the malady it seeks to regulate.[54] By contrast, other forms of speech are high-value, and the liberty to engage in them is a fundamental liberty. As a result, content-specific regulation of high-value speech must satisfy strict scrutiny or some comparable standard. The Supreme Court formulated that key distinction in *Chaplinsky v. New Hampshire*.[55] Here, I would argue that the kind of analysis conducted by the Supreme Court, for example, in its analysis of obscenity, is applicable to the regulation of hate speech and that the Court should extend its analysis of obscenity to the realm of hate speech (not as Absolutists have argued, the effective deregulation of obscenity by the courts).

I would argue that hate speech invective is of such low social and political value as to be without major redeeming importance and hence not worth protecting. Here, as with the judgment of obscenity, I believe that context and intent are important to the assessment of locutions, texts, and symbols. Works, locutions, or courses of action will need to be judged as a whole. Here the standard, I think, becomes one of the reasonable person and their reasonable perception of prevailing contextual standards.

As with obscenity, I would exempt from the category of the proscribed, works that are judged to be of overriding historical, scientific, artistic, or political value, notwithstanding their racial messages. Again, works must be judged a whole. This is, I think, in line with Mill's general desire to preserve and not destroy the patrimony of ideas available to society, while trying to ensure that the best examples of ideas are kept, not the irredeemably low. Again, it should be bourn in mind here that hate speech tends to silence the historically marginalised by stifling the expression of their views or preventing their views from receiving a fair hearing. If hateful words or symbols retard, rather than advance deliberative values in society, then they should count as low-value speech, and their regulation should be subject only to the bar of the

---

[54] Heyman, "Spheres of Autonomy," 688-714.
[55] US 315 (1942), 568. Some forms of expression, among them obscenity and fighting words, do not convey ideas and thus are not subject to First Amendment protection.

proportionality of the measure adopted to the nature of the harm being tackled. Hate speech is of such low value in promoting deliberative values in society, in comparison to its attempt to suppress the deliberative values of minorities, that it can, I think, be judged a reasonably apportioned measure.

Conclusion

Having reviewed the respective positions of the Absolutists and the Criticalists, concerning First Amendment jurisprudence, I have opted for a *via media* position between those two opposing camps. The via media position adopted is, I think, supported by the work of J. S. Mill, furnishing us with an expanded conception of liberty that stresses the value of "positive liberty" as well as "negative liberty." The unpacking of a broader notion of liberty and an array of critical interests at stake, gives us sufficient grounds for justifying the imposition of criminal sanctions on certain forms of hate inspired speech in civil society.

EDUCATION AS THE KEY FOR A GLOBAL SOCIETY IN PEACE AND FREEDOM

Elmar Kuhn

Is our global society on the right way or has it lost its internal compass and orientation? Is a university the right place to change the worlds future? An intercultural attempt to understand the mechanism of contemporary societies.

This article is about "Education is the key for a prosperous Europe in peace and freedom". But that's only half of the truth. The other half is "the inevitable role of ethics and religions for the future of global development".

Let's bring to our inner eyes the image of an ordinary sausage. Like all sausages in the world – Plato would say it is it "eidos" of every "morphe" of a real existing sausage – also our sausage in the brain has two ends. And these ends are dead ends, no filling is inside, its not well tasting and only necessary to keep the sausage closed.

It's the same with societies. The well tasting part of society is the good and tolerant mixture of politics, economics and religions. Neglecting this triangle of interdependences causes a lot of troubles. As we see in the middle east and also in huge parts of Asia like Pakistan or Myanmar, picking out politics and religions, especially one religion only, brings struggles, intolerance and bad economic development. That leads to extremism and poverty. It doesn't matter which religion politics choose for to marry with, Islam, Hinduism, Buddhism…. When this happens, we see the fall down of economy, the end of a free public dialogue, the persecution of Christians, Hindi or Muslims by the major religion in the state. So this is one of the dead ends of the sausage, a dead end for the development of civil society.

The other dead end of the sausage is a society, where politic is mainly interested in economy, and where economical and financial necessities rule the society. In Europe for example there has been 70 years of peace – in the European union.

Law, Ethics & Society

The rest of Europe felt into wars and poverty. The welfare of the European Union was built up by the equidistance of politics, economics and religions in plural. In this climate of freedom, solidarity and tolerance a society grew up with economic welfare, cultural and social activities and visionary concepts for a better future.

In 2007 the world financial crises ended a lot of these dreams and showed, that this equidistance of politics, economy and religions was destroyed. One player was kicked off from the civil society playground: The religions.

What happened: More and more our society was set into freedom with no limits. Everything was allowed, a process which started with the sexual revolution in the 1970s. It was a process determined by the scripts of Wilhelm Reich *"Sexuality in the clash of cultures. The socialist restructuring of men"* from 1936[1]. This book was rediscovered and implemented by the student revolt of 1968. Reich's main idea is that one must destroy the family in order to destroy the capitalist social order, that is, the social order with the right of freedom and property.

More and more the part of the religions failed to become an equal part in society. And the growing Muslim population in Europe after 1970 was not helpful. In contrary: Because Islam promotes religious laws (the Sharia) as unchangeable part of the political system, Muslims couldn't arrange with the secular politics in Europe. They failed to understand the role of religions as integral but not dominating part in the European society. Instead of bringing Muslim spiritual traditions and values into the European context, with tolerance and respect towards secular and Christian ways of life, they organized their own parallel society inside Europe and urged ultimately politics to respect everywhere their halal dietary laws.

In Vienna of today the secular and Christian pupils in school and kindergarten have to eat only halal school meals: pasta asciutta, Wiener Schnitzel or pork sausages (like the old traditional Viennese sausages you can buy on every corner in Vienna) were no longer allowed. It's up to the reader to

[1] W. Reich, Sexualität im Kulturkampf. Zur sozialistischen Umstrukturierung des Menschen, (1936) Kopenhagen

136

adapt this European example to the US. And maybe you will find similar trends, and this might lead to a better understanding of the hidden and obvious fears of American politicians of today.

By this example of urging the own religious standard to everybody but at the same time rejecting the political system, the role of religions in the European civil society system was minimized. No longer religious and ethical expertise's were asked for their advice, politics and economy joined to lead Europe by themselves. But this brought us to the other dead end of the sausage.

You can get what you want – if you can pay

In our global society we lost ethical standards, because an unquestioned libertinism is the general rule in society. Allowed is what you want and what you can pay for. Euthanasia? If you pay you get it in.

Sexual orientation? Do, what you want. Well there is nothing bad with respect for homosexuals or transgender. But do we really need 60 different gender identities[2], which are offered by Facebook to its users? There is no longer an ethical standard worthwhile for everybody's general orientation. Exemptions are a question of tolerance, but no obligation to offer all possibilities to society as a normal way of life.

Another example are the genetic manipulations which go on in international laboratories, so that the creation of a child according to your own wishes will be reachable within a decade – if you can pay for!

But about all this we could discuss. Out of the question are two things: The **freedom of will** and the **value-orientated education.**

First question: the freedom of will

I remember a British medical doctor. As catholic he didn't accept to assist in the abortion of a child. Because of this he was not allowed to hold surgery hours any longer. That happens, if a society without religious values loses all orientation about

---

[2] Vgl. http://de.wikimannia.org/60_Geschlechtsidentitäten

fundamental human rights. This example shows that the free-dom of believe comes into troubles in Europe today. If only the wishes of economic driven hospital agenda count, the free will and faith of the doctors are eradicated.

Second question: the value-orientated education

1) Religious education is getting to be debatable today in many western orientaded states, and the direction is clear: Exclude religions from school and university! In-stead of this politics initiates: nothing. No cultural ethics, no tolerance education, no value orientated lectures. So pupils go through their school career without ethics and discussion to form a proper personal identity with values and believes. So these pupils are open for anybody who gives them orientation. This might be an event culture with no content or even fundamentalist religious believes. Young Muslims like young Christians are let alone with the main questions of her life: What I am, what's the meaning of my life? Whereto I go? Moreover, all ques-tions to which ethics alone is not able to give satisfactory final answers. Disorientation instead of self-confidence is the result. The inability to call sth. into question makes young people vulnerable for fundamentalists who offer seemingly "easy ways" for a meaningful life.

2) Reducing pupils and students to working robots: This means, if the financial and industrial sector (the economy) urges politics to change the curricula of schools and uni-versities to the direct needs of companies, all general educational matters get lost. In schools this means no hu-manistic education, no value education, no creative lectures and no training of free intellectual spirit and emo-tional competence.

This sounds dangerous to our global civil society, but in edu-cational systems in Asia this is getting reality. Our western economical welfare is directly connected to free will, rational discussion and different believes. This necessarily leads to the main principles of tolerance and respect. I fear the day when politics or companies dictate what they believe what should be tolerated and what not. As Böckenförde, the German high-judge and professor of law, always told:

> *The liberal, secularized state lives from conditions which it cannot guarantee itself. ... As a liberal state it can only exist on the one hand if the freedom it grants to its citizens is regulated from within, by the moral substance of the individual and the homogeneity of society. On the other hand he cannot guarantee it with the means of legal constraint and authoritative commandment, without giving up its freedom and - on a secularized level - to fall back into the claim to totality from which it led in the confessional civil wars.*[3]

But who is able to guarantee this moral substance of the individual if not the state?

Sure, it's not religion out of its social structure. The errors of confessional persecutions and war in our past tells us that religions and confessions are not able to guarantee this freedom. The state himself depends to decisions of majorities. And we know, how intolerant the state can act as he showed us in communism and fascism. And we see the intolerance growing in European politics of today.

Who then can guarantee the value of life and individual believes?

First, we have international organisms like the United Nation with, for example, the human rights declaration. But this declaration is not accepted by major parts of the world, not by the Muslim world and not by the Chinese.

Second, we have the arts: artists were always under the warners for an open and tolerate society. But also, they failed if the political power was to strong.

Third we have the academic life: the elite of a society should be able to warn against violations of individual rights. But often the academics failed to do so.

---

[3] Böckenförde, Ernst-Wolfgang (1976): Staat, Gesellschaft, Freiheit. S. 60

Law, Ethics & Society

So who is left?

As I believe: the **Religions in Plural**, their revelations and their theologies all together are able to identify and guarantee an education to freedom. Therefor they would have to come together, not as church structures, but as theologians and spiritual leaders. Together and as common partners of politics and economy they could advice wisely. So, I hope that the world religions will be able to find a common language for peace. By his peace talks in Assisi Pope John Paul II. began such a process. If religions dare to speak with one tongue to fundamental aspects of civil society, then they would be able to fulfil their role in a fruitful equidistance of politics, economics and religions for a peaceful and prosperous society. The "document on human fraternity for world peace and living together", the so-called Abu Dhabi declaration from February 4th 2019, signed by Pope Francis and Ahmad Al-Tayyeb, the Grand Imam of Al-Azhar university in Cairo, is a first step into this direction under others this interreligious document states:[4]

> The firm conviction that authentic teachings of religions invite us to remain rooted in the values of peace; to defend the values of mutual understanding, human fraternity and harmonious coexistence; to re-establish wisdom, justice and love; and to re-awaken religious awareness among young people so that future generations may be protected from the realm of materialistic thinking and from dangerous policies of unbridled greed and indifference that are based on the law of force and not on the force of law." And to the misunderstandings and problems between eastern (oriental) and western (industrial nations) the document frames, that "good relations between East and West are indisputably necessary for both. They must not be neglected, so that each can be enriched by the other's culture through fruitful exchange and dialogue. The West

---

[4] cf. http://w2.vatican.va/content/francesco/en/travels/2019/outside/documents/papa-francesco_20190204_ documento-fratellanza-umana.html

Education as Key for Global Society

can discover in the East remedies for those spiritual and religious maladies that are caused by a prevailing materialism. And the East can find in the West many elements that can help free it from weakness, division, conflict and scientific, technical and cultural decline. It is important to pay attention to religious, cultural and historical differences that are a vital component in shaping the character, culture and civilization of the East. It is likewise important to reinforce the bond of fundamental human rights in order to help ensure a dignified life for all the men and women of East and West, avoiding the politics of double standards.

The real surprise is, that also the Islamic side declares its will to unroll this document's ideas toward all educational sectors:

Al-Azhar and the Catholic Church ask that this Document become the object of research and reflection in all schools, universities and institutes of formation, thus helping to educate new generations to bring goodness and peace to others, and to be defenders everywhere of the rights of the oppressed and of the least of our brothers and sisters.

This document shows us, what is really important for the welfare, freedom and peace of our global world: That a global society in peace and freedom undoubtedly is connected to the educational sector. What might be the contribution of schools and universities to a global and peaceful civil society development?

The answer is easy: Many campuses especially in US show to us how strong the impact of an education campus could be for society. If it is true – like I tried to point out – that the lack of ethical education produces workers but no critical civil society members. In contrary, open minded, creative and daring campuses understand education as a chance to change society. Young students get the smell of visionary cooperation for a better, stronger and more solidary society. For to ensure this, an interdisciplinary approach is necessary for each campus in future who will contribute to an open society. The cooperation of different departments, interreligious and intercultural efforts have to be made, actors of civil society should be invited, international connections must be initiated, and last but not least arts and artists are to be integrated.

Whoever is studying at a modern campus in a global co-operating and interacting Campus breaths the air of a new und strong civil society. Education is the key for a peaceful and welfare, a free and visionary world. But the indispensable background of each person, institution and religious representative working in the educational sector are the main principles of humanity: Tolerance and Respect as keywords for a strong, open-minded, peaceful and prosperous society.

GLOBAL ECOLOGY AND SUSTAINABLE DEVELOPMENT: A STUDY IN GANDHIAN PERSPECTIVE[1]

Manish Sharma

Introduction

"Everybody talks about the weather, but nobody does anything about it." This quote from Mark Twain is very relevant today. The environmental pollution multiplies manifold, arising out of millions of smoke-emitting vehicles, running with frequent traffic jams on the matchingly inadequate roads, with struggling parking space and overcrowding of people.

This has almost reached the peak in New Delhi (INDIA), making it the one of the polluted city of the world. The situation in other metropolitan cities, namely Mumbai, Calcutta, Chennai and many other industrial cities of India has also become very grim. It has been deteriorating without manageable controls despite a lot of talks, seminars, conferences, warnings, precautions but with inadequate, ineffective results.
Due to unplanned mechanization, haphazard urbanization, uncontrolled population growth and clustered living due to poverty and unhealthy sanitations around, this has been a deteriorating curse inflicted on humankind in India and elsewhere.

Amidst universalisation of the issue of environmental degradation on global levels, its acute state in India cannot be ignored. India's environmental problems are gaining global significance because of the rapid and offensive speed of urbanization and lack of infrastructure.

Further, in a published study in the Journal Environmental Research Letters, it has been observed that the rise in CO_2 level will accelerate the jet stream – a high-altitude wind blowing from west to east across the Atlantic. It will speed up eastbound flights but slow down west-bound flights. Therefore, transatlantic aircraft will spend an extra 2,000 hours in

---

[1] First published in E-Journal *Global Processes* Vol. 1/2018, p. 213. Published with consent of GPJ. Revised.

the air every year. Further, transatlantic flights will burn an extra $22 million worth of fuel annually, which means this will increase the fuel costs to airlines, potentially raising ticket prices, and it will worsen the environmental impacts of aviation as it will emit an extra 70 million kg of CO2. According to the research, this might only be the tip of the iceberg.

The present paper is an attempt to analyze the impacts on environment because of misbehaving with the environment and how the same can be safeguarded from a Gandhian perspective and the new developments coming out of new researches alongwith the suggestions for a safe and Green Third Millennium.

Root and Principles of Gandhian Philosophy

The fundamentals of Gandhian philosophy are truth, nonviolence, and asceticism. His life and thinking revolved around his relentless quest for truth: that is also the literal meaning of the term Satyagraha.

Ahimsa (nonviolence) literally means non-harm, but to Gandhi nonviolence was much more than the absence of violence: it was a fully defined way of life.

According to Gandhi, ahimsa refers to nonviolence in action, speech, and thought. He believed that truth and nonviolence were intertwined, overlapping and interrelated ideas, and that truth can only be achieved nonviolently.

The concept of Satyagraha gave practical realization to the ideals of truth and nonviolence. According to Gandhi, Tapasya or ascetic self-sacrifice was necessary to achieve the highest level of truth.

Gandhi was very much influenced by Jainism and Buddhism.

Jainism looks at nature as a living entity and exhorts human beings to continually purify themselves by respecting the diverse life forms. In contemporary times, Jainism has been interpreted in such a way as to strengthen the relation between man and earth, a clear case of deployment of religion for ecology.

Hinduism also looks at nature and all life forms with equal reverence. Gandhi's voice of environmentalism was not the

Global Ecology: A Gandhian Perspective

lone voice at the turn of the Twentieth Century. Rabindranath Tagore represented nature in his poems and works. Shantiniketan, the institution that he founded, was another example of nature-friendly study and living.

Gandhi drew on a number of Western thinkers, who, although were not against the modernist project, romantically cherished the pre-industrial order. John Ruskin, for example, was critical of industrialisation in that it had sapped human sensibility and destroyed the harmonious relationship humans had with nature.

Gandhi, it must be noted, was a critic of the contemporary industrial civilization. He was an admirer of John Ruskin's criticism of Victorian era industrialization and urbanization in Britain. It was by reading Ruskins's book, 'Unto the Last', that Gandhi first realized the importance of manual labor. He was also influenced by Leo Tolstoy's idea of agriculture as the prime occupation of man.

In his own influential volume, Hind Swaraj (Indian Self-Rule), Gandhi argues that what we perceive today as civilization is an illusion, and that a so-called civilization that is unkind to outsiders will also maltreat the insiders.

Importantly, though a critic of modernity, Gandhi was not against technology. What he opposed were the inequalities and hierarchies of power among men, and the blind subjugation of nature to man, resulting from the estrangement of technological development from morality. Modern civilization has come about by doing violence to nature, understood as man's property.

Today's generation bears witness to the adverse effects of this tussle between men, modernity and nature.

From Survival to Ecology

Gandhi did not come to develop his integrated vision from original insights into nature and its working. Instead he was exploring how social change could be brought about through least harm to other human beings as well as to nature. Gandhian environmental activists like Chandi Prasad Bhatt and Sunderlal Bahuguna of the Chipko movement or even Medha Patkar and Baba Amte of the Narmada movement began their activism over questions relating to the livelihood issues of the marginalised sections of society.

Their struggle for protecting the livelihood resources eventually led to a form of environmentalism that made it possible for them to see the interconnections among environment, development, survival, sustainability and peace.

Gandhi was not an environmentalist who, while acknowledging the interconnection among all forms of life, was unconcerned about the survival of the human species. In fact, ecological concerns emerged from his focus on a basic needs model of social order that would not exploit nature for short-term gains but take only from it what is absolutely necessary for human sustenance.

Gandhi had to concede that life involves a certain amount of violence to nature even if it is unintended. What we can do is to minimise it to the maximum extent. Ecological Implications of Gandhi's Critique of Modernity for Gandhi, industrialisation and profit- generation were at odds with moral progress.

He said: *"The incessant search for material comforts and their multiplication is an evil. I make bold to say that the Europeans will have to remodel their outlook, if they are not to perish under the weight of the comforts to which they are becoming slaves."*

Further, with a prophetic vision, Gandhi warned: *"A time is coming when those who are in mad rush today of multiplying their wants, will retrace their steps and say; what have we done?"*[2]

If we look at the current debate on climate change, the manner in which the West is frantically trying to persuade the emerging countries to reduce their carbon emissions and the billions of dollars being spent by developed countries to slow the pace of climate change, it seems Gandhi's prediction has come true.

Although from the early seventies we were made aware of the environmental perils through books like Small is Beautiful (Schumacher, 1973) and Limits to Growth (Meadows et

---

[2] Quoted in Khoshoo and Moolakkattu, 2009.

al. 1972), it took more than two decades for the world to understand the gravity of the situation.

Meaning of Development & Sustainable Development

When we think about development, we are reminded of developed countries, their living standard, per-capita income
and gross national income. Developed countries have good
industrialization, good infrastructure and can be said that everything is well managed and very good than why are they
researching for sustainable development.

Development. It is process of progress or change in current system for comfort. In literal terms, development is about
improving the wellbeing of society/people.

Raising living standards and improving education, health, and
equality of opportunity are all essential components of economic development. Ensuring political and civil rights is a
broader development goal. Economic growth is an essential
means for enabling development; If development is sufficient
modern world should be satisfied with such type of development. but in itself it is highly imperfect proxy for progress.

Modern world and scientist thought that:

• The world has an unlimited supply of resources for human
   use;

• Nature is for human being and can be used any limit and any
way.

Sustainable Development. Sustainable development
means to "fulfil the present needs without compromising the
needs of future generation." Mahatma Gandhi's way of living
is the best example of sustainable development for world.

The theme of sustainable development has evolved with
the evolution of human civilization. The very beginning of human society and its onward march is woven critically around
this concept which has assumed significance for the survival
of the modern civilization and planet earth. Whenever human
civilization receded from the path of sustainable development
the danger to its survival was ensured. With the advent of industrial revolution in Europe began the era of unsustainable
development. The unleashing of creative energies of people

during that period led to the spectacular progress in the field of science and technology. The tapping of energy from coal and the application of new methods of production gave rise to unprecedented productivity.

While industrial revolution released humans from the fetters of feudalism and bigotry it put new chains around them in the form of materialism and materialistic appetite. The mind which became free from bondage of bigotry and exploitative feudal mode of production became subservient to machinery and greed. Driven by the credo of mass production the modern western civilization chose the path of violence subjugating the territories of the peoples of Asia, Africa and Latin America and appropriating their resources. Conquest and exploitation of the human and material resources beyond the boundaries of Europe became the guiding aspect of that civilization. The policies and values associated with that path led to the indiscriminate consumption of energy and resources of the planet earth and gave birth to an imperial mindset. By 1980s it was realized that such an approach would degrade the environment beyond repair and cause unimaginable consequences to the very existence of the planet.

An institutionalized approach in the form of The World Commission on Environment and Development under the Chairmanship of Harlem Brundtland was set up to find remedies to the problem. It produced a report in 1987 entitled "Our Common Future" which stressed on the ability of mankind to make development sustainable.

Gandhian Sustainability & Environmentalism

Mainstream Western ideas of scientific and technological development have historically been of decisive importance. So much so that from the era of the Industrial Revolution onwards, an incalculable amount of senseless harm has been inflicted upon the environment, largely in the name of progress and development.

However, the very idea of development has today become problematic. As commonly used by the mainstream media, the term "development" mainly refers to economic development, improved infrastructure, and achieving higher standards of living. This brand of development often blatantly disregards the profound humanitarian and environmental concerns about progress as historically observed, about development as we know it.

If we are to continue as a species on this planet, it stands to reason that development must not be taken to mean the irresponsible and irreversible plundering of natural resources and of the environment. It is clear that, while we must have some form of development, it had better be sustainable. This study views our treatment of the natural environment as a consequence of our worldview and of our morality and argues that Gandhian philosophy provides a viable (and authentically Indian) conceptual foundation on which to build genuinely sustainable development.

Gandhian values need to be accepted as the guiding principles underlying all our development planning. Moreover, since Gandhian values have worldwide appeal, so should their application to important, burning issues of ecology and sustainability.

Mahatma Gandhi & Sustainable Development

Mahatma Gandhi's familiar figure has become a symbol of peace and nonviolence to the whole world. He was a leader and a social reformer of extraordinary stature and authority. However, it is not common to think of Gandhi as an environmentalist. Although, admittedly, he wasn't an environmentalist in the modern sense (the major environmental problems of the present emerged in the post-Gandhi era), yet the Gandhian ideals – including, centrally, the idea of Swaraj or self-rule – enable a practical of sustainable development that can be implemented without compromising the quality of life. Indeed, Gandhi's oft-quoted view that "the Earth provides enough to satisfy every man's need, but not any man's greed" may stand as a one-line ethical summary of modern environmentalist thinking.

Gandhi was a practitioner and ardent advocate of vegetarianism. He also practiced "nature cure," a traditional Indian form of medicine that is now achieving a semblance of some acceptance in the West. He was a dedicated practitioner of frugality, of recycling and reuse, and a trenchant critic of various aspects of modernity. Most major Indian environmentalists today are influenced by the precepts of Gandhi's Satyagraha – nonviolent resistance, which in some extreme cases may even include fasting unto death – in opposing the political status quo.

In spite of his attachment to nature, Gandhi was not chiefly preoccupied with problems of nature or the environment.

For example, the dangers posed by the man-eating tigers of Kumaon (made famous by the narratives of Jim Corbett, British-Indian hunter and tracker turned conservationist, author of Man-Eaters of Kumaon) would have left less of a moral impression on Gandhi than instances of political or social injustice, lawyer by training and moralist by calling that he was. Reportedly, the English historian Edward Thomson once remarked to Gandhi that wildlife was rapidly declining in India, to which Gandhi replied with sarcasm, "Wildlife is decreasing in the jungles, but increasing in the towns."

In the words of the environmentalist Ramachandra Guha, "the wilderness had no attraction for Gandhi." In his writings, Gandhi does not emphatically celebrate the harmony or untamed beauty of nature; his focus is the study of men, of their mores and morals, of the human condition.

So, yes, there are some obvious limits to calling Gandhi an "environmentalist" without qualification. Yet his immense influence on the life and works of many of India's best-known environmentalists must not be overlooked. It is arguably its Gandhianism that gives modern Indian environmentalism its depth, strength of character, authenticity, and global appeal.

Gandhi, who considered the earth a living organism, understood nature and existence in terms of a Cosmic Law that entails that the universe is a single self-coherent all-encompassing entity, organized and animated by a cosmic spirit wherein all life and all existence are one. As a proponent of the monistic (non-dualist) Indian philosophical system of Advaita, he believed in the essential unity of man and nature.

He wrote, *"I believe in the advaita (non-duality); I believe in the essential unity of man, and for that matter, of all that lives. Therefore, I believe that if one-man gains spirituality, the*

Global Ecology: A Gandhian Perspective

world gains with him, and if one man fails, the whole world fails to that extent."

He held evolution to be impossible without the cooperation and sacrifice on the part of all species, human and nonhuman alike. Gandhi synthesized his philosophical and spiritual principles out of his deep knowledge of the religious traditions of Hinduism, Buddhism, Jainism, Christianity, and Islam. His social, economic and political ideas developed within a conceptual framework that assumed the internal interconnectedness and interdependence of the universe in its entirety. In this context, the well-known Gandhian prescription of "simple living" attempts both to curb human overreaching and greed, and to prevent the mindless exploitation of natural resources.

Gandhism and the **Gandhian vision** of sustainable development emerged as a critique of the Western-centric dominant model of development with its misplaced emphasis on the promotion of individual growth and selfadvancement, the harnessing of Nature, the achievement of technological sophistication, the spurring of urbanization and the increased use of markets for the distribution of economic goods and services.

Gandhism challenges the basic assumptions that the Western model of development makes about the use of Nature and natural resources, the meaning of progress, the ways in which society is governed and also about how public policy is made and implemented.

The discussion of Mahatma Gandhi and Sustainable Development would be incomplete without referring to the burning issue of water scarcity in the world.

Twenty first century has been described as the most water stressed century in the world. Water scarcity across the world may cause conflicts among nations. If not controlled and dealt with in a fair and equitable manner the water scarcity problem may give rise to another world war reminiscent of other world wars over resources and other trading and commercial interests. It is in this context that Mahatma Gandhi's ideas need to be recollected and put into practice. During our struggle for independence he referred to the water famine occurring in the Kathiawar region of Gujarat ruled by many princes.

To address the issue of acute shortage of water he advised all the princely States to form a confederation and take long term measures for planting trees in vast tracts of land. He opined that afforestation on a large scale constituted the most effective step to face the water crisis.

The twenty-first century world need to follow his words with utmost seriousness. The British rulers who treated forests as a source of revenue hardly understood their relevance from the point of view of ecology and sustainable development. Their approach was a byproduct of the exploitation of natural resources regardless of its consequences for the common people and environment.

Tuning himself with the common people whom he called "the dumb millions" he also suggested in a prayer meeting in Delhi in 1947 for harvesting rain water and using it for irrigational purposes to avoid famines and food shortages.

The M.S. Swaminathan Commission for Farmers in its report submitted to the Prime Minister in 2006 recommended to harvest rain water for addressing the problem of irrigation affecting our farmers.

Mahatma Gandhi was far ahead of his times in grappling with challenges to planet earth arising out of a life style which multiplied wants and desires and left no stone unturned to satisfy them. At a time when mankind is facing the dangerous prospects of getting annihilated due to accelerating pace of global warming it is important to rediscover Gandhiji's ideas and put them into practice. It is heartening that in many parts of the world people are getting inspired by his ideals and taking appropriate action.

It was best reflected in the initiative taken in Germany to establish Green Party and pursue policies consistent with nature and ecology. One of the founders of Green Party Ms. Patra Kelly admirably summed up the impact of Mahatma Gandhi in forming the party when she wrote the following: In particular area of our work we have been greatly inspired by Mahatma Gandhi. That is in our belief that a life style and method of production which rely on endless supply of raw materials and which use those raw materials lavishly, also provide motive force for violent appropriation of raw materials from other countries. No 1/2018

In contrast, a responsible use of raw materials as part of an ecologically oriented life style and economy reduces the risk that policies of violence will pursue.

Such a vision provides the remedy to create a new civilization the foundation of which is based on discipline, restraint and morality. It is heartening to note that the recent literature being brought out in the western world is eloquently following the vision of Mahatma Gandhi.

A book, *Surviving the Century: Facing Climate Chaos*, edited by Professor Herbert Girardet and brought out by the World Future Council stresses on measures suggested by Mahatma Gandhi in the beginning of the twentieth century. The book argues for an approach which would speak for the earth community. It suggests that such an approach can be devised if we become nonviolent, respect nature, follow the path of sustainable development and ensure justice to the poor. All those aspects remained central to Mahatma Gandhi's life and work.

There is slow but sure realization that by following Gandhiji's ideals we can survive the century. The line of argument which attempts to speak for the earth community essentially recaptures the immortal and eloquent words of Mahatma Gandhi that earth has enough for fulfilling everybody's need but not anybody's greed.

These words constitute the sum and substance of sustainable development. There is no alternative to such a world view. *The Time Magazine* in its 29th April 2007 issue came out with 51 *Global Warming Survival Guides*. The 51st Guide earnestly suggests sharing more, consume less and simplify life. In other words, the Time Magazine, one of the mouth pieces of the western world, is turning to Mahatma Gandhi to save the world from the danger of extinction caused by global warming. It is a measure of Mahatma Gandhi's enduring and deeper significance in the context of attempts to protect the planet earth. It is therefore indispensable to rediscover his writings and comprehend them to further the cause of sustainable development.

Law, Ethics & Society

The Gandhian vision of Sustainable Development can be spelt out in a 'Ten-Point Charter':

- Humankind would act in a manner that it is a part of Nature, rather than apart from Nature.
- Materials available on the earth are not used with an element of greed.
- Human beings practice non-violence not only towards fellow human beings but also towards other living organisms and inanimate materials, because overuse of such materials also amounts to violence.
- Women are respected, and are made partners in, and are given their rightful place in all spheres of human endeavour.
- Bottom-up shared view is preferred to the top-down authoritarian overview.
- Conservationist and sustainable life-saving approach prevails over the unsustainable, consumerist, self-destructive approach.
- Human beings care for and share with the poor and the destitute in society, as a moral obligation towards them.
- The human race thinks about how much is enough for a simple, need-based, austere and comfortable lifestyle.
- All development, as far as is possible, leads to local self-reliance, and equity with social justice.
- Ethics and self-discipline in resource use is an overriding criterion of development.

It needs to be recognized that the Gandhian vision aims at fulfilling human material and non-material needs, advancing social equity, expanding organizational effectiveness and building human and technical capacity towards sustainability.

The objectives of sustainability require the protection of the natural resource base upon which future development depends.

To Gandhi, valuing Nature and non-human life forms in an intrinsic way, has also to become an integral part of

Global Ecology: A Gandhian Perspective

development. The Gandhian model of development is aimed not just at protecting Nature but at creating an ecological society that lives in harmony with Nature.

This calls for reconciling economic activity with social progress and environmental protection.

In the Gandhian model, the promotion of human well-being does not have to depend upon the destruction of Nature.

The Gandhian model represents an important example of the new environmentalist approach. It seeks to reconcile the ecological, social and economic dimensions of development, now and into the future, and adopts a global perspective in this task.

It aims at promoting a form of development that is contained within the ecological carrying capacity of the planet, which is socially just and economically inclusive. It focuses not upon individual advancement, but upon protecting the common future of humankind.

Gandhi challenges industrial societies not only to reduce the resource intensity of production (sustainable production), but also to undertake new patterns of consumption that reduce the levels of consumption and change what is consumed and by whom (sustainable consumption). This would create the conditions necessary for equitable development.

Gandhian Principles & Action Plans for Sustainable Futures

The need of the hour, at the present juncture, is to acknowledge the contemporary relevance of the following six Gandhian eternal Principles and to develop suitable Action Plans to realize them, as emphasized by the Global Greens, an international network of Green parties and political movements at the Global Greens Conference in 2001:

- Ecological Wisdom
- Social Justice
- Participatory Democracy
- Non-Violence/ Ahimsa
- Sustainability
- Respect for Diversity

Law, Ethics & Society

Conclusion

New Global Economic System some economist suggests that anew economic system at global level is necessary for long term survival of the human race. The present economic system is characterized by maximum flow of money, maximum profit, maximum production, maximum consumption, and maximum resources use.

This frontier economy as it is called now, should be replaced by space ship economy. A space ship economy or sustainable economy promotes Reduce, Reuse & Recycle.

Conservation, of renewable resources, product durability and a clean and healthy environment. People live within the limits imposed by earth. Future patterns of developments should be made much less material-intensive. Broken goods should be repaired, rather than replaced.

Sustainable economy can be achieved and succeed only with new policies, new political directions, education and awareness. The most fundamental changes would have to be an ethical shift promoted by parents, teachers, and government agencies.

Government can help by framing new laws that are conducive to the attainment of sustainable society with sustainable economy can come from combination of personal and governmental efforts.

From a Gandhian perspective, the present environmental mess, ranging from deforestation, soil and biodiversity loss, to pollution and climate change, is not a disease but only a symptom. A good doctor treats the disease and not the symptom. The disease is the very concept and patterns of growth and development that are being followed everywhere.

We can say that Gandhi's environmentalism fitted in with his overall vision for India and the world that sought to extract from nature what is absolutely necessary for human sustenance. His ideas on environment are intimately linked with all his ideas relating to the polity, economy, health and development.

His asceticism and simple living, a rural-centred civilisation based on village autonomy and self- reliance, handicrafts and craft-centred education, emphasis on manual labour and absence of exploitative relationships are infused with elements of an ecological vision.[3]

Even his approach to gender did not attempt to break the connection with nature, but to man- euver within it and provide some space for women to uplift themselves.

It is therefore no wonder that Gandhi is a major inspiration for many environmental movements worldwide, particularly for those who link their movement with larger concerns for human sustenance and development. He would not be an inspiration for environmental radicals whose approach to environment allow little space for human sustenance and livelihood issues.

Although he was not anthropocentric in his approach, he was not prepared to allow the question of human survival to be sidelined in discussions on environment. Instead he showed how a total sustainable way of organizing human affairs could be evolved that left a lighter human footprint on this earth and showed how man could live in harmony with nature.

Small wonder, his famous statement "the Earth has enough for everyone's need, but not for anyone's greed," has become a slogan for contemporary environmental movements.

References

Gupta, I. (2015). *Sustainable Development: Gandhi Approach*. OIDA International Journal of Sustainable Development 8(7), 27-32.

Kumar, D. J. (2011). *Gandhian Economic Thought and Sustainable Development. Indic Economic Thought in Pursuit of Happiness and Sustainable Development: Its Relevance and Application Draft*, Retrieved on 12.9.2016 http://www.devf.org/Documents/Symposium/Gandhian%20Economic%20Thought%20and%20Sustainable%20Development-Jeevan%20Kumar%20D.pdf.

---

[3] Jones, 2000.

Law, Ethics & Society

Kumar, j. (2011). *Gandhian Values for Sustainable Futures*, Retrieved on 12.9.2016 from http://www.countercurrents.org/jkumar121011.htm.

Moolakkattu, J. S. (2010). *Gandhi as a human ecologist. Journal of Human Ecology*, 29(3), 151-158.

Nishtha Sood, N. (2016). *Mahatma Gandhi as Environmentalist and Sustainability Precursor*, Retrieved on 12.9.2016 from http://www.ecorama.org/gandhian-philosophy-ofsustainable-development-12.

Saravanamuthu, K. (2006). Emancipatory accounting and sustainable development: a Gandhian–Vedic theorization of experimenting with truth. Sustainable Development, 14(4), 234-244

Sasikala, A.S. (2015). *Gandhi and Ecological Marxists: A Study of Silent Valley Movement*, Retrieved on 12.9.2016 fromhttp://www.gandhiashramsevagram.org/gandhiarticles/gandhi-and-ecological-marxists-a-study-of-silent-valley- movement.php.

Satya Narayana Sahu, S.N. (2016). *Mahatma Gandhi and Sustainable Development,* Retrieved on 12.9.2016 from http://magazines.odisha.gov.in/Orissareview/2016/August/engpdf/7-15.pdf.

The Law of Heraldic Arms

Paul Borrow-Longain

Introduction

The Law of Heraldic Arms governs the legal right to the possession of an Achievement of Arms[1], as well as their use and
display within certain jurisdictions. Each jurisdiction, even
within the United Kingdom of Great Britain and Northern Ireland, has a different legal standing for their governance: the
right to display arms within England & Wales is distinctly different from Scotland. The law of Arms is in turn different from
our continental European cousins independent of their Sover-
eigns in most countries mentioned herein descending from
the Queen-Empress[2] Victoria and her consort Prince Albert,
the Prince Consort (formally His Serine Highness Prince Albert of Saxe-Coberg and Gotha). Within this paper, we shall
be discussing a limited number of counties within Europe and
their distinctive application of the laws of Arms in their legal
jurisdictions, as well as the governance of Arms within the
United States of America as an example of how they are handled within a Republic with no historical precedence of
granting Armorial Bearings[3] to its citizens.

Governance of the granting, assumption (within jurisdictions which allow) of Arms and the subsequent use and
display of such Achievements of Arms had to be implemented
as their initial use was to act as a manner to identify Knights
on the battlefield and subsequently during jousting competi-
tions, as the armour rendered the wearer unrecognisable.
Therefore, it was imperative that no two Knights were display-
ing the same Achievement of Arms.

The law of Arms, as the above suggests, dates back to
the 14th century with the first written mention of the same being by the renowned Italian legal scholar Bartoulus de
Saxoferrato who lived between 1313 and 1357. In his treatise
De Insigniis et Armis, he presented an in-depth academic

---

[1] An Achievement of Arms is the term used to describe the full heraldic
achievement which in its whole consists of shield, supporters, crest, and
motto.

[2] The Prime Minister of the day of the United Kingdom was instrumental in
having the Queen proclaimed Empress if India due to the fact her daughter
was the Empress of Germany.

[3] Armorial Bearings are defined as the heraldry consisting of a design or image depicted on a shield.

discussion on both the law of Arms as well as a number of the pertinent problems within trademark law.

While the law of Arms is part of the law of the land in countries whom govern the granting, assumption and use of heraldry, it is not part of common law within England or countries whom derive laws from English law.

Right to Armorial Bearings

The right of an individual or corporate body, be they an institution of academic learning; a religious institution (including in the person who holds a religious seat - such as an Archbishop); or an incorporate body such as a private or public corporation, to bear such Armorial Achievements must be found ultimately within law of Arms in such jurisdiction as which they reside.

Within jurisdictions where the granting, assumption and subsequent use of such heraldic symbols are commonplace, the right to said Arms is borne by the virtue of ancestral right or by a new grant to the user from their jurisdiction's governing authority. In relation to ancestral right, historically in the male line, though modern times have seen the same in the female line, this means decent from an individual who received a grant of Arms via Letters Patent[4] from their governing authority. Since the early use of heraldry this has been from the Crown.

Realms of HM Queen Elizabeth II

In relation to the Realms of Her Majesty Queen Elizabeth II, the Crown's prerogative of granting Armorial Bearings to her subjects and corporate bodies within said Realms is delegated by Letters Patent to a number of distinct governing bodies. Within England & Wales the delegation is to H.M. College of Arms in London; in Scotland it is to the Office of the Lord Lyon in Edinburgh; and within Canada, it is to the Canadian Heraldic Authority Under the direction of the Queen's representative in Canada, the Governor-General. Her Majesty's other Realms, such as New Zealand and the Commonwealth of Australia, do not currently have their own heraldic authority. However New Zealand has a dedicated Officer of Arms (a Herald) based in New Zealand who is part of the Royal Household as a member of H.M. College of Arms. There is a long running debate within the Commonwealth of

---

[4] Letters Patent is the name given to the official document authorising the grant of an Achievement of Arms.

Australia, primarily spearheaded by the Australian Heraldry Society for clarification on the legal basis for the College of Arms, which is legally constituted by the Crown in right of England & Wales, to grant arms to Australians, especially under the position as Crown in right of the different States and Territories that constitute the Commonwealth of Australia.

Canada—Since H.M. The Queen of Canada signed the Letters Patent creating the Canadian Heraldic Authority any Canadian citizen or corporate body can petition for a grant of new arms or registration of existing arms, assuming they meet the requirements. Eligibility for a grant of arms is based on an individual's contributions to the community, although the exact criteria for grants or registrations have not been published, as is the case throughout the Queens Realms.

A significant number of grants have been presented to individuals whom have been recognised with State Honours for their achievements, such as through admission to the Order of Canada, and who are therefore entitled to an Achievement of Arms[5].

In relation to individuals and institutions who already possess legitimate Achievement of Arms, they may request the Canadian Heraldic Authority to have their arms registered. There is no cost associated with application for registration.

Direct descendants of an individual granted Armorial Bearings are entitled to use said Arms, with suitable marks of difference. Within Canada the right is held by both male and female offspring.

Scotland—Within Scotland there are two legal ways to hold Armorial Bearings. The first being to inherit them and the second via a new grant of Arms from the Office of the Lord Lyon.

In relation to inheritance of Arms, the Law is rather straightforward and different from England & Wales. Within Scotland a coat of arms is considered an incorporeal heritable property and therefore can only belong to one person at a time. For this reason, the younger children of an armiger have no direct right to inherit the arms (unless and until all elder branches die out) and therefore why they must matriculate their fathers' arms with a mark of difference with the Office of the Lord Lyon. The eldest son inherits his fathers Arms as

[5] The Canadian Heraldic Authority charge a nominal fee to those successful in their petition for an Achievement of Arms.

they are in according to any limitations of the grant or of tailzie (entail[6]).

In relation to a new grant of Arms If you are Scottish of are of Scottish descent and not living in a country where there is a heraldic authority, and subject to the Office of the Lord Lyon considering you a 'worthy and virtuous person', a grant of Armorial Bearing is possible via one of the following three routes:

- ❖ If you can prove that you are heir to someone who at some time properly matriculated a Scottish coat of arms, then you can petition the Lyon Court to matriculate these in your name;
- ❖ If you have no armigerous direct forebears, you can petition for a new Grant of Arms;
- ❖ If you live in, say, America and have no property in Scotland or residence there, it may be possible to petition for arms in the name and memory of a long-deceased Scottish ancestor, then establish a cadet[7] matriculation.

Once recorded in the Lyon Register, these arms have the full protection of the laws of Scotland, and the armiger becomes one of Scotland's 'noblesse'[8].

England & Wales—Within England & Wales there are two legal ways to hold Armorial Bearing. The first being to inherit them and the second is via a new grant of Arms from H. M. College of Arms in London.

In relation to inheritance the children of a holder of legally granted Arms may use their fathers Arms, with a suitable mark of difference called Cadency Marks, during their father's lifetime. Upon his passing the eldest son will inherit his father's Arms, without any Cadency marks, while the other sons continue to use their fathers Arms with the marks of difference.

In the case of daughters, they may use their father's Arms on lozenge. While they are unmarried, she displays her arms on a lozenge or an oval. When she marries, a lady may unite her arms with those of her husband; this is called marital arms. The combined Achievement of Arms is called Impaled

---

[6] A legal component often found within an individuals Last Will and Testament.

[7] A junior branch of a family.

[8] This term does not mean that the individual has achieved the status of being ennobled.

Arms[9]. In the case where one spouse belongs to the higher ranks of an order of chivalry[10], and thereby entitled to surround his / her arms with a circlet of the order, it is usual to place them on two separate shields tilted towards one another. In modern times a married woman may also display either her own arms, or her husband's arms, alone on a shield with a small differencing mark to distinguish her from her father or husband.

Cadency marks may be used to identify the arms of brothers, in a system said to have been invented by John Writhe in about 1500. Small symbols are painted on the shield, usually in a contrasting tincture at the top. The standard Cadency Marks are as follows:

- ❖ The eldest son (during the lifetime of his father) has a label[11].
- ❖ The second son has a crescent.
- ❖ The third a mullet.
- ❖ The fourth a martlet.
- ❖ The fifth an annulet.
- ❖ The sixth a fleur de lis.
- ❖ The seventh a rose.
- ❖ The eighth a cross moline.
- ❖ The ninth a double quatrefoil.

Arms are only transmitted through a female line when there is a failure of male heirs[12]. A woman with no surviving brothers, or whose deceased brothers have no surviving issue, is an heraldic heiress. Providing that she marries a man who bears arms, the children of their marriage may include the arms of her father as a quartering in their own shields. This is how elaborate shields of many quarterings come about.

You'll sometimes see that an heraldic heiress will request her future husband to petition for an Achievement of Arms in their own right, subject to them meeting the requirements, so that any future children will inherit a quartered Arms. Therefore, keeping her fathers Arms in use.

The second way that Arms can be held is if the holder has legally petitioned H. M. College of Arms in their own right.

---

[9] Impaled meaning placed side by side in the same shield, with those of the man on the dexter and those of his wife on the sinister.

[10] An Order of Chivalry includes, for example, the Order of the Garter: Order of the Thistle; Order of Merit; and the Order of the British Empire.

[11] a horizontal strip with three pendent drops.

[12] The holder of the Achievement of Arms has no sons to inherit.

Law, Ethics & Society

They enact the power delegated to them by the Sovereign and therefore all Grants come from the Sovereign of the United Kingdom.

While the complete process leading to the issuance of a Letters Patent granting Armorial Bearings is not fully known, the first step is to submit a petition to His Grace The Duke of Norfolk as Earl Marshal of England. This petition is not written by the applicant but by one of the Officers of Arms acting as his Agent. There are no fixed criteria of eligibility for a grant of arms, however things such as awards or honours from the Crown, civil or military commissions, university degrees, professional qualifications, public and charitable services are all taken into account.

Republic of Ireland

The legal prerequisite to have been granted, or have been hereditary inherited, an Achievement of Arms is not required within the Republic of Ireland. Where a heraldic symbol (Achievement of Arms, flag, standard, banner, badge or any such similar device) existed pre-1552 or at any time after if they belong to the Gaelic tradition may continue to use such heraldic symbols.

In relation to new grants from the Office of the Chief Herald of Ireland, the Office accepts petitions for grants of arms from:

i.   A citizen of Ireland or a person who has an entitlement to become a citizen.

ii.   A person resident in the State for at least the five-year period immediately before the date of the application.

iii. A public or local authority, corporate body or other entity which has been located or functioning in Ireland for at least five years.

iv.   An individual, corporate body or other entity not resident or located in Ireland but who or which has substantial historical, cultural, educational, financial or ancestral connections with Ireland.

Kingdom of Spain

Withi-n the Kingdom or Spain, the power to grant a new Achievement of Arms is legally restricted to the Spanish Sovereign. The Cronistas de Armas (Chroniclers of Arms) have the power to certify arms within the jurisdiction of their office. Currently the only such jurisdiction that carry out certification of Achievement of Arms is the Province of Castile and Leon.

Kingdom of Denmark

During the Absolutist era (1660 to 1848) the Arms of Denmark's nobility were granted by the King's herald. However, the Office was dissolved in 1849 and ever since the only way for a Danish subject to acquire an Achievement of Arms is through assumption. Therefore, the individual designs their own or commissions an artist to design on their behalf.

Kingdom of Norway

Within the Kingdom of Norway there has never been a granting and regulatory authority for Achievements of Arms to their subjects for personal Arms, nor has one been proactively requested in their legal system. Since the Middle Ages Arms have simply been assumed by those who want them.

Federal Republic of Germany

Since 1918 personal Arms have generally been assumed by anyone wanting them, as was the general case during the times of the German Empire, the former German States and in the Holy Roman Empire. There is an option to register the Arms.

It is worth noting at that in the Federal Republic of Germany the Arms relate to a family, and so a name, and not to an individual. The right to the arms passes from the original bearer to those of his legitimate direct descendants by a male line.

The right to arms is now considered analogous to the right to names, expressed in the Bürgerliches Gesetzbuch, section 12. This interpretation was confirmed in 1992 by the Federal Court of Justice of Germany. Therefore, if an individual has the right to certain arms, that right is protected by the courts.

Pre-1918 Practice in the Holy Roman Empire & the German States

In the Early Middle Ages Emperor Karl IV's Marshal of Arms Bartolus de Saxoferato (Berthold Eisensax) stated "it is practice in the Holy Empire that everyone will use the arms he wants". While it is impossible to know exactly how many Germanic families held, or used, Armorial Bearings an estimate of three million is generally accepted. However, it was only a matter of a few thousand whom paid the fee to register them with a version of heraldic authority called a Hofpfaltzgraf.

A Hofpfaltzgraf could be a person, a corporate body, or an organisation. Most of the Germanic noble families held the position as an hereditary title. The University of Vienna also had the legal right to appoint a "Doctor Laureus" to carry out the same job as the Germanic noble families in this regard.

Some of the Hopfaltzgrafen had the authority to confer ennoblement to individuals within their jurisdiction, however many who did not have this legal right still conferred nobility if they were suitably financially compensated by the individual in question. This compensation was shared between themselves and the Holy Roman Emperor and record keeping was not considered overly advantageous.

By the time the Holy Roman Empire ceased to exist 1806 almost four thousand families and other entities claimed Hofpfaltzgrafen status, though their legal standing is certainly open to significant interpretation. Most of the records relating to Arms 'granted' during this period of time no longer exist because of a combination of factors including age and conflict related damage as well as parchment being recycled during the 30 Years War. No correct official record was kept and those that were kept suffered the same fate as the grantees originally Letters Patent.

After the fall of the Holy Roman Empire, Hofpfaltzgrafen became a nominal title while their previous powers were transferred to State Herald's Offices called Heroldsaemtern. Regrettably these were not established everywhere. Where the State Herald Offices were created, they concerned themselves generally to questions relating to nobility, Noble Arms and civic Arms. Most German States had no Heralds Office. Three exceptions are The Kingdom of Prussia who maintained a Herald Office from 1888 to 1918, the Kingdom of Bavaria who maintained one from 1899 to 1918, and the Kingdom of Saxony which maintained one from 1806 to 1918.

South Africa

Under South African law, which is Roman–Dutch, all citizens have the right to assume and bear arms as they please, provided they do not infringe the rights of others. The Bureau of Heraldry[13] has the power to register coats of arms to protect against misuse, but registration of arms is voluntary.

Kingdom of Sweden

---

[13] This authority has recently been used by individuals wanting an officially granted Achievement of Arms without paying the higher fees associated with other authorities. However, there us is still subject to the laws within their country of residence, so are arguably worthless unless they live in a country without heraldry having legal protection.

Within the Kingdom of Sweden corporations and government offices are entitled to Armorial Bearings if legally granted and registered with the Swedish Patent and Registration Office, which is subject to approval by the National Herald and the Heraldic Board of the National Archives of Sweden. Once this is completed the Achievement of Arms is legally protected by Swedish law.

Achievement of Arms of common citizens (referred to as burgher arms), however, are less strictly controlled. These are recognised by inclusion in the annually published Scandinavian Roll of Arms[14]. Therefore, anyone can assume Arms within the Kingdom of Sweden.

Finland
Within Finland there is currently no significant control on the assumption and subsequent use of heraldry. It should be noted that Achievements of Arms are not very popular within the country, which probably explains the lack of a granting authority and regulation.

Portugal
Currently Portugal has no granting authority for Achievements of Arms and therefore individuals are free to assume Arms.

Russian Federation
Within the Russian Federation, any individual is, in general, free to assume Arms, though there is some regulation regarding the Arms of nobility, State and Municipal Arms.

Republic of France
Within the Republic of France, any individual, corporate entity or municipality is entitled to assume Armorial Bearings as no heraldic authority currently exists within the Republic. For historically issued Arms which have been inherited, the protection is just the same.

Law of Arms as Part of General Law
Within the jurisdictions that we are discussing within this paper the degree by which general law recognises Arms certainly differs, though the granting of an Achievement of Arms confers certain legal rights to the grantee[15], or heirs, of the Letters Patent. Within a given heraldic jurisdiction no two

---

[14] A document that lists the Achievements of Arms of individuals *et al.*
[15] Original individual or organisation who received the grant.

individuals or corporate bodies may use the same Achieve-ment of Arms. However, this protection is not extended between heraldic jurisdictions, and therefore it is both possi-ble and legal for an individual, for example in Germany, to use the same Achievement of Arms as an individual in England & Wales.

Although the common law courts do not regard Achieve-ment of Arms as property, armorial bearings are a form of real property. They are generally described as *tesserae gentilita-tis*.[16] Armorial Bearings are generally granted to descend from the original grantee by their children, by both males and fe-males, within the male line. In layman's terms this simply means that all the children of a grantee can use their fathers Achievement of Arms with suitable marks of difference, while the right to those Arms only pass to the children of the sons of the original grantee.

While the above is generally true one must take account of a number of possibilities. The first being that there is no surviving male heir to the original grantee. In this situation if there is a daughter (known as a heraldic heiress) and assum-ing their sons have the legal right to bear Arms, they may quarter their mother and father's Arms.

The second possibility is that the grantee only has a nat-ural born son, meaning a son born out of wedlock, and therefore no heraldic heir. I'm this situation the son may inherit his father's Arms with a suitable mark of difference[17], normally a black border around the outside of the shield.

A continuation of the discussion into the law of Arms as part of Common Law requires us to discuss each jurisdiction in turn, due to their unique differences.

Ireland—In the Republic of Ireland, the granting of Armorial Achievements to Irish citizens in governed by the Office of the Chief Herald of Ireland, an office dating back to 1552 when it was established under the English Crown as the Ulster King of Arms and converted to the Chief Herald's Office after the enactment of the 1937 Irish Constitution.

With the creation of the Irish Free State,[18] many func-tions had passed under the Irish Free State (Agreement) Act 1922 to the Provisional Government of the Irish Free State as of April 1922, however the pre-existing office of the Ulster

---

[16] insignia of gentility.
[17] An additional component of the Achievement of Arms to separate it from others.
[18] Formed when Ireland separated from the United Kingdom.

King of Arms continued unchanged until 1943. On the 1st April of that year the Office of the Chief Herald of Ireland as part of the Genealogical Office was created.

While the Office of Chief Herald of Ireland now has legal force derived from the National Cultural Institutions Act 1997, Section 13, which was enacted in May 2005. This enables the Board of the National Library to "designate a member of its staff to perform the duty of researching, granting and confirming coats of arms and such member shall use the appellation Chief Herald of Ireland or, in the Irish language, Príomh-Aralt na hÉireann, while performing such duties". Section 13 was intended to legitimise the granting of arms in Ireland, however its enactment caused significant debate as to whether any grants made since 1943 were valid.

This should have been of significant importance to the Government or Ireland as, in 1945, a grant was issued granting an Achievement of Arms to the State. There remains a degree of concern regarding the true effectiveness of said bill. Individual members of the Seanad Eireann[19] including Senator Brendan Ryan introduced the Genealogy & Heraldry Bill (2006). The Bill was later withdrawn on 12 December 2006 with the consent of the sponsoring senator and was subsequently referred to the board of the National Library for consideration by John O'Donoghue - Minister for Arts, Sport and Tourism at that time.

In September 2007 a notice was added to the National Library website noting the suspension of the new granting of Achievement of Arms until the questions around the legality of their granting was further clarified. Subsequent to the receipt of legal advice, the Board of the National Library was "satisfied that it can exercise the heraldic powers conferred on it by the 1997 Act", and therefore the Office of the Chief Herald of Ireland recommenced the process of granting Armorial Bearings to individuals and Corporate Bodies entitled to them. The Board did, however, note that "doubts exist regarding the legal basis of heraldic functions exercised in the State prior to the establishment of the Board" and that "with minor amendment, the wording of the Act could be made more succinct".

While the issue of the legality of grants of Achievement of Arms by the Chief Herald may have been resolved in the most part, there aren't any penalties to discourage anyone from designing and subsequently using a new coat of arms.

---

[19] Irish Senate and upper house.

Law, Ethics & Society

Such arms would be protected by the current copyright law of Ireland.

Kingdom of Spain—In relation to the Kingdom of Spain there is no current governing law and therefore authority.

Kingdom of Denmark—In Denmark the unlawful use of an Achievement of Arms and / or other insignia of Danish and foreign authorities is a criminal offence under the Danish Criminal Code §§ 132-133. There is no legal protection for Non-official Achievements of Arms (eg. Those which have been assumed). Having stated that fact any specific rendition of an Achievement of Arms (when considered as a Trade-mark) is already protected through current copyright law.

Most if not all of the insignia used by cities, towns and regions are regulated by the Heraldic Consultant to the Danish State, which is an office constituted under the Danish National Archive. Registration by the Heraldic Consultant to the Danish State is a prerequisite for protection of all official Danish insignia and is governed by the Danish Criminal Code's §§ 132-133. Protection of all insignia in relation to trademark law requires registration by the Danish trademark authorities. However, if an insignia is registered by the Heraldic Consultant, trademark rights are automatically acquired.

Kingdom of Norway—In relation to the national arms as well as the Royal Arms and Arms for use by the Ministry of Foreign Affairs, they are governed by a department of the Norwegian Government. When it comes to the subject of Arms for branches of the Armed Forces they fall directly under the jurisdiction of the relevant heads of the branch of the Norwegian Armed Forces. Municipal Arms are governed by The National Archives of Norway as their heraldic authority. Public arms are protected by the Norwegian Penal Code, article 328, which also governs the unauthorised use of foreign public Arms.

Federal Republic of Germany—Since the formation of the Federal Republic of Germany in 1918 following the end of the First World War heraldic affairs are handled under the Civil Law. Personal arms are protected as a part of the name, if the Achievement of Arms is officially recorded and subsequently published. There are several "heraldic societies" which have been granted a legal license by the local Lower Court, the Revenue, and the Chamber of Commerce. Each of these

Law of Heraldic Arms

legally constituted societies has to be formally established and obey various rules set down by the aforementioned authorities which include the requirement to maintain detailed records, publishing an armorial as well as keeping genealogical records for each Achievement of Arms it registers.

When an individual approaches one of the societies, they will review Arms against the rules of heraldry and retain the authority to demand the individual make changes in order for them to be registered. However, the only action the society can take if the individual refuses is to, in turn, refuse to register the Arms.

For individuals who do not wish to approach one of these societies, it is possible to register your arms via the professional services of a solicitor. The individual is still required by law to publish the registered arms, and the solicitor would probably not be in a position to certify that they accorded with the rules of heraldry. If a legal professional's work does not meet the rules of heraldry, they are regarded in law as a trademark.

In relation to the use of civic arms, governance is slightly different. Most municipal constitutions state that the town or community may use arms should it wish. If the municipality requires a new Achievement of Arms, they are required to be designed by a heraldist or heraldry society. The next phase required sees the Arms being scrutinised by the State Archive. Upon their approval the Arms become legal. If a community uses an Achievement of Arms without going through this process, they are therefore unofficial and subsequently illegal.

Canada—The Canadian law of arms is now regulated by the Canadian Heraldic Authority since 1988. This is because of a Letters Patent signed by H.M. The Queen[20]. This document is the legal basis for protection of heraldry within Canada.

The Letters Patent being:

ELIZABETH THE SECOND, by the Grace of God of the United Kingdom, Canada and Her other Realms and Territories QUEEN, Head of the Commonwealth, Defender of the Faith.

(Great Seal of Canada)

---

[20] HM The Queen acted as Sovereign of Canada which is legally separate from her Sovereignty of her other Realms.

Law, Ethics & Society

TO ALL TO WHOM these Presents shall come or whom the same may in anyway concern,

GREETING:

WHEREAS it is desirable and Our Privy Council for Canada has advised that Letters Patent do issue authorizing and empowering Our Governor General of Canada to exercise or provide for the exercise of all powers and authorities lawfully belonging to Us as Queen of Canada in respect of the granting of armorial bearings in Canada.

NOW KNOW YE that We, by and with the advice of Our Privy Council for Canada, do by these Presents authorize and empower Our Governor General of Canada to exercise or provide for the exercise of all powers and authorities lawfully belonging to Us as Queen of Canada in respect of the granting of armorial bearings in Canada.

IN WITNESS WHEREOF, We have caused these Our Letters to be made Patent and for the greater testimony and validity thereof, We have caused Our Great Seal of Canada to be affixed to these Presents, which We have signed with our Royal Hand.

GIVEN the fourth day of June in the year of Our Lord one thousand nine hundred and eighty-eight and in the thirty-seventh year of Our Reign.

BY HER MAJESTY'S COMMAND

(signature Brian Mulroney)

PRIME MINISTER OF CANADA

Canada, unlike other Realms of Queen Elizabeth II, also provides full equality to women in terms of inheriting and transmitting arms.

And additional protection granted to all armigers[21] within Canada is that they have the opportunity to file for trademark protection of their Achievement of Arms under the Trade-Marks Act, Under para. 9(1) (n.1).

---

[21] An individual who holds Armorial Bearings legally.

"any armorial bearings granted, recorded or approved for use by a recipient pursuant to the prerogative powers of Her Majesty as exercised by the Governor General in respect of the granting of armorial bearings, if the Registrar has, at the request of the Governor General, given public notice of the grant, recording or approval".

On request, the Canadian Heraldic Authority can arrange for the trade-mark registration of a heraldic emblem in the Public Register of Arms, Flags and Badges of Canada. A fee is payable for this service which is currently in the order of $500 per emblem, payable to the Receiver General of Canada. The protection is valid for 15 years. It's important to note that each component of the grant, badge, flag, standard and coat of arms are considered separate emblems, and the fee is payable for each one you with to apply for protection on.

Once the process for awarding of Armorial Bearing to Canadian citizens is completed, the grant documents are recorded in the Public Register of Arms, Flags and Badges of Canada and the notice of the grant is published in the Canada Gazette, Part I, under the section "Government House[22]".

South Africa—Within South Africa The Bureau of Heraldry has the power to register coats of arms to protect against their misuse, however it is important to note that registration of one's Armorial Bearings is on a purely voluntary basis.

There is no legal protection for Armorial Bearings unregistered, and, should an individual who has had their arms registered, consider your arms as infringing, there could be a legal case made.

Kingdom of Sweden—Within the Kingdom of Sweden in relation to corporations and official bodies and offices The National Archives Heraldry Board, which was established under Swedish statute 2007:1179, is the current highest heraldic body within the Kingdom. The board is chaired by the National Archivist and includes three other officials, referred to as deputies, which is made up of the State Herald (who acts as secretary), the National Archives Jurist and the National Archives Heraldic Artists. This board only convenes as needed, which in recent years has been once or twice a year, and governs the award and subsequent use of heraldry in relation to corporations and official bodies and offices.

---

[22] Home of Her Majesties representative in Canada, the Governor-General of Canada.

Law, Ethics & Society

In order to register new municipal arms, a municipality must submit its proposal to both the National Archives Heraldry Board and to the Swedish Patent and Registration Office for registration. Once the board has completed its consultation process and a warrant of arms has been presented to the petitioner, the Achievement of Arms may then be registered and implemented for use by the municipality.

Apart from municipal arms, heraldic arms registered by counties as well as by the Swedish military and other government bodies are also handled by the same authorities.

In relation to Arms of individuals, they do not have the same, or any legal protection under the Swedish legal system, unlike Arms of the Swedish Nobility and official bodies. The Swedish Collegium of Arms, operating under the Swedish Heraldry Society, is responsible for reviewing and registering burgher arms. The only protection available in this situation is if the Arms are registered as a legally enforceable logo.

As has already been stated, Burgher arms are not required to be registered, and so they are not protected under Swedish law. The Swedish Heraldry Society has stated that the most common way of obtaining recognition of burgher arms is by inclusion in the annually published Scandinavian Roll of Arms (Skandinavisk Vapenrulla). These were first published in 1963 and currently includes over 400 Swedish family coats of arms, as well as Armorial Bearings from the other Scandinavian countries.

Once an individual has made a submission to the Swedish Heraldry Society, the proposed arms are reviewed by the Swedish Collegium of Arms, who in turn publish their decisions in the Scandinavian Roll of Arms.

Finland—For all intense and purpose there is no heraldic legal system within Finland.

Portugal—Since the fall of the Monarchy of Portugal and the creation of the Republic, no centeral heraldic authority has been institutionalised, though there have been a number of sector-specific heraldic authorities.

In 1930, the Ministry of Interior appointed the Heraldic Section of the Association of Portuguese Archeologists as the authority to monitor the use of municipal heraldry with Portugal. This section also serves as heraldic adviser for other entities, however with no formal authority.

In 2004, H.R.H. Don Duarte Pio, Head of the Royal Family of Portugal, established The Institute of the Portuguese

Nobility to be the heraldic authority for the personal and family coats of arms of the descendants of the old Portuguese nobility. It was founded to be a replacement for the previous Council of Nobility. While the organisation is a private institution and therefore has no formal powers granted by the State, as it is not an official authority. However, it should be noted that its decisions in these matters are usually accepted by the Portuguese courts of Justice and by other official authorities.

It is important to note that other private institutions exist which are frequently required to act as heraldic advisers for both public and non-public entities. Two of the better known ones are the Portuguese Institute of Heraldry and the Portuguese Academy of Heraldry. However, like the aforementioned organ-isation, these institutions have no formal heraldic powers.

During the Monarchy (until 1910) the heraldic authorities of the Kingdom were the officers of arms and the Nobility Register Office. The Portuguese Monarchs had officers of arms at their service since approximately the 14th century, though there is learned opinion that they might have existed earlier. It's interesting to note that the first known holder of the office of Portugal King of Arms was most likely an Englishman named Harriet, who was in office during the reign of H.M. King John I.

At that time the granting of Armorial Bearings was not limited to the Monarch. Several nobles not only assumed their own Arms, but also granted arms to individuals under their authority. Therefore, external to the Monarch there have been a number of princes and other members of the nobility also had private officers of Arms working in their service. This practice came to an ended in 1476, when H. M. King Afonso V decreed that all grants of arms were to be made through the Portugal King of Arms.

The heraldic laws put in place by H. M. King Manuel I in 1521 regulated the heraldry as well as strictly regulating the organisation of the corporation of Officers of Arms of the Portuguese Monarchy. The corporation was headed by a Principle King of Arms whose role was to be fulfilled by the already existing Portugal King of Arms.

The corporation of the Officers of Arms came to include three Kings of Arms, three Heralds and three pursuivants. The three kings of arms were named after the three constituent states of the Portuguese Crown, namely the Kingdom of Portugal, the Kingdom of Algarve and the State of India, while the heralds after their respective capital cities and the pursuivants after a notable town of each of the states. When the

Law, Ethics & Society

Portuguese Court was moved to Brazil, the India King of Arms was renamed America, Africa and Asia King of Arms in 1808, though this was extremely short lived, and the Office was returned to the original title in 1825.

The Nobility Register Office was responsible for keeping the registers of all the Achievement of Arms of the Kingdom of Portugal. Meanwhile the High Armorer had the heraldic responsibility of keeping a roll of arms for the King's immediate consultation.

From the late 17th century the role of the the Officers of Arms became increasingly more ceremonial. Therefore, the offices were often filled by individuals with little or no heraldic knowledge. From that point onwards the responsibility for the heraldic authority function fell mainly on the Nobility Register Office.

Russian Federation—Within the Russian Federation, there is very little legal protection, regulation and quasi-state monitoring of the assumption and subsequent use of Armorial Bearings.

The Heraldic Council of the President of the Russian Federation is the official body that advises the President, and therefore the State, on heraldic matters. This includes the use of official symbols, and also is in charge of preventing their use by non-authorised individuals and bodies. It also helps local and regional governments devise coats of arms for their own identity and use.

The State Heraldic Register was founded with the decree of former President Boris Yeltsin № 403 dated March 21, 1996 and was founded with the primary defined as "with the aims of the systematisation and ordering of the use of official symbols and distinguishing signs."

The Heraldic Council also discusses matters relating to heraldry and researches heraldry in Russia. Part of this body of research is held by the State Heraldic Register which it has authority over.

Republic of France—Within the Republic of France the law recognises both assumed and inherited arms, considering them under law to be equivalent to a visual representation of a name, and given the same protections.

There is no central registry of arms currently in use within the Republic, and in the case of a disputed the matter has to be handled within the French legal system, who will make a judgement based upon the individual who can prove the longest right to the blazon.

England & Wales—Armorial Bearings within England & Wales are granted by the authority of the Sovereign. We can date the Royal control of Achievement of Arms from approximately 1530, when the Visitation Commission directed Clarenceux King of Arms to "reform all false armory and arms devised without authority".

The control over all heraldic matters within England & Wales is delegated to the Kings of Arms, namely Garter Principle King of Arms, Clarenceux and Norroy & Ulster. They have the duty, responsibility and privilege to interpret the laws of arms, and are empowered by the Sovereign, to grant arms in the name of The Sovereign.

In England & Wales, the law of arms is regarded as a part of the laws of England, and the common law courts will take judicial notice of it as such. However, the law of arms is not part of the common law and the common law Courts have no jurisdiction over matters of dignities and honours, such as armorial bearings, or peerages.

In England & Wales the jurisdiction of deciding rights to arms, and claims of descent, is held in the Court of Chivalry. As the substance of the common law is found in the judgments of the common law Courts, the substance of the Law of Arms can only be found in the customs and usages of the Court of Chivalry.

When the Court of Chivalry first obtained jurisdiction over armorial bearings is not known. It may be that when heraldry was first introduced, men took what arms they pleased. Nevertheless, by the first half of the fourteenth century, the Court of Chivalry began exercising jurisdiction in heraldic cases within England & Wales.

Scotland—The important difference between Scottish and English heraldic law is that in Scotland it is a matter of statute rather than civil law. Since a coat of arms may only be used if recorded in the Public Register of All Arms, approved by the Lord Lyon, no two individuals can bear the same arms at the same time, even by accident. To pretend to arms not so granted brings the matter under statute law and there may be proceedings in the Lyon Court, which is fully part of the Scots criminal justice system. Anyone who has stained-glass windows, dinner services, silver cutlery or anything else made carrying arms they do not legally possess, may find the whole lot confiscated and a fine imposed.

Law, Ethics & Society

The relevant Scottish laws, generally known as the Lyon King of Arms Acts, were passed in 1592, 1669, 1672 and 1867.

The law of arms as understood in Scotland consists of two principal parts, the rules of heraldry (such as blazoning[23]), and the law of heraldry. A coat of arms is incorporeal heritable property, governed, subject to certain specialities, by the general law applicable to such property. The possession of armorial bearings is therefore unquestionably a question of property. The misappropriation of arms is a real injury, actionable under the common law of Scotland.

Legally, it is the blazon which is important, and which is inherited, rather than the design as such, so it can be thought of more as a patent than a logo. Therefore, there may be differences in detail between depictions of arms.

United States—A Special Discussion

Considering the author is a Director of The College of Arms Foundation which is a registered 501(c)3 within the United States of America[24] he is very familiar with the growing interest in heraldry amongst Americans, and especially those with Scottish and English ancestry. We therefore present a concise overview on the legal standing of heraldry within the United States of America.

In the United States, protection of Achievement of Arms is for the most part limited to specific units of the United States Armed Forces, with a few exceptions. President George Washington, the first President of the United States of America held the belief that he was against the establishment of a national heraldic authority, although this did not stop him making use of his own ancestral arms.

Therefore, Personal Achievement of Arms may be assumed by any individual or corporate entity, however the right to these blazons is not protected by law in any way. It is possible that a coat of arms could be successfully protected as a trademark, however in general such protection is reserved for commercial use and not as a heraldic coat of arms.

The University of Texas at Austin has registered its emblem and Achievement of Arms for use in its capacity as an institution of higher education. Such protection presumes a specific graphic design or work of art, while blazon is a description which may be widely interpreted artistically.

---

[23] The language that is used to describe the Achievement of Arms in writing.
[24] The American legal structure for a charity.

Law of Heraldic Arms

A specific coat of arms could be protected by copyright as a pictorial, graphic or sculptural work. The usual requirements of originality and artistic creativity would need to be met; neither notice nor registration is required but may be advisable.

It is important that Americans with ancestral roots in Scotland, England & Wales or Canada can apply to their heraldic authorities for a grant of Arms. This is a root that many Americans choose each year.

WILLIAM TYNDALE'S PUBLICATION OF THE NEW TESTAMENT IN THE ENGLISH VERNACULAR

Craig Paterson

> I have here translated the new Testament for your spir-
> itual edifying, consolation and solace: Exhorting
> instantly and beseeching those that are better seen in
> the tongues than I, and that have higher gifts of grace
> to interpret the sense of the Scripture, and meaning of
> the Spirit, than I, to consider and ponder my labour,
> and that with the spirit of meekness. And if they per-
> ceive in any places that I have not attained the very
> sense of the tongue, or meaning of the Scripture, or
> have not given the right English word, that they put to
> their hands to amend it, remembering that so is their
> duty to do. For we have not received the gifts of God
> for ourselves only, or for to hide them; but for to be-
> stow them unto the honouring of God and Christ, and
> edifying of the congregation, which is the body of
> Christ.[1]

In 1408, following express instructions from the Crown in The *Constitutions of Oxford*, the English polity prohibited all vernacular translations of the Bible.[2] John Wycliffe's earlier 1380's English manuscript edition of the Bible had been subject, over the years, to many purges by the authorities.[3] For well over 100 years, oral transmission, in effect, became the safest way to pass on the New Testament to the common people, whose English text many Lollards (followers of John Wycliffe) memorised and recited in large sections.[4]

---

[1] From the Prologue of William Tyndale's first attempt, in 1525, to print his English New Testament. Powerful words addressed to a people told that the Bible could only be printed and copied in Latin, not their native tongue.

[2] Thomas Arundel, Archbishop of Canterbury, held a council at Oxford, which decreed that the Bible should not be translated nor read in English. See David Daniell, *William Tyndale: A Biography* (New Haven, Conn.: Yale University Press, 1994), ch. 8.

[3] Written in the Middle English of the period, and a great achievement in many ways, it is, nevertheless, an awkward translation as it follows the Latin word order and doesn't flow very well.

[4] David Diringer, *The Book Before Printing: Ancient, Medieval and Oriental* (London: Hutchinson, 1953), 528-31.

Law, Ethics & Society

In the early 1520's Martin Luther's writings began to circulate in England. The authorities feared the links that could be established between the Lollards' religious views and the fervour of Luther's anti-clerical views. The bishops burned books, bibles, and people to try and prevent the 'seditious disease' of private religious judgment from spreading in England. This prohibition was vigorously enforced by Cardinal Wolsey, Primate of England, and the Lord Chancellor, Sir Thomas More, in an attempt to prevent what they saw as the grave threat of English 'Lutheranism.' Both Wolsey and More were opposed to Scripture being studied by the untutored and were deeply opposed to ordinary people being able to determine the meaning of Scripture for themselves. Direct mediation by the Church was considered absolutely necessary lest the flock fall astray into error and unbelief.[5]

Despite their best efforts to suppress Luther's writings from entering England across the Channel, many of Luther's texts in fact reached English shores. Lollards and Lutherans were in contact as early as 1520 when John Hacker of Coleman Street, in London, distributed banned books at Burford. John Stacey and Lawrence Maxwell in the adjacent London parish of Alder Manbury also became distributors of imported Lutheran books.[6] On 12 May 1521 many of Luther's books, having been rounded up, were burned at St. Paul's churchyard in London. Bishop John Fisher, a vociferous opponent of Luther, claimed that this Martin Luther "hath stered a mighty storme and tempeset in the chirche."[7] John Foxe, a contemporary spectator of events and protestant martyrologist, writes of these ordinary men who were book distributors that, "few or none were learned, being simple labourers and artificers, but as it pleased the Lord to work in them knowledge and understanding by reading a few English books such as they could get in corners."[8] By October 1526 the ecclesiastical and civic authorities in London were so alarmed as to commence

[5] William A. Clebsch, "The Earliest Translations of Luther into English," *Harvard Theological Review* 56 (1963), 75-86.
[6] *Ibid.*
[7] A. G. Dickens, *The English Reformation* (New York, N.Y.: Schocken Books, 1964), 28.
[8] *Ibid.*, 30.

an examination of every priest and tutor in all ecclesiastical wards to find and destroy seditious religious books.[9]

In 1521, John Skelton, a regarded poet of the time, described popular religious attitudes fermenting in the air in his poem of that year. In *Colyn Clout*, Skelton specifically linked Lollard sympathies with Luther's writings:

> And som have a smacke/Of Luthers sacke/And a brennynge sparke/Of Luthers warke/And are somewhat suspecte/In Luthers secte/And some of them barke/Clatter and carpe/Of that heresy arte/Called Wytclyfista/The devylyshe dagmatista.[10]

It is upon this scene, of religious unrest and ferment, spurred on by the availability of radical Lutheran works, either translated into English from the German or read in German, that an Oxford scholar, William Tyndale (Tindale; Tyndall; Tindall), was to make a deep and lasting mark, further spreading the desire for change in the English Church in a manner that was already being seen on the Continent of Europe.[11]

Martin Luther's writings had already fuelled fervour for change in Europe with his dissenting theological texts and his publication in 1522, in Basel, of his German New Testament, translated directly from the Greek.[12] Luther's German New Testament was a "publishing phenomenon" in every sense. Several of Europe's growing network of printers, who were forward thinking enough to perceive demand, and prepared to undertake personal risk, sought to prepare an edition of the text. Some eighteen editions of Luther's German New Testament appeared in print between 1522 and 1525.[13]

This phenomenon would not have been possible prior to the development and spread of print technology (moveable type, paper, presses) in Europe in the early 16th century. Only

---

[9] For more on systematic book hunting see William Estep, *Renaissance and Reformation* (Grand Rapids, Mich.: Eerdmans, 1986), 251-4.

[10] *Skelton Poems*, ed. Robert S. Kinsman (Oxford: Clarendon Press, 1969), 111, quoted in Dickens, *The English Reformation,* 33.

[11] Daniell, *Tyndale*, ch. 1.

[12] Estep, *R & R*, 135-7.

[13] Lucien Febvre and Henri-Jean Martin, *The Coming of the Book* London: Verso, 1976), 287-304; Elizabeth Eisenstein, *The Printing Revolution in Europe* (Cambridge: Cambridge University Press, 1893), ch. 6.

print technology, first deployed, with success, by Johannes Gutenberg[14] in 1455, could have hoped to create sufficient output, and present a comparatively uniform and readable text available to a greater body of people. Scale, speed, and comparative uniformity of text presented the Reformers with an unparalleled opportunity to communicate with sympathisers on a scale hitherto unprecedented in history.[15]

Printing, then, was in many ways a catalyst by which reformers could hope to write, print, and distribute texts in sufficient quantities and with comparative speed to impact the marketplace of ideas that was fermenting in Europe at the time.

Printing had not simply made texts more widely available, however, as the printing process itself gave rise to the ability to set moveable type in such a way as to greatly assist comparative philological scholarship.[16] A vitally important text to appear in print, one that significantly influenced the interpretative practices of Luther and then Tyndale, was Desiderius Erasmus's Greek/Latin Parallel New Testament, printed by John Froben of Basel in 1516. This was the first non-Latin biblical text to have appeared for centuries and greatly spurred on the interest of new emerging scholars to rediscover and read the Greek *textus receptus* that informed St. Jerome's original translation of the Latin Vulgate in the 380's. Erasmus's publication was the first major attempt to ascertain what the writers of the New Testament had actually said in the tongue they had used to think and write with.[17] Even Erasmus's text was, nevertheless, viewed with great suspicion as it seemed to question the authority of the Vulgate as the guiding standard for biblical exegesis. Once the Greek New Testament became more readily available, and more scholars could read Greek, translators of the Bible started to

---

[14] Gutenberg demonstrated the power of the printing press by selling copies of a two-volume Bible (*Biblia Sacra*), a Latin Vulgate, for 300 florins a copy.

[15] *Ibid.* Also Estep, *R & R*, 96-8.

[16] See Alexander Nesbitt, *The History and Technique of Lettering* (London: Constable, 1950), 49-52.

[17] Johan Huizinga, *Erasmus and the Age of Reformation* (London: Paedon Press, 1952), 87-100.

break with the settled conventions of the Latin Vulgate tradition.[18]

The Lollard background, the impact of Martin Luther, the availability of new scholarship in the Greek and a determination to go back to sources, allied to the availability of print technology and distribution networks, informed the impetus behind William Tyndale's desire to translate and print a New Testament in the English tongue for the benefit of the English people.[19]

Tyndale's background in scholarship at Oxford University, allied to an adventurous and ardent temperament, were ideally suited to the task of eventually translating the New Testament into English. When the new humanist learning reached Oxford towards the end of the reign of Henry VII, the university became a centre of Greek studies for eager young scholars from every quarter of the kingdom. Tyndale studied under the tutelage of gifted scholars like William Grocyn, Thomas Linacre, William Latimer, and John Colet.[20] He had a natural gift for languages and by the age of 21, in 1515, he had mastered eight languages, including Hebrew and Greek. It was during his Oxford years that the young Tyndale became a Lollard sympathiser and supporter of religious reformation. Tyndale believed strongly in the principle of *sola scriptura*: that the basic truths of Christianity are so clearly expressed in the Bible that all should be able to read and interpret it for themselves in their native languages.[21]

In 1521, having taken holy orders, Tyndale became tutor to the family of Sir John Walsh, a Lollard sympathiser, and used his time there to study reformation texts, especially the writings of Luther, and also Erasmus's scriptural exegesis.[22]

Tyndale left Walsh's Gloucestershire home in 1523 to move to London and to preach dissenting doctrines. He also moved to London with the hope of finding backers for his fermenting plan to publish a translation of the Bible in English.

---

[18] See Eisenstein, *Printing Revolution*, ch. 6.
[19] See again the opening quotation of this paper. Further, see Brian Moynahan *God's Bestseller: William Tyndale, Thomas More, and the Writing of the English Bible* (New York: St. Martin's Press, 2002), chs. 4 & 5.
[20] *Ibid.*, ch.1.
[21] Daniell, *Tyndale*, ch. 2.
[22] *Ibid.*, ch. 3.

Law, Ethics & Society

Although Sir Henry Monmouth became a key benefactor of Tyndale's while in London, it proved impossible to advance the project in England, even with Monmouth's financial assistance, for the Bishop of London, Cuthbert Tunstall, openly opposed any such publication plan.[23]

Unlike other parts of Europe, the printers in England, at the time, were far fewer in number, and none dared defy the civil and ecclesiastical authorities that had unambiguously placed a ban on any such printing. It would certainly have cost a printer his livelihood, or even his life, to so defy the authorities in such a way. Spies would likely have detected and reported any attempt at surreptitious printing. Such was the grip of the authorities over printing in England that there was thus no practical possibility of Tyndale printing his vernacular translation in England.[24]

Unable to find the resources to support his efforts to translate and publish an English New Testament in England, Tyndale travelled to mainland Europe in 1524 and studied in Hamburg and then Wittenberg. It was during his stay in Wittenberg that Luther encouraged Tyndale to forge ahead with his own translation project. Further, it was through Tyndale's association with Luther, with financial backing from England, that Tyndale was able to finish his translation work in 1525 and persuade a Cologne printer, Peter Quentell, to take on board the task of publishing the text.[25]

Quentell was to produce a scholarly quarto edition of the translation and started to embark on the project but the Dean of Frankfurt put pressure on Quentell and forced him to abandon his contract to print the text. The Frankfurt authorities came and seized the sheets already printed. Cardinal Wolsey had used his ecclesiastical connections abroad to thwart this first attempt of Tyndale to publish his translation.[26]

All that now remains of this earlier 1525 attempt to print his translation, is the unique *Cologne Fragment* now owned by the British Library. Until the 19th century all of the sheets

---

[23] *Ibid.*, ch. 4.
[24] Frederick Bruce, *History of the Bible in English* (Cambridge: Lutterworths, 2002), 24-9.
[25] *Ibid.*
[26] Moynahan, *God's Bestseller*, ch. 5.

were presumed to have been destroyed. In 1834, however, a number of the Cologne sheets were discovered bound into another work. This fragment contains 31 leaves, and includes Tyndale's Prologue, a woodcut of St. Matthew, and chapters i-xxii of St. Matthew's Gospel, including marginalia. It was printed in black Gothic type on paper supplied by a local Cologne mill.[27]

Forced to flee from Cologne with his assistant Willian Roye, Tyndale sailed up the Rhine and headed for the city of Worms. In Worms he was introduced to another printer Peter Schoeffer. Schoeffer agreed to print the text, providing costs were defrayed and in early 1526 printed an octavo format edition of the text using bastard (Schwabacher) types. Some 3000 to 6000 copies of the translation were believed to have been printed. Unlike the earlier quarto edition, the text of the 1526 octavo edition lacked the preface and the marginalia.[28] The exclusion of prefatory matter and marginalia was designed to keep typesetting costs down. Also designed to keep paper costs down to a minimum was the decision to print in octavo rather than quarto format thus using half the sheets of paper that would otherwise have been needed for a quarto. The smaller format was also considered more suitable for a highly controversial work as it could more readily be concealed and hidden from the authorities when smuggled into England.[29]

Word of the second attempt to print the translation also found its way back to the English authorities and they attempted to guard against its importation. Despite the high alert status of the port authorities, it was smuggled into England by merchants in various bales of merchandise. The first copies of the 706 page text began to arrive on English soil during the early months of 1526.[30]

Of the several thousand that were printed, there are only three surviving copies of the 1526 edition left. One copy is owned by the British Library (lacking the title-page) and one

[27] Roland H Worth, *Church, Monarch and Bible in Sixteenth Century England* (Jefferson, NC: McFarland, 2000), 24-5. See also Daniell, *Tyndale*, ch. 5.
[28] Daniell, *Tyndale*, ch. 6.
[29] Bruce, *History of the Bible*, 32-4.
[30] Moynahan, *God's Bestseller*, ch. 7.

Law, Ethics & Society

complete copy is owned by the Württemberg State Library in Stuttgart. Another incomplete copy (missing 59 leaves) is owned by St. Paul's cathedral, London.

Why are there so few copies left in existence? The English authorities hatched several tactics to try and thwart the dissemination of the text. First, some text were intercepted at the import stage at the ports. Second, some texts were surrendered on fear of punishment by the authorities. Third, Cardinal Wolsey ordered that a search be made in many places where copies were suspected to be hidden, requiring that London, Cambridge, and Oxford be searched. Fourth, the authorities went to the Continent and tried to close down the distribution of the text. In February 1526, Henry VIII and Cardinal Wolsey addressed letters to various authorities in Antwerp, Barrow, Zealand, Ghent, Bruges, Brussels, and Louvaine, asking them to pursue and destroy all copies of Tyndale's New Testament. Fifth, Wolsey, acting through front men, decided to use money to purchase a large consignment of the text and had them prominently burned outside St. Paul's Cathedral.[31]

During the late 1520's and the early 1530's the text was continuously hunted down and destroyed. Henry and his Cardinal were incensed at Tyndale's publication, more so when Tyndale took to writing charged polemical texts against the Church and the King.[32] Several unsuccessful attempts were made to arrest him while in Germany and the Low Countries.

During his time on the Continent, Tyndale embarked on an exchange with Sir Thomas More, a strong defender of the establishment line and embarked upon a further plan to translate the Old Testament from the Hebrew. Thomas More in his, *A Dialogue Concerning Heresies*, fervently opposed Tyndale's use of Greek translation to challenge the biblical basis for key claims of the Catholic Church.[33] Tyndale was adamant that the Latin Vulgate was misleading as a basis for English translation. He translated key words directly from the Greek

---

[31] Daniell, *Tyndale*, ch. 6; Moynahan, *God's Bestseller*, ch. 7; Bruce, *History of the Bible*, 24-36.
[32] His *Parable of the Wicked Mammon* and his *The Obedience of a Christen Man,* both published at Antwerp in 1528.
[33] Published in London in 1529.

to mean different things from the Latin Vulgate: 'senior' instead of priest, 'congregation' instead of 'church,' and 'love' instead of 'charity.' More found his choice of words to be highly subversive and dangerous for the English polity because they might hold sway with the 'untutored' and cause political unrest akin to the changes taking place on the European Continent.[34] During 1534 and 1535, Tyndale went on to published two more editions of his New Testament, editions that included typographical corrections (for example, Moses instead of Noses; beggar instead of neggar), scholarly revisions to his text (for example, his use the word 'elder' as a better translation from the Greek instead of the word 'senior'), and the addition of additional scholarly marginalia.[35]

Tyndale's, forthright, and yet deeply poetic, translation of the New Testament brought to the very front of political discourse the significance of textual interpretation for the whole future and direction of the English Church. It is difficult to imagine any more important book, in the whole history of the English language, that carried with it such politically charged implications.

Tyndale was a dangerous figure to the authorities because the printing of his translation threatened the interests of the established order. Consequently, he became a man hunted in the manner of a fugitive, and, despite being supported and respected by many reformers, could not escape the reach and wrath of the English king and his supporters forever. In 1536, he was eventually betrayed for a reward, arrested, tried, and finally burned for heresy at Vilvorde, near Brussels, at the behest of Charles V, Holy Roman Emperor (a strong supporter of the Papal authority in Church governance).[36] His dying words were recorded by Fox as, "Lord! open the king of England's eyes."

Tyndale's downfall was, in large measure, due to the antipathy felt towards him by King Henry VIII. Henry had earned the title *Fidei Defensor* (Defender of the Faith) from Pope Leo X in 1521 because of a polemical tract, *An Assertion of the Seven Sacraments,* he had published against the doctrines of

---

[34] Bruce, *History of the Bible*, 23-6.
[35] Daniell, *Tyndale*, ch. 12.
[36] *Ibid.*, ch. 15.

Martin Luther.[37] While Henry VIII eventually brought about his own split from Rome, he was to all intents and purposes still largely a Romanist at heart, and was still very antithetical to Lutheranism. The Pope may subsequently have been replaced by Henry as Supreme Head of the English Church, but he still remained opposed to the use of the vernacular. It was 1539 before Thomas Cromwell, Henry's later Secretary of State, and Thomas Cranmer, Henry's Archbishop of Canterbury, were finally able to exhort and persuade the King to permit the display of an approved vernacular copy of the Bible in parish churches.[38]

Few texts have engendered so much passion and controversy. Tyndale had embarked upon a course of action from which there could be no going back. Tyndale's achievement was considerable, and his legacy ran very deep, for his work did not die with him. His translation was reprinted many times (for example, in a bi-glot printing using Erasmus's Latin text) and other translators, following after him, borrowed extensively from his text.

Subsequent translations of the New Testament have been heavily indebted to his literary style and the quality of his translation. He had a gift for vivid phrases which have passed into common English parlance: 'The salt of the earth,' 'No man can serve two masters,' 'The spirit is willing, but the flesh is weak,' and 'Let us eat and drink, and be merry,' are notable examples. Tyndale also coined new words that found their way into the common English vocabulary. Words such as 'Passover,' 'peacemaker,' 'scapegoat,' and even the adjective 'beautiful,' owe their appearance to Tyndale's genius for word-crafting.[39]

The Coverdale Bible, the first complete Bible to be printed in English was published in 1535 as a result of directly incorporating Tyndale's translation of the New Testament with Myles Coverdale's and John Roger's English translation of

---

[37] Published in London in 1521. Henry characterised Luther as a "... venemous serpent, a pernicious plague, an infernal wolf ... an infectious soul, a detestable trumpeter of pride, calumnies and schism, having an execrable mind, a filthy tongue, and a detestable tongue."

[38] Bruce, *History of the Bible,* ch. 6.

[39] Daniell, *Tyndale,* ch. 13.

the Old Testament from German and Latin sources. This Bible was still not authorised, being printed in Antwerp. A further revision, the Matthew's Bible, this time from the original Hebrew for the translation of the Old Testament, was undertaken by Rodger's and was published, again in Antwerp, in 1537.[40] In 1539 the so called 'Great Bible' was published and was the first Bible expressly authorised and permitted for public display and use in England. It is ironic that the King of England finally consented to the public use of a text he had tried so hard in the past to suppress, especially as the New Testament translation, albeit with alteration, was largely derived from the work of William Tyndale.[41]

In 1604, at a conference between the Bishops and the Puritans at Hampton Court, a new revision of the Bible was proposed, and this was welcomed by King James I. Fifty translators were appointed to work in six groups, each responsible for a section of the text. They were to follow the Great Bible as much as possible, correcting any errors. Their work was submitted to a committee for final editing and was published in 1611. Because James I had commanded it, it became known as the King James Version or the Authorised Version. For more than 300 years it remained the most widely read book in the English language. Even today, the Authorised Version is what many English-speaking people think of as "The Bible." When thinking of the immense influence exerted by the KJV through the English-speaking world, however, it is fitting indeed to remember that Tyndale's translation is the source of much of the poetic beauty present in that edition, for "Nine-tenths of the Authorized New Testament is still Tindale, and the best is still his."[42]

---

[40] *Ibid.*
[41] *Ibid.*
[42] Bruce, *History of the Bible,* 96.

Law, Ethics & Society

Tyndale NT Bibliography

Cologne Fragment

1.   *The newe Testament as it was written and caused to be written by them which herde yt. To whom also oure saveour Christ Jesus commaunded that they shulde preache it unto al creatures.* Quarto. [Cologne: Peter Quentell, 1525].

2.   Edward Arber, ed., *The first printed English New Testament: translated by William Tyndale.* Photo-lithographed from the unique fragment, now in the Grenville collection, British Museum: edited by Edward Arber. London: [The Selwood printing works], 1871. (Includes Prologue and Matthew 1-22 from the 1525 Cologne quarto).

3.   Pollard Alfred W., ed., *The beginning of the New Testament translated by William Tyndale 1525*: Facsimile of the unique fragment of the uncompleted Cologne quarto edition. Oxford: The Clarendon press, 1926.

1526 Printing

4.   *The newe Testament as it was written and caused to be written by them which herde yt. To whom also oure saveour Christ Jesus commaunded that they shulde preache it unto al creatures.* Octavo. Worms: Peter Schaffer, 1526.

5.   *The New Testament of our Lord and Saviour Jesus Christ.* London: S. Bagster & Sons, 1836. Reprint.

Tyndale's New Testament in English

6.   *The New Testament of our Lord and Saviour Jesus Christ*. By William Tyndale, the martyr. The original edition, 1526, being the first vernacular translation from the Greek: with a memoir of his life and writings. To which are annexed the essential variations of Coverdale's, Thomas Matthew's, the Genevan, and the Bishops' Bibles, as marginal readings. Andover, Mass. and New York: Gould & Newman, 1837.

7.   Scholz, Johann Martin Augustin, ed., *The English hexapla, exhibiting the six important English translations of the New Testament Scriptures.* London: S. Bagster & Sons, 1846.

8.   New *Testament. Tyndale's first edition, supposed to have been printed at Worms by Peter Schaffer in 1526*; a facsimile on vellum, illumined, reprinted from the copy in the Baptist College, Bristol. London: Francis Fry, 1862.

9.   *The New Testament of our Lord and Saviour Jesus Christ: published in 1526*. Being the first translation from Greek into English, by that eminent scholar and martyr, William Tyndale. Reprinted verbatim: with a memoir of his life and writings, by George Offor. Together with the proceedings and correspondence of Henry VIII, Sir T. More, and Lord Cromwell. London: Samuel Bagster & Sons, 1836. Reprinted 1871.

10. *The Newe Testamente, M. D. XXVI.* Lexington, Ky., Anvil Press, 1955.

11. *The New Testament 1526.* London: D. Paradine Developments, 1976.

Law, Ethics & Society

12. Cooper, W. R., ed., *The New Testament: the text of the Worms edition of 1526 in original spelling*. Translated by William Tyndale, edited for The Tyndale Society by W.R. Cooper, with a preface by David Daniell. London: British Library, 2000.

1534 Printing

13. *The newe Testament, dylygently corrected and compared with the Greke by Willyam Tindale: and fynesshed in the yere of oure Lorde God A.M.D. & xxxiiii in the moneth of Nouember*. Octavo. Imprinted at Antwerp by Marten Emperowr, Anno M.D. xxxiiii.

14. Taverner, Richard, ed., *The Nevv Testament in Englysshe: after the Greke exemplar*: dilygently translated and corrected by Rycharde Tauerner. Quarto. London: Thomas Petyt, for Thomas Berthelet, 1539.

15. Wallis, Hardy N., ed., *The New Testament, translated by William Tyndale, 1534*. A reprint of the edition of 1534 with the translator's prefaces and notes and the variants of the edition of 1525. Edited for the Royal Society of Literature by N. Hardy Wallis. Cambridge: Cambridge University Press, 1938.

16. *The newe Testament of oure Sauyour Jesu Christ*. Octavo. London: [Publisher unknown], 1548.

17. *The Newe Testament of our Sauiour Jesu Christe*. Octavo. London: Printed by S. Mierdman for John Daye, 1551.

18. Wilson, R. Mercer, ed., *Tyndale's commemoration volume, reproducing substantial parts of Tyndale's revised Testament of 1534*, with some of the original woodcuts. London: Lutterworth Press, The United Society for Christian Literature, 1939.

19. Sawer, John Wesley, ed., *Tindale's triumph, John Rogers' monument: the Newe Testament of the Matthew's Bible, 1537 A.D.* (i.e. 1534 text). Houston, Tex. : J. W. Sawyer, 1989.

20. Daniell, David, ed., *Tyndale's New Testament, translated from the Greek by William Tyndale in 1534, in a modern-spelling edition.* New Haven, Conn.: Yale University Press, 1989.

21. *The New Testament, translated by William Tyndale on CD.* Sola Scriptura Publishing, 2001.

22. *Bible in English (990-1970)* [Online]. Proquest Publishing.

1535 Printing

23. *The New Testament yet once again corrected by William Tyndale.* Printed in Antwerp by Martin de Keyser and published by Godfrey van der Haghen, 1535. (the "GH" edition, of which only four copies survive).

24. H. Guppy, ed., *William Tyndale and the earlier translations of the Bible into English.* Manchester: John Rylands Library, 1925. Reprint of 1535 printing.

Latin-English Bi-glot

25. *The new Testament in Englyshe [Tyndale 1534] and in Latyn accordyng to the translacyon of doctour Erasmus of Roterodam.* Anno. M.CCCCC.XXXVIII. Octavo. London: Prynted in Fletestrete by Robert Redman, 1538.

Law, Ethics & Society

26.   *The new testament in Englishe after the Greeke
      translation annexed wyth the translation of Erasmus
      in Latin*. Octavo. London: Thomas Gaultier, 1550.

27.   *The new testament in Englishe after the Greeke
      translation annexed wyth the translation of Erasmus
      in Latin*. Octavo. London: Thomas Gaultier, 1552.
      Reprint of 1550.

THE CONTRIBUTIONS OF INTERNATIONAL LAW & NON-GOVERNMENTAL ORGANIZATIONS IN FACILITATING THE PEACEFUL REUNIFICATION OF THE KOREAN PENINSULA

Milka Ristova & Sanja Angelovska

Introduction

The first contact with the programme goals of HWPL from Seul Rebuplic of South Korea was back in 2014 when I (Milka Ristova) was offered a collaboration for participating in the process of creating and signing the Declaration for peace and preventing war worldwide. While working on the declaration there was certainly no doubt about the need of the new mechanism of the international law for implementation of the international law in maintaining world peace. The foundation of this declaration it is the maintaining sustainable peace is only possible with conflict resolution by the law.

The use of the international law and the rich experience of the International Organizations are of great interest to every country member of UN.

With the internalization of the protection of human rights and accepting the fact that its protection it is not only in the domain of the national law moreover a legitimate aim to the international community the need of the Declaration is justified.

This document should secure maintaining of political goals that shell be resolved with a mediation of the system of international law in the frame of the UN.

Aside from the fact that lasting peace in the Korean Peninsula is long and hard process still the citizens of both Koreas' have the right through all the forms of a peaceful resolution to maintain their legitimate goals.

Through the peaceful activities, a hope is being felt that there will be historical and internationally law assumptions for the realization of the justifiable aim and that is the peaceful reunification of Korean Peninsula.

One of the most important goals of the international law is its enforceability. That is like that starting from charter of the UN Article1: To maintain international peace and security, and to that end: to take effective collective measures for the prevention and removal of threats to the peace, and for the suppression of acts of aggression or other breaches of the peace, and to bring about by peaceful means, and in conformity with the principles of justice and international law, adjustment or settlement of international disputes or situations which might lead to a breach of the peace.

To become effective the system of international law in resolving disputes among two countries it is of great importance to the values which its norms and principles are protected and these are enforceability, freedom, interests, goals, etc. They are embedded in all law acts and principles for all the countries. Their compulsory implementation is guaranteed by law sanctions, forced and protective measures, which it is demonstrated that in practice they are not efficient.

HWPL as a peaceful organization, supported by thousands of peaceful people and organizations worldwide has declared itself to a peaceful dispute resolution. Patiently studying the general and specific conditions that lead to the dispute, with fully respecting the interests of all the sides in the dispute. That is a long-term process, but it is for sure more efficient when it comes to disputed questions and maintaining lasting peace. For that purpose, it was adopted law act Declaration of the Peace and Cessation of War (OPCW).

View of Political Leaders of South-Eastern Europe for the SEE Process of Democratization

We attended High-Level Meeting of Former Political Leaders in Europe to Spread the Culture of Peace and Call for Support for the Peaceful Reunification of the Korean Peninsula with the same purpose as said in its title. To provide support for the achievement of peace and stability in Korea peninsula. We are so excited that a new era has opened in relations between North and South Korea, after the historic meeting between the leaders of the two countries. Dialogue is a political form from which should bring the Korean people closer together, which is unnaturally divided in two states. A nation that speaks the same language, shares the same tradition, customs, culture, folk dance, but also historical victories and defeats. But most important of all they also connect private kinship and friendly relationships, which are all long suspended.

For several years now we've been following the HWPL Man Hi Kim's peace-building activities and his associates who fervently support the Korean people and therefore we truly support him and his deed, because it is a noble act.

The Declaration of Peace, uniting the Korean Peninsula, is in the right direction of achieving lasting peace and prosperity not only to citizens of Korea, but in the world as a whole. The process of peaceful resolution should take place according to the example of the processes of democratization of countries in Eastern Europe and the unification of Germany. The changes in Eastern Europe and the foundation of the common justice. Having said this with due respect to the invited guest speakers – former presidents and functioners from South-Eastern Europe who shared their experience and knowledge how their countries overcame hard times during dispute and war times. We all have agreed to the great importance and role that international law has to play in these situations.

We also agreed that since 1948 international law was many times on test, and few times has failed. In order not to happen that again, we practitioners and peace-builders with expertise in international law and conflicts (especially their psychology foundation) are willing to act proactively and prevent any possible non-peaceful acts.

Working and advocating for peace and security means working and looking for a peaceful resolution including here also the case of Korea, because there is always such a solution.

The Case of Republic of Macedonia

Our country, the Republic of Macedonia, in this process was

Law, Ethics & Society

separated peacefully from Yugoslav federation, and proclaim independence. We are a democratic society where we built coexistence between Christians, Muslims and other communities, to wake up in peace and understanding. The cost is the process of transition when we moved to a market economy, from a one-party system to pluralism, and to the rule of law. Citizens seek economic justice and equality before constitution and laws. They seek economic justice and peace. That time we encountered many difficulties, but the most difficult of all are these two questions:

1. The emergence of nationalism, which seriously puts into question danger to the inner cohesion of the society and the risk of conflict. We needed a lot energy to get rid of intolerance for all people in a multinational and a multiconfessional society. Although there were some challenges, the people of Macedonia demonstrated a capacity of overcoming that and instead work for peace and coexistence. Here, we need to highlight that using a permanent dialogue as a tool become our practice, for overcoming interethnic questions. For the time being we are successfully doing I and we are trying to become members of NATO and the EU.

2. However, the most difficult problem is the absurd problem, which is with our southern neighbour the Republic of Greece, which has issues with our constitutional and historical name Republic of Macedonia. Therefore, we are here as persons who in their professional career served law and justice, and moreover peace work. We want to affirm the principle of cooperation and peaceful negotiations in the most difficult issues in the interests of peace. This peaceful initiative should be guaranteed under the International Law and with international guarantees. Just one reminder one of the core values of international law is the right of self-determination. Most of the experts world-wide would agree with us that we've express good will in the negotiation process so far.

We do expect that through the intensive negotiations that are going for the 3 decades old dispute a resolution will be a bilateral treaty for friendship and cooperation.

Activities for Peace by the NGO Sector

On 26 April 2016 in Skopje was found a peaceful committee in the Republic of Macedonia for signing and supporting of implementation to the Declaration for peace and preventing war in the world. Created by HWPL and IWPG from Seul, South Korea. Many non-governmental organizations and NGO activists especially the youth signed the declaration. The campaign is still going on. The Macedonian citizens are supporting the initiative for the peaceful reunification of Korea.

Following the rule of international law, we know much work is being done by the non-governmental organizations. Governments sign agreements, peace accords but organizations advocate for peace through different tools such as empowerment, arts, and dialogue as its highest form of communication for the humankind.

Consider as important and high-level accomplishment for peace-builders is dialogue. Dialogue cannot be led with trust as a foundation. In the case of Korea, this is essential. People of Korea have to learn how to take conditionally said the best of the past and learn how to share it. This can be done only with a sincere engagement from the peace-builders, people who believe in and work for peace, and people who`s passion is peace. There should be a generic strategy on how to overcome and accomplish this. We know states as actors in the peace process are the main actors but without nongovernmental support, this will hard to be settled or even more implemented.

When we say strategy, we mean peace-building strategies including here concrete peace-building activities. Organization from both Koreas and of course international ones with a joint collaboration should be working on this. Starting at grass root level from primary schools – programmes for children and youth, then including profiles working in the educational system. Furthermore, the process shell be going including adults with offering a concrete psychological support to ones who were directly affected by the

Law, Ethics & Society

Korean War. We know that post-traumatic disorder is much present among the population who suffered any form of violence including war. With such a strategy and work on the non-governmental organizations directly supported by state institutions and including here international organizations, a result can be achieved. The reunification of both Koreas will become an inevitable and much-needed step forward towards building a peace at the Korean Penninsula but moreover an example to the world.

It is also the case with our country Republic of Macedonia. After signing the Ohrid Framework Agreement back in 2001, supported and facilitated by the international community, many non-governmental organizations have been supporting the peace-activities through their work. It is the case nowadays the case. Once, societies become fragile and the trust among communities is broken it takes decades to rebuild it.

The actual atmosphere of the peace process between North and South Korea gives a good impulse to the process of reunification itself. With a consistent support from the international community a peace is possible and much wanted. The peace-building activities in the concrete case are more preventing in order to rebuild a society with a strong cohesion since there are no obstacles for it. People share so many things in common. Language, customs, norms, habits, the same territory. With this context the process becomes simple than we can imagine.

Toward the Process of Peaceful Reunification of the Korean Peninsula

Following the subtitle at the round -table Empathy for Peace, we empathize with the actual situation of Korea. Considering the fact that international law most and overall considers human life—we also know that too many lives have been badly affected by this dispute over the last 70 years.

That is why the process needs to more holistic. We greet this kind of gathering of experts in different fields in order to work on peaceful reunification of Korea, to that instance where the process will become normal, wanted and inevitable.

In the meantime, state actors should work along with civil society starting with programmes for children and youth at grass root level. By national and international peace agreements and their full implementation peaceful reunification is possible. International law will be implemented and there won't be any need for using its tools such as humanitarian intervention.

In this process with our friends from Korea, with support from women, youth and all layers of the bureaucracy for the peaceful reunification of the Korean peninsula. To cultivate the culture of peace!

For sure that is going to be a long and complex process of peaceful negotiations of the interested sides and political leaders from South and North Korea, thus negotiation should be led patiently in the interest of the Korean people.

In the process the norms of the international law are of immense importance.

BLOCKCHAINS & CYBERCURRENCIES CHALLENGING ANTI-TRUST & COMPETITION LAW[1]

Stephan U. Breu

Abstract

Blockchain technology has come to most people's attention through Bitcoin as the leading cryptocurrency today. But the technology can be used for a lot of other applications as a way to store decentralized data and information. Blockchains are filing their records through a continuously growing number of single "blocks" which are linked and secured using cryptography. Typically, such blockchains are managed by a peer-to-peer network using a specified protocol for validating new blocks. By storing data across an international network, this new technology is operating independently of any government or central bank as it is not residing in a specific area of influence of any given regulation or jurisdiction. Also, there is the question as to which court has jurisdiction in context of blockchain disputes based on the international and anonymous structure. These systems also offer a high level of anonymity to their participants. Given these scenarios, it has to be considered that blockchains with shared use of distributed ledgers by several competitors might be a considerable risk under antitrust and competition laws. To get full value for future blockchain applications, a deep cooperation and collaboration on a common platform by all participants – that often will also be competitors – will be necessary. Although collaborating to achieve an outcome more efficiently is generally not sanctioned by antitrust laws, there are still potential antitrust concerns to be considered. And finally, due to the automatic and irreversible execution of blockchain transactions, one has also to think about technical precautions for enforcing any possible court decisions. All these challenges

---

[1] Originally published in the *International Research and Practice Journal Law* (Law and Digital Economy), No. 1, (01) 2018, p. 12. Revised.

Law, Ethics & Society

for the future will ask for a strong self-regulation of the market participants in the digital marketplace.

Introduction

Today's society is much influenced by rapid changes in the digital world. A number of new technologies have a sustainable influence on human relations, economics and society as a whole. In this environment new techniques like blockchains are becoming more and more prominent. The blockchains are using a peer-to-peer network and are managed autonomously and the information is secured in a decentralized way. These new technologies, in combination with cryptocurrencies, are offering new ways of transferring value without being confronted with compliance regulations of an established financial system and it is very difficult to identify involved parties for law enforcement and security organizations. The inherent decentralizing aspects of blockchains make it difficult to define the appropriate jurisdiction. Solving this aspect is not only important for rules and regulations regarding compliance and misuse of cybercurrencies but also regarding possible violation of antitrust and competition law. As published in the *Harvard Business Review* early 2017[2] the future increased value and importance of many blockchain applications will require a close cooperation and deep collaboration of multiple stakeholders in the system. All participants on all levels of the process have to adopt and follow a common platform and procedure which will lead to industry consortia.

In general, antitrust law is not rejecting collaborations between competitors as long as the outcome is such as it would be unlikely to be achieved independently or the efficiency of the processes are substantially increased. But as soon as information sharing comes to competitively sensitive information like costs and future prices, it can become a serious antitrust offense. Also, exclusive commitments to a single consortia or exclusion of certain competitors from accessing the distributed ledger have to be defended with sound

---

[2] Marco Iansiti, Karim R. Lakhani, "The Truth About Blockchain", published in the *Harvard Business Review* January/February 2017
https://hbr.org/2017/01/the-truth-about-blockchain

reasons not to fall under competition law violation. As antitrust and competition law violation can create criminal exposure or costly investigations by law enforcement agencies any stakeholder in a blockchain consortia should consider potential antitrust risks. Accepting that we are only seeing the first developments of these new markets also allows us to start discussion about necessary steps to adapt regulations and compliance policies on an international level and establish a basic understanding of blockchains and cryptocurrencies in as many jurisdictions as possible. Thus, given these scenarios this paper aims to start discussing the possible frictions between blockchain stakeholders and antitrust and competition law as we might foresee them today for the coming impact of blockchains on the economy and our society.

What is Blockchain Technology

Blockchain has become more and more prominent in the last years. It is basically an algorithm with decentralized data storage, lacking a central administrator, and where the participants know nothing about each other. Best known as the technology behind bitcoin as the leading cryptocurrency, it is mostly understood as distributed ledger technology which is widely used today. Bitcoin and its underlying blockchain technology were first introduced by Satoshi Nakamoto in his paper "Bitcoin: A Peer-to-Peer Electronic Cash System"[3]. The whole software for cryptocurrencies is open source and keeps the ledger of all transactions ever occurring on public files. The records of all transactions are secured on the computers that build this ledger, but not the whole ledger on all but only small blocks with references to other blocks on all these computers worldwide, linked and secured using cryptography. This means, any alternation of any block cannot be done without alternation of all subsequent blocks which makes the system permanent, efficient and verifiable. So, each transaction and its identification is validated by at least three parties involved in maintaining the whole system and "mining" new blocks of information containing data relating to the actual

---

[3] Nakamoto Satoshi, "A Peer-to-Peer Electronic Cash System", published in November 2008 https://bitcoin.org/bitcoin.pdf

transaction. By solving mathematical problems presented by the system these blocks are added to the existing blockchain, so all members of the system have access to the data. If a transaction is not verifiable with the existing blockchain the new blocks will not be integrated and so the integrity of the system is guaranteed. Distributed ledger technology has been described as potential secure and efficient solution for several applications[4][5][6].

It is also widely expected that blockchains will track integrity and provenance of other special products like pharmaceuticals, diamonds or seafood in future. Blockchain will change the way of exchanging data and the ability to transact globally in various fields, including financial services. Beside the public blockchains, like the one used by bitcoin, there are new applications like consortium blockchains where the consensus process is limited to predefined nodes of the blockchain i.e. participants and members of the consortia. The access to the blockchain can be public or restricted or even hybrid. In a fully private blockchain the write permission is kept by one organization but it might be possible to have public reading permission or even that could be restricted to certain stakeholders of the blockchain. In contrast to the public blockchains, consortium or private blockchains can easily change rules and entries in the ledger and even revert processes. But having a central entity controlling the blockchain and being capable of interfering with the algorithm, especially for the challenges discussed in this paper, any action regarding antitrust and competition law is much easier to enforce as the responsibilities are more clearly defined compared to distributed ledger technology.

---

[4] Robert Plant, "Can Blockchain Fix What Ails Electronic Medical Records?" published on April 27, 2017 in the *Wall Street Journal* https://blogs.wsj.com/experts/2017/04/27/can-blockchain-fix-what-ails-electronic-medical-records/

[5] Nathaniel Popper, Steve Lohr, "Blockchain, A Better Way to Track Pork Chops, Bonds, Bad Paenut Butter?", published March 4, 2017 in the *New York Times* https://www.nytimes.com/2017/03/04/business/dealbook/blockchain-ibm-bitcoin.html

[6] Rachel Arthur, "From Farm to Finished Garment: Blockchain Is Aiding This Fashion Collection with Transparency", published May 10, 2017 by *Forbes* https://www.forbes.com/sites/rachelarthur/2017/05/10/garment-blockchain-fashion-transparency/#4975681774f3

Jurisdictional Competence for Blockchains

Any possible legislative regulations on blockchains and cryptocurrencies are difficult to maintain. For a state it is very difficult to implement regulations that have to be followed in a system that is outside its sphere of influence and action. An autonomous system maintained and managed by the users themselves over which no stately organization has any influence and control. Bitcoin with its underlying blockchain has already started to create a supranational economy in which the classical idea of a legal person is obsolete[7] whereas the supranational law is not really designed to address these new developments yet. Within this new digital economy there is no technical necessity for the stakeholders to be attached to any jurisdiction. In traditional law, and in absence of any agreement stating otherwise, blockchain disputes are normally settled by state courts. But the structure of blockchains are giving nearly insoluble problems to such state courts. How can the jurisdiction be determined if the participants of the blockchain are anonymous and the data storage is virtually everywhere? How can any state court have the required technological expertise and efficiency to sufficiently understand the mechanism of blockchains and decide any dispute fast enough compared to the rapidly proceeding blockchain applications?

As the courts and states have enormous problems to tackle in these new scenarios, self-regulation of the market participants will play an important role. One part of a consumer-friendly self-regulation could be dispute settlement by an arbitral tribunal. Such arbitral processes could also be individually tailored for stakeholders in a specific blockchain application. As a legal classification of the stakeholders in blockchains or cybercurrencies is very complex and supranational law is not really suitable for these challenges yet, regulations will for some time mainly concentrate on interactions between stakeholders of the blockchains. Blockchains

---

[7] Dima Starodubcev, "Bitcoin created a supranatinsl economy", published March 17, 2016 on coinfox.info http://www.coinfox.info/news/persons/5109-dima-starodubcev-bitcoin-created-supranational-economy

Law, Ethics & Society

and cybercurrencies might have to be officially recognised as unregulated technologies as there are no legally ascertainable providers with the distributed ledger technology and the system itself is a publicly accessible technology and service. Another opinion on this jurisdictional issue is: "that at a simple level, every transaction potentially comes under the legislative umbrella of wherever the node exists whether in respect of financial services or data protection."[8]. Whereas the author also states that this means that blockchains would then need to be compliant with a potentially unwieldy number of legal and regulatory regimes. Given this, the locus of a relevant "act" could be unclear as the transactions may have occurred simultaneously in a few different places, which again makes it nearly impossible to determine the competent jurisdiction. The unsolved questions regarding competence of jurisdictions in these new challenges of the new digital economy will also soon concern antitrust and competition law considerably as blockchain technology and its surrounding architecture will develop into new spheres and have considerable impact on our daily life.

Possible Frictions of Blockchains with Antitrust & Competition Law

If we want to have a closer look into possible frictions of blockchain applications with antitrust and competition law, we have to consider several anticipated blockchain applications that are discussed today. To take full advantage of the potential of a lot of blockchain applications - be it in distributed ledger technology, blockchain consortia or private blockchain - there will be necessary a deep cooperation and collaboration of the stakeholders of such blockchains. A blockchain is demanding a unified and common platform and processes to maintain its structure. As long as such cooperation and collaboration mainly focuses on making the processes involved more efficient, or combine them for an achievement that the

---

[8] Gregory Brandman, Samuel Thampapillai, "Blockchain – Considering the Regulatory Horizon", published July 2016 by University of Oxford, Faculty of Law, *Business Law Blog*
https://www.law.ox.ac.uk/business-law-blog/blog/2016/07/blockchain---considering-regulatory-horizon

independent participants could not achieve individually, there is basically no violation of antitrust and competition law. Blockchain applications are today predicted for various areas interacting with economical processes and governments agencies. Widely discussed are applications such as healthcare, supply chains, stock trading, land registry, or e-voting. These applications are still underdeveloped today but have attracted considerable attention. As the report on a recent survey by IBM's Institute for Business Value highlighted: "[blockchains] are likely to radically change how organizations operate, generate revenues and respond to customers, partners and competitors alike"[9].

Anticipating the level of cooperation and collaboration of stakeholders of such blockchains one cannot neglect the positive effects on economic progress; yet stakeholders in such blockchain consortia should be careful considering potential violations of antitrust and competition law. Especially exchange of current and future pricing of a product or other similar competitively sensitive information could rapidly be deemed price fixing which is one of the most serious offenses under antitrust and competition law. Within a blockchain all information shared between the stakeholders should help the consortia to achieve legitimate goals and not violate laws and regulations. As the European Commission state: "common standards, agreed to and applied by participants in a market, will generally be pro-competitive, as they allow for promote "economic interpenetration"[10]. As stakeholders in blockchains could not only be partners and suppliers but also competitors it needs to be ensured that adopted rules within the blockchain are not limiting competition among stakeholders or with other organizations. Regulations like exclusive commitment to one blockchain or exclusion of other competitors from access to the distributed ledger would ask for sound arguments to upkeep such regulations against antitrust and competition

---

[9] IBM Institute for Business Value, "Forward Together: Three ways blockchain Explorers chart a new direction", published as *Global C-suite Study*, 19th Edition https://www-01.ibm.com/common/ssi/cgi bin/ssialias?htmlfid= GBE03835USEN

[10] Para. 263 of the European Commission's *Guidelines on Horizontal Cooperation Agreements*, (2011/C 11/01).

law[11]. Some publications even suggest that distributed ledger technology is facilitating cartel management for groups that do not trust each other but have to cooperate[12]. Very challenging problems in the future could be blockchains that are operating through learning by doing and are independently optimizing prices and profits by using the data stored within its ledger. Such processes are not yet governed by antitrust or competition law as there are no anticompetitive agreements or intentions between the stakeholders, but the outcome is profit maximization without benefit for the consumers. As the antitrust and competition law today is mainly focused on violations that have already occurred and can be proved by clear collusion and misuse of market power, in the future, antitrust and competition law should also become more proactive to cover the asymmetric between information available to regulators and blockchain industry.

The Future of Blockchains

As mentioned before, the potential of blockchains can only be presumed today. As all stored data in distributed ledger cannot be corrupted, they are cryptographically validated data. To quote Leanne Kemp, CEO of Everledger, from the IBM Institute for Business Value report: "At its core, blockchain is a shared ledger that allows participants in a business network to transact assets where everyone has control but no one person is in control"[13]. So blockchains will be used to validate and secure almost everything in the future. As mentioned, validated supply chains will be available to the consumers, healthcare data will be managed in blockchain consortia

---

[11] David Kully, Joe Dewey, "Bitcoin tech may be the future, but it raises serious antitrust questions" published May 25, 2017 by the *Hill* http://thehill.com/blogs/pundits-blog/technology/335140-is-bitcoin-tech-the-future-or-will-they-violate-antitrust-laws
[12] Izabella Kaminska, "Exposing the "If we call it a blockchain perhaps it won't be deemed a cartel? tactic", published May 11, 2015 in the *Financial Times* https://ftalphaville.ft.com/2015/05/11/2128849/exposing-the-if-we-call-it-a-blockchain-perhaps-it-wont-be-deemed-a-cartel-tactic/
[13] IBM Institute for Business Value, "Forward Together: Three ways blockchain Explorers chart a new direction", published as *Global C-suite Study*, 19th Edition https://www-01.ibm.com/common/ssi/cgi-bin/ssialias?htmlfid=GBE03835USEN

models, and financial trading platforms will be managed through blockchains. Smart contracts will facilitate, execute and enforce agreements through blockchain technology and will guarantee proper fulfilment of the agreement and secure storage of data. This technology will make the use of intermediates and middleman more and more neglectable. Government services will be offered digitally like Land-Registry, E-voting, Notary Public Services, Passports, ID's, and Licenses which will be tamper-proofed and access to personal assets will be secure and readily available i.e. bitcoin and other cybercurrencies. The coming years will show an enormous development of blockchain technology impacting all aspects of life on a day to day basis. The main challenge for regulators and society is an increasing asymmetry between the blockchain industry, its stakeholders and the legal system and consumer. Today's approach by various governments to implement more and more legal restrictions on the internet will not prove sustainable[14]. All regulations and restrictions should consider the specific aspects of blockchains and cryptocurrencies and not diminish the potential positive effects of economic growth and innovation. The only way to have a sustainable effect on security and legitimacy of blockchains and cryptocurrencies lies in a balanced emphasis of law enforcement and government means of control and individual freedom of civil society.

Conclusion

Blockchains and cybercurrencies are opening a challenging new development for legislative regulations and law enforcement in general but antitrust and competition law in particular. The decentralized and autonomous technology and structure of blockchains and the complete independence of any state institutions and controls poses unseen challenges to both governments and international institutions. As a blockchain does not fall under any given governmental regulation or competence it could be viewed as agnostic to any jurisdictional

---

[14] UNESCO Global Report 2017/2018 "World Trends in Freedom of Expression and Media Development", published 2017 by UNESCO
http://www.unesco.de/fileadmin/medien/Dokumente/Kommunikation/EN_WTR_2017_Executive_Summary_web.pdf

rules and must most probably been accepted as unregulated sooner or later. Blockchain consortia with self-learning software will go beyond the market structure as we have it today. The blockchain software will trigger decisions and actions automatically and without interference of blockchain participants. Antitrust and competition law violations will not be possible to attribute to an intention of a blockchain participant but will be managed by a neutral software and proof of violation will be difficult to provide. Such scenario will force antitrust and competition law enforcers to become more proactive in their planning and operational modus. Capacity building has to be emphasized to keep the asymmetry of information between regulators and industry as small as possible. As competence of state courts is difficult to assign to disputes with blockchains, implementation of self-regulation by the market players are necessary to support. Finally, any regulations and standards have to be internationally coordinated and have to stay flexible to react to any development of these technologies which asks for ongoing international analysis and monitoring of evolution and market changes.

References

1. Nakamoto Satoshi, "A Peer-to-Peer Electronic Cash System", published in November 2008
    https://bitcoin.org/bitcoin.pdf
2. Christopher Boog, Banjamin Gottlieb "Disputes in the context of blockchain appli-cations" published by Schellenberg Wittmer, Attorney at Law, Newsletter June 2017
    http://www.swlegal.ch/CMSPages/GetFile.aspx?disposition=attachment&nodeguid=9cbbaf0f-8781-431f-8702-6673a2b29ac5
3. Gregory Brandman, Samuel Thampapillai, "Blockchain – Considering the Regulatory Horizon", published July 2016 by University of Oxford, Faculty of Law, Business Law Blog
    https://www.law.ox.ac.uk/business-law-blog/blog/2016/07/blockchain—considering-regulatory-horizon
4. Dima Starodubcev, "Bitcoin created a supranational economy", published March 17, 2016 by coinfox.info

http://www.coinfox.info/news/persons/5109-dima-starodubcev-bitcoin-created-supranational-economy

5. Sergii Shcherbak, "How Should Bitcoin Be Regulated?", published Spring/Summer 2014, Volume 7, Issue 1, in European Journal of Legal Studies http://www.ejls.eu/15/183UK.pdf

6. Ronald Mulder, "How Blockchain Can Save the Free Market", published September 25, 2016 by Medium.com https://medium.com/intuitionmachine/how-blockchain-can-save-the-free-market-80b8800931f9

7. David Kully, Joe Dewey, "Bitcoin tech may be the future, but it raises serious antitrust questions" published May 25, 2017 by the Hill http://thehill.com/blogs/pundits-blog/technology/335140-is-bitcoin-tech-the-future-or-will-they-violate-antitrust-laws

8. Tom Rees, "Regulating Bitcoin: how new frameworks could be a catalyst for cryptocurrencies", published April 16, 2017 by The Telegraph http://www.telegraph.co.uk/business/2017/04/16/regulating-bitcoin-new-frameworks-could-catalyst-cryptocurrencies/

9. Michael Milnes, "Blockchain: Issue in Competition & Consumer Law", published Mai 26, 2016 https://www.linkedin.com/pulse/blockchain-issues-competition-consumer-law-michael-milnes

10. Wendy McElroy, "De Facto Federal Legislation of Cryptocurrencies is Nigh", published July 11, 2017 by bitcoin.com https://news.bitcoin.com/federal-legislation-cryptocurrency-nigh/

11. Primavera De Filippi, "We Must Regulate Bitcoin. Problem Is, We Don't Understand It", published January 3, 2016 by wired.com https://www.wired.com/2016/03/must-understand-bitcoin-regulate/

12. Matt Nixon, "Bitcoin Foundation seeks legal protection from US currency regulation", published August 30, 2017 by Independent http://www.independent.co.uk/news/business/news/bitcoin-foundation-legal-protection-us-currency-regulation-llew-claasen-cryptocurrency-bit-licence-a7919401.html

13. Guy Rolnik, Asher Schechter, "How Can Antitrust Be Used to Protect Competition in the Digital Marketplace?" published September 26, 2016 by

ProMarket.org
https://promarket.org/digital-market-not-going-correct/

14. Andy Extance, "The future of cryptocurrencies: Bitcoin and beyond" published September 30, 2015 by nature.com
https://www.nature.com/news/the-future-of-cryptocur-rencies-bitcoin-and-beyond-1.18447

15. James P. Gerkis, Serafima Krikunova, "Bitcoin and Other Virtual Currencies: Approaching U.S. Regulatory Acceptance", published Spring 2014 in Administrative & Regulatory Law News, Volume 39, Nr. 3
https://www.americanbar.org/content/dam/aba/publica-tions/administrative_regulatory_law_newsletters/spring_2014_vol%2039-4.authcheckdam.pdf

16. Marco Iansiti, Karim R. Lakhani, "The Truth About Blockchain", published January/February 2017 Issue Harvard Business Review
https://hbr.org/2017/01/the-truth-about-blockchain

17. Vitalik Buterin, "On Public and Private Blockchains", published August 7, 2015 on Ethereum Blog
https://blog.ethereum.org/2015/08/07/on-public-and-pri-vate-blockchains/

18. Financer Worldwide Magazine, "Potential cryptocur-rency regulation", published March 2015
https://www.financierworldwide.com/potential-cryptocur-rency-regulation/#.WdX74bpuKUk

19. Ameer Rosic, "5 Blockchain Applications That Are Shaping Your Future", published November 28, 2016 in the Huffington Post
https://www.huffingtonpost.com/ameer-rosic-/5-block-chain-applications_b_13279010.html

20. IBM Institute for Business Value, "Forward Together: Three ways blockchain Explorers chart a new direc-tion", published as Global C-suite Study 19th Edition
https://www-01.ibm.com/common/ssi/cgi-bin/ssi-alias?htmlfid=GBE03835USEN

21. Izabella Kaminska, "Exposing the "If we call it a block-chain perhaps it won't be deemed a cartel?" tactic", published May 11, 2015 in the Financial Times
https://ftalphaville.ft.com/2015/05/11/2128849/expos-ing-the-if-we-call-it-a-blockchain-perhaps-it-wont-be-deemed-a-cartel-tactic/

22. Bernard Marr, "Practical Examples of How Blockchains Are Used In Banking And The Financial Services

Blockchains & Cybercurrencies

Sector", published August 10, 2017 in Forbes
https://www.forbes.com/sites/bernard-
marr/2017/08/10/practical-examples-of-how-
blockchains-are-used-in-banking-and-the-financial-ser-
vices-sector/#739f63f11a11

23. Mathias Bucher, "Banking 3.0: Wie Blockchain die
Bankenwelt neu gestaltet", published August 28, 2017
by Lucerne University of Applied Sciences and Arts

24. https://blog.hslu.ch/retailbanking/2017/08/28/banking-3-
0-wie-blockchain-die-bankenwelt-neu-gestaltet/

25. Blockchain Technologies "Smart Contracts Explained",
published on company website 2016
http://www.blockchaintechnologies.com/blockchain-
smart-contracts

26. Reenita Das, "Does Blockchain Have A Place In
Healthcare", published May 8, 2017 in Forbes
https://www.forbes.com/sites/reenita-
das/2017/05/08/does-blockchain-have-a-place-in-
healthcare/#145fbd671c31

27. Mike Orcutt, "Who Will Build the Health-Care Blockchain?", published September 15, 2017 in MIT
Technology Review
https://www.technologyreview.com/s/608821/who-will-
build-the-health-care-blockchain/

28. Robert Plant, "Can Blockchain Fix What Ails Electronic
Medical Records?" published on April 27, 2017 in the
Wall Street Journal https://blogs.wsj.com/ex-
perts/2017/04/27/can-blockchain-fix-what-ails-
electronic-medical-records/

29. Nathaniel Popper, Steve Lohr, "Blockchain, A Better
Way to Track Pork Chops, Bonds, Bad Peanut Butter?",
published March 4, 2017 in the New York Times
https://www.nytimes.com/2017/03/04/busi-
ness/dealbook/blockchain-ibm-bitcoin.html

30. Rachel Arthur, "From Farm to Finished Garment: Blockchain Is Aiding This Fashion Collection with
Transparency", May 10, 2017 by Forbes
https://www.forbes.com/sites/rachelarthur/2017/05/10/g
arment-blockchain-fashion-transpar-
ency/#4975681774f3

PREVENTIVE DIPLOMACY AS A KEY FOR THE REDUCTION OF ASYMETRIC CONFLICTS

Zoran R. Vitorovic

Abstract

This paper focuses on preventive diplomacy in order to increase confidence and diffuse tensions between the parties of a conflict. Since the concept of preventive diplomacy has become binding on all members of the UN, they must build trust and partnership relations in order to reduce the prospects of violent conflict between states by applying PD. The paper also deals with why states have not yet managed to find a solution to form the Global Village, a key vision in seeking to combat conflict and crisis.

Introduction

In the multipolar world of today, which is slowly growing, one of the models for easing and reducing the incidence of asymmetric conflicts is certanly use of preventive diplomacy. The basic idea was promoted by the first UN General Secretary U Tanta. The idea is that, at the very least, by recognising and paying attention to the appearance of «smoke" we may be able to prevent the outbreak of «fire and conflict". This focus on prevention was discussed at numerous international conferences.

It was not until 1971, however, when the expert of psychodynamics of ethnic conflict, Professor Joseph Montville[1], pointed out the importance and essence of preventive diplomacy (PD) as a mechanism for preventing the emergence of conflicts, that PD really became an integral part of global processes. This was the reason why I addressed this concept of Preventive Diplomacy in a book issued in 2003[2] under the same name.

In that book I am pointing out that this concept moves beyond the diplomacy of everyday situations which are linked by "vertical lines" inside of one society, and "horizontal lines"

---

[1] Joseph Montville, Director of the Department for Preventive Diplomacy, the Center for International Strategic Studies from Washington, formulated one of the PD application models.

[2] Zoran Vitorovic, "Preventivna Diplomatija", book, Ars Libry, 2003, Beograd, Srbija.

Law, Ethics & Society

through the so-called "bridges of interest groups" between two states, that can be in some form of conflict.

People of the same ideas connect first through informal groups, after that when the number of informal group members increases, they begin to put pressure on the top of the pyramid in the society or state administration. This bonding takes place in various spheres of sports (sports diplomacy), and in literature, science, culture, politics.

The basic motives for all those involved in these informal groups are spreading the idea of communion, unity of diversity, and ultimately (at the end) the prevention of conflict. One of the ultimate consequences of the use of preventive diplomacy is the change of existing structures in power, and another is a stronger connection with the same-minded «on the other side of the state border."

When the so-called "critical mass" is formed, it begins to act like a torrent of a river flowing in one direction. At a later stage, this torrent, by the nature of the dynamics of the groups involved in social processes, chooses the leaders. In the beginning, everything is structured in so-called informal social groups, and in the end, the political entity is born in the form of a party or movement. The most obvious example is the case of "Solidarnosc" in Poland which ultimately chose Leh Valens as leader.

However, like any idea born on healthy ground, the ways in how preventative diplomacy has been used and pursued often looks like a case of Nobel's Dynamite. The dynamite was supposed to help people to overcome easily the natural obstacles. However, it was used more in conflicts and wars rather then more upstream for genuine peaceful preventative purposes. More clearly explained, it all looks like the story about a little Indian who came back from the forest. Dad, the tribal chief asked him, "Son, I see that you had try to send smoke signals, but I did not understand the message." The little Indian replied "I did not send anything; my blanket was on fire".

Today, the practice of how preventive diplomacy is used, often seems to look like story of small Indian.

It's enough to point out the cases of «Arab Springs" that began with the goals of getting rid of power from dictatorial and authoritarian regimes, and at the end of the day all switched to chaos and destabilization of Libya, Egypt and Iraq. The same has happend in a Ukraine, after "Majdan", where a dispute started with a protest and finaly ended with a civil war.

Preventative Diplomacy

American strategists were the first who had used the program of preventive diplomacy to develop mechanisms of the so-called non-violent regime change. On other side, great superpowers like China or Russia did not sit with crossed hands and wait. They also began the develop and implement numerous models of preventive diplomacy in order to achieve their own desired geopolitical aims. The importance of preventative diplomancy concepts can be seen in the number of centers that have been established in America, China, the Russian Federation, Saudi Arabia, Jordan, Morocco, and Indonesia.

Characteristics of Modern Asymetric Conflicts and their Sources

Global Village - Yes, but How?
Accelerated developement of technology and artifical inteligence, known as a fourth industrial revolution (automation, digitalization and robotics), poses numerous challenges in front of humanity. One is a clear move to an interconnected Global Village in which there will no longer be places for be isolated societies. This was discussed in 1995 when the first United Nations Conference on Human Rights was held at the United Nations in Vienna. At that time, the basic guiding idea was «how the Global Village should be built" in view of the galloping process of developing technologies that force us in that direction.

All subjects of the international community, from the permanent members of the Security Council - China, Russia, Great Britain, France and USA - to the representatives of the countries of Latin America, Asia and the Arab world, agree that this is "the direction of the future development of the Earth's globe." At the UN conference, it was necessary to define the minimum human rights as the basis on which the national, regional and international legal order would be developed.

Regardless of the good will to seek a peace settlement, UN member states failed to agree on the baseline values of the future Global Village. The adopted declarations and conclusions of the UN Human Rights Conference have not only been «Lukewarm" and non-binding, but also emerged at a time at the beginning of a whole range of regional, national and intranational conflicts which took place for the next 20 years, after the end of the conference. Each side has tried to convince the other, in practice, that their concept of Global Village was the only correct one. Behind the formal proclaimed aims, very soon it was clear that the ultimative priority for states was in geostrategic and geopolitical interests.

The lines of deep divisions were not only between the states, but also within the national political-business structures and establishments inside countries. In the end, in 2017, everything "exploded" when it was definitely clear for everyone that behind the scene is a tectonic conflict between the owners of huge capital. They are split into main groups - one is still for the option that Global Village must be build on a form of transnational, regional, social structures in which national states will "drown". On other side are all those who still belive that regional organisations could be functional and effective only with a stronger presence, in the decision-making processe, of national states.

An additional stroke was the knowledge that when the world was confronted wiht a Global financial crisis (2009), huge state interventions resulted in many countries like Russia and China and in Western economies.

This was a shock for many Western analysts who until that moment had repeated, like a mantra, that the time "of the state's interference with the economy is going to pass, and that it is enough to release the free market could on their own succeesfully regulate all financial problems and crisis." In the end, it became clear that Global multipolar Society is slowly growing up and that liberal capitalism must be essentially reformed in a basic ground.

Talking about five priorities for the current 2017 year the founder of the World Economic The Davos Forum, Professor Klaus Schwab, stressed that "for the leaders of the global elite urgent priority must be reform of existing structure of liberal market capitalism".[3] Professor Schwab says:

> It is most important to constructively think about the future and to catch up with existing problems. Instead of hacking and expanding pessimism, it is more important to examine what specific measures should be taken to overcome the problems. One thing is clear: market capitalism has to change, to improve, but we simply do not have a better system for the development of democracy.

> Representatives of the elite and political leaders had made a lot of mistakes because they had been

---

[3] Klaus Schwab, www.weforum.org/agenda/2017/03/klaus-schwab-new-narrative-for-globalization

concentrating on the needs in contexts of short-term (daily) solutions. Instead of that, they should be dedicated to activities that will lead to the fulfillment of long-term vision.

Subregional Structures Versus National States?

One of the asymmetric conflicts which is present around the world has been created as a reflection in the processes of Global integration - conflicts between national countries versus sub-regional structures.

For example, the idea of the great (and perhaps the last) visionaries of the common European Union - Miterand and Koll - to develop the EU "first through the strengthening of the euro currency and then through the integration of common European values" is largely in crisis and retreat.

What happened? Best explained by EU Parliament President Martin Schulz (WEF Davos 2017)[4], who said:

> The primary goal, when building the EU and insisting on the freedom and rule of law, was to prevent the emergence of authoritarian or dictatorial regimes. Unfortunately, in some countries like Poland or Hungary, is the emergence of authoritarian regimes, and that's contrary to the basic values on which the EU was built.

Martin Schulz emphasizes that:

> The EU is not a federal state and the EU Commission is not a federal government. The EU is an alliance of sovereign states. The EU is neither pro-Germany nor pro-France! Our institutions are clearly defined by agreements that all 28 members have accepted and signed. So, decisions are made unanimously, and it does not matter if a country is 'small' or 'big', economically stronger or weaker, all members are equal. The EU is a joint project of all member states.

The "double standards" of the political representatives of EU member states are explained by Schulz with the words «And now, one minister comes to a meeting in Brussels, he actively

---

[4] WEF Forum, ibid.

participates in the work of the Commission or the Parliament, and then when he returns home, for   domestic audience he says I have nothing to do with it. They decided there in the EU! It's scandalous! Here, we all participate in the decision-making process and then they 'do not know anything.' That's exactly why we have lost confidence of citizens in the EU institutions!".

In the meantime, some countries like the United Kingdom through a referendum of citizens decided to "exit from the Common Europe". In other words, the clashes between supranational organizations (EU, Mercosur, ASEAN, etc.) and national states has been intensifying.

Let's take as a second example China. It has, along with active participation in the organization of ASEAN countries, started with developing the Shanghai Cooperation Organization and the project "Road and Ring of Silk in the 21st Century" as a model for the realization of Chinese interests from Asia to Europe. From the above examples of double standards - political representatives of the members of the European Union and China's geopolitics - it is evident that the policies that most countries are following are related more to national priorities instead of readiness to develop Sub-national state structures.

Islamic (Religious) Radicalism as a Rebellion & Renaissance or a Muslim Society?

One of the factors that further reinforces all aspects of asymmetric threats to peace and stability is the global strengthening of radical, Islamic fundamentalism. The reasons for this are numerous, from the socioeconomic to the average Muslim's sense of "inferiority" in relation to the West or Asia.

The reflection of the power of Islamic radicalism has been felt by the peoples of Iraq, Libya, Syria. Instead of building up a prosperous society system after the "Arab Spring" - with more democracy, rights and freedom - civil wars have exploded. The so-called secular Islamic states are slowly becoming either a warlike conflicts places with incalculable consequences, or like Algeria, in order to calm the emotions of the population to establish more radical political structures of power.

However, this phenomenon, which many, first of all in Europe, had looked at a specific form of Autism ("it happens somewhere there"), with a growing migrant crisis began seriously to "move" on the domestic European terrain.

Preventative Diplomacy

With the "tsunamis" of the refugees in Europe came (covert) the whole brigade of fighters of Islamic fundamentalists, whose presence began to become more and more present with a numbers of terrorist strikes, known as "bites of green axes". From Berlin, Marseilles, Paris, Brussels, London, Mancester, the brigade pointed out a problem which can never be solved by the use of classic police military models.

The only way out is to actively involve all politicians, intellectuals, religious leaders from the Arab Muslim world in the process of suppressing these radical fundamentalists. At the same time, it is essential that the international community, in the form of a new "Marshall Plan", urgently invests huge amount of money in stabilizing economic and social problems from the Mugreb to the Persian Gulf.

The Spread of Conflicts as a Rescue for the Strongest Economies?

The former President of the EU Parliament, Martin Schulz, is one of few world's leading politicians who underlies the hypocrisy of modern political thought and the ethics of those who made decisions using "double" standards, spinning and inversions. That is why many analysts wonder: "do we live in a times when the emergence of a crisis of liberal capitalism is sought in regional, local and subregional conflicts" that most favor military-industrial lobbies and is their ultimate goal "stabilizing the economies of the world's strongest powers using the fascist principle - Strengthening of the war Machineries, provoking wars and cheap post-war take-up of natural resources?".

According to my analyis, the greatest enemy of any modern political leader is he - himself. More precisely, a mirror in which every morning he looks at. If everyone would start to treat the world individually from that perspective, without having a double or triple moral, I am convinced that the current global asymmetric crisis would burst apart like soap foam. It is enough that people, ordinary citizens, start direct communication and start to build, right now and immediately, one better future and things will quickly "get into normality".

Take as example a residential block in one building in Bosnia, after the war. When three tenants agreed (in 2002) to reconstructruct and repair the entrance, all the floors, galleries, the parking space and the windows on the building, without waiting for the municipal authority - it was very fast, in two days all done. Three started the action during the day, the neighbors from all flats of the given entrance joined (in total,

42 people). After two day the entrance and stairs were shining – like new.

The inhabitants of the neighboring entrance saw that "it is nice, everything is shining there", with the comments "we are not any less incompetent than the neighbors" they self-organized and also brought everything in order for two days. After that, actions were transferred to the neighboring buildings like viruses. Within 7 days, the whole quart looked like it was recently built, and tenants began to behave far more responsibly towards their immediate surroundings.

If this was possible to be done at the level of the whole quart, a mutnational, after war in Bosnia, surely the same can be done at the level of the state of Bosnia and the whole Western Balkan as a region. The important point is a will, readiness for the concrete action of individuals, and that people are connected about common needs and interests, without waiting for the municipality, the canton, the state. This is a major example of preventive diplomacy in practice.

Concluding Remarks

Observing the Global Village, it seems that the fear and general insecurity of the citizens are dominant. The increasingly reflection of the old ideological conceptions with the present deeper crisis of global liberal capitalism does not give hope that the use of "sincere" preventive diplomacy will give positive results for the Global Peace.

Maybe it is already too late for preventive diplomacy. If the day is known by the morning, the world is at the doorsteps of greater global conflicts and wars. The question is when this will start, how and in which forms?

If this is a case, then the best definition of complete humanity is recorded in a single cartoon: The cartoon shows the monkeys, in front of monkey is a neanderthal, in front of the neanderthal is a modern man. From the other direction is a man coming back from 23th century. He looks on a group and says: "Pease, lets go all back. We ruined everything what we could!".

INTERNATIONAL LAW UNDER ATTACK BY GEOSTRATEGIC TENSIONS BETWEEN LEADING NATIONS[1]

Stephan U. Breu

Introduction

We life in a time where major actors of international geostrategy change their approach to International Law in a drastic manner. Historically, International Law has a primarily regulatory function for the purpose of facilitating international cooperation and giving it a predictable pattern on the basis of binding rules. One of the main objectives of International Law is to create the conditions for international peace and stability. International Humanitarian Law, often also called Law of War or Law of armed Conflicts, is an important part of the International Law concept.

Encouraging the development of international law as a way to regulate international relations has been a major objective of the United Nations since its very beginning. Within the UN Structure the United Nations Security Council (UNSC) is charged with the maintenance of international peace and security. As the permanent members of the UNSC are understandably the major actors and opponents on geopolitical level they are following opposing strategies on various topics. Not really accepting the chains of the International Law we notice a strong mindset in the governments of these countries to return to the concept of "Power of the stronger" or "Because we can". If necessary, they are introducing new concepts like "Humanitarian Interventions" and use these concepts one-sided which is not foreseen in International Law without prior approval by the UNSC.

Of course, International Law cannot be ethically perfect. As it is law and law needs to be clearly defined and not easily adaptable to the benefit of one party. Whereas the severity of

---

[1] First published in the Collective Monograph "Topical Issues: Problems of Modern Law and Economics in Europe and Russia, Vol.II", p. 44, Yustitsinform Moscow, 2018. Published with the consent of the author.

penalties can be considered under ethical approaches, the crime as such has to be conclusively defined. It can be considered one of the greatest achievement of mankind that we were able to give us at least a basic legal framework to create an environment that enables nations, corporations and humans to work towards the goal to co-exist peacefully and promote economic and social progress for all.

The tendency of major geopolitical actors to fall back on the "Power of the stronger" concept of the past is drastically undermining the trust and confidence of the whole mankind into the International Law as basic for a peaceful and sustainable future. Through acts of war against other sovereign nations, annexation of land through hybrid warfare or one-sided abandonment of signed treaties under International Law these actors are pushing the cooperation between nations towards a difficult position.

The community of values is only in focus between closed allies and as soon as the own goals are confronted with such values one can put them easily aside. As we see today values should be transported to other nations and societies by force only and not by living an example. Propagation of such community of values as well as regime changes through outside forces or proxies are deemed to fail as it is not based on social development and perverted if the originators show by their actions that they do not care themselves for such values to reach their goals.

To secure a more peaceful future of mankind and enable a sustainable development of economic and social structures it is very important to return to a level of accepting at least the most important regulations of International Law. Denying diplomatic work and following his own agenda without compromise will not help progress of mankind but throw us back to an instable and unsecure world with much more crises areas and warzones. We should never forget that we need peace and prosperity well to progress towards a better world for everybody.

International Law under attack

International Law governs relations between states and

simplifies international cooperation, providing certainty through the establishment of binding rules. It provides a basis for peace, stability and the protection of human beings. Within a context of ever-increasing interdependence, it is constantly evolving[2].

Much of International Law is consent-based governance. This means that a state member is not obliged to abide by this type of international law unless it has expressly consented to a particular course of conduct. However, the United Nations Security Council (UNSC) is the only UN body with the authority to issue binding resolutions to all member states.

An important part of International Law is International Humanitarian Law (IHL). International Humanitarian Law is a set of rules that seeks, for humanitarian reasons, to limit the effects of armed conflict. It protects persons who are not, or are no longer, participating in hostilities, and imposes limits on the means and methods of warfare. IHL is also known as 'the law of war' or 'the law of armed conflict'[3].

Distinction must be made between IHL, which regulates the conduct of parties engaged in an armed conflict (*jus in bello*), and that part of public international law set out in the Charter of the United Nations that regulates whether a State may rightfully resort to armed force against another State (*jus ad bellum*). The Charter prohibits such use of force, with two exceptions:

- cases of self-defence against an armed attack;
- when the use of armed force is authorized by the United Nations Security Council.

Not mentioned in the Charter are so-called "humanitarian interventions", a concept favoured prominently by NATO members to explain aggressive armed actions against sovereign nations without a mandate from UNSC, for example in Serbia or Syria. Legally the discussions around the

---

[2] Swiss Confederation/Federal Department of Foreign Affairs FDFA, Factsheet
https://www.eda.admin.ch/eda/en/home/foreign-policy/international-law.html
[3] International Commitee of the Red Cross, Legal Factsheet "What is International Humanitarian Law", published December 2014
https://www.icrc.org/en/download/file/4541/what-is-ihl-factsheet.pdf

rightfulness of the concept of humanitarian interventions reminds me of the historical discussions and disputes about tyrannicide as humanitarian interventions mostly include the objective of a forced regime change in sovereign nations.

The origins of the current order of International Law were formed as long ago as the "Peace of Westphalia" in 1648. Prior to 1648 it was common to define the rightfulness of a war by judging the purpose and legitimacy of it. This theory of power interruptions can also be found in the writings of the Roman orator Cicero and the writings of St. Augustine.

Until the mid-19th century, relations between nations were regulated by treaties and agreements unenforceable except by force, and not binding except as matters of honour and faithfulness. This led to calls for regulation of the acts of states, especially in times of war.

One of the first instruments of modern international law was the Lieber Code, passed in 1863 by the Congress of the United States, to govern the conduct of US forces during the United States Civil War[4]. It is considered to be the first written recitation of the rules and articles of war. In the years that followed, other states subscribed to limitations of their conduct, and numerous other treaties and bodies were created to regulate the conduct of states.

United Nations & the United Nations Security Council (UNSC)

Encouraging the development of international law as a way to regulate international relations has been a major objective of the United Nations since its very beginning.

Within the UN Structure the United Nations Security Council (UNSC) is charged with the maintenance of international peace and security. Its powers include the establishment of peacekeeping operations, the establishment

---

[4] The Lieber Code of April 24, 1863, also known as Instructions for the Government of Armies of the United States in the Field, General Order № 100, or Lieber Instructions, was an instruction signed by US President Abraham Lincoln to the Union Forces of the United States during the American Civil War that dictated how soldiers should conduct themselves in wartime. Its name reflects its author, the German-American legal scholar and political philosopher Franz Lieber. https://ihl-databases.icrc.org/ihl/INTRO/110

of international sanctions and the authorization of military action through Security Council resolutions. It is the only UN body with the authority to issue binding resolutions to member states. Its effectiveness is compromised by the United Nations Security Council "veto power" which give the power to each of the permanent members of the United Nations Security Council to veto any "substantive" resolution.

As the permanent members of the UNSC are understandably the major actors and opponents on geopolitical level they are following opposing strategies on various topics. Not really accepting the chains of the International Law we notice a strong mindset in the governments of these countries to return to the concept of "Power of the stronger" or "Because we can". Meaning that all the progress in international peaceful cooperation of nations and people originating way back in the "Peace of Westphalia" in 1648 and developing during hard times and two World Wars are only considered valuable as long as it is serving their own agenda.

The UN Charter provision for unanimity among the Permanent Members of the Security Council was the result of extensive discussion where all parties involved favoured the principle of unanimity. Mostly the motivation was not by a belief in the desirability of the major powers acting together but by a concern to protect their own sovereign rights and national interest. The veto was forced on all other governments by the five veto holders during the negotiations building up to the creation of the UN and was established in order to prohibit the UN from taking any future action directly against its principal founding members.

Today we are again in a situation that the veto power makes the UNSC unable to act in various cases. As the permanent members of the UNSC are understandably the major actors and opponents on geopolitical level they are following opposing strategies on various topics. This might be a severe pain seen from an ethical point of view but on legal terms the situation is quite clear. Even under the concept of the responsibility to protect populations from genocide, war crimes, ethnic cleansing and crimes against humanity (also referred to as "RtoP") it is undoubtedly so that "only the UNSC can authorize the use of force, under Chapter VII, Article 42, of the

Charter. "Coercive military force can be utilized in various forms, through the deployment of United Nations-sanctioned multinational forces for establishing security zones, the imposition of no-fly zones, the establishment of a military presence on land and at sea for protection or deterrence purposes, or any other means, as determined by the Security Council."[5]

It is true that international pressure is mounting on the UNSC Veto Powers especially after the adaption of the "Responsibility to protect" principles. France is advocating the other Veto Powers to forswear veto when a clear majority of UN member states supports actions to mitigate the risk of a mass-atrocity crime. As ongoing blocking of decisions by the UNSC are threatening and jeopardizing the credibility and legitimacy of the UNSC and the effectiveness of the UN or its bodies of law. On the other side it is quite hard to believe that the other Veto Powers would follow the French proposal on a voluntary basis as all members are using their veto under circumstances where they really believe that a proposed resolution will cause more harm than good from their point of view.

"Humanitarian Interventions" under International Law

As we have seen an armed intervention in a sovereign nation can only be legally undertaken through a unanimous decision of the UNSC. Humanitarian intervention is a concept that is mostly favoured by NATO members and the Western hemisphere to give a reason to use force despite a missing resolution from the UNSC under Chapter VII of the Charter of the United Nations. Legally the concept is designed to circumvent the UNSC by invoking a right not foreseen in the UN Charters. The concept is also contradicting long established legal basics in International Law like the regulation, that any sovereign nation can act freely within their own borders (Treaty of Westphalia) which is also upheld in the UN Charter

---

[5] Report of the Secretary General United Nations General Assembly Security Council, "Responsibility to protect: timely and decisive response" July 2012 http://www.responsibilitytoprotect.org/UNSG%20 Report_timely%20and%20decisive%20response(1).pdf

of 1945, where article 2 (7) stats that "nothing should authorize intervention in matters essentially within the domestic
jurisdiction of any state".

As we have seen above even taking in account the concept of the "Responsibility to protect" still only the UNSC can
authorize the use of force, under Chapter VII, Article 42, of the
Charter. This is clearly stated and does not give any option
for unlawful actions of war against sovereign countries and
UN members.

Even looking at humanitarian interventions from an ethical and moral point of view leaves us with the question who
has the position as moral agent to decide what is allowing
such an intervention. There are strong disputes around the
world that this concept is a modern manifestation of Western
colonialism or is using humanitarian pretexts to pursue otherwise unacceptable geopolitical goals and to evade the non-
intervention norm and legal prohibitions on the use of force.
This argument is also supported by the fact that military campaigns like the one against Serbia or the one favoured by a
lot of Western military or politicians against Syria are justified
with humanitarian reasons but there was not reaction by the
same global players during the slaughter in Rwanda and in
the war zones in Yemen or Sudan which are not prominently
covered on television in the western countries. Avram Noam
Chomsky writes that "Humanitarian interventionism goes only
one way – from the powerful to the weak" and condemns the
targeting of the concept of national sovereignty by humanitarian interventionism.

Maybe also following these arguments the "so-called
right of humanitarian intervention" has been condemned as
having no basis in international law during the Havana G-77
summit in 2000.[6]

Taking into account these opinions from representatives
of different groups and societies around the world we have to
accept once again the "community of values" defined and upheld by Western civilization has no exclusive position with
mankind. The position as moral agent for the world is lost

---

[6] Group of 77 South Summit, Havana 2000, Declaration of the South Summit.

especially when major geopolitical players are circumventing International Law to follow their strategic goals or try to initiate regime changes as in Syria or Iran, only naming the last examples. Also signed treaties are not respected as soon as they seem not to fit in the present agenda as we have seen with the annexation of the Crimea or the nuclear treaty with Iran.

Whom are we transferring the moral position as moral agent to decide which humanitarian intervention is legal or unlawful if not the UN and its bodies? Such decision should never become a weapon for one geopolitical power to follow its aims ruthless without consent of the whole mankind. It is hard to bear the suffering of human beings from genocide, war crimes, ethnic cleansing and crimes against humanity knowing that there are limited possibilities to stop such crime. But knowing that all Veto Powers in the UNSC are at the end only opposing a resolution if they are really concerned that it will cause more damage than good we might really have to settle for this minimalistic point of consent for legitimation of such rigorous external intervention in the sovereignty of nations.

Conclusion

International Law and International Humanitarian Law are challenged strongly by the major geopolitical actors in the last years. Negating the need of nations to have sovereignty without external influence, reliable treaties and agreements and protection from strong opponents through the world-wide community of nations, the leaders of these actors tend to fall back into the time before the "Treaty of Westphalia" where the concept of "Power of the stronger" was reigning the world.

For a peaceful co-existence of mankind and sustainable economic and social development we need reliable treaties and agreements which are resilient. Interventions from external powers against sovereign nations should be the very last exception. Such interventions on humanitarian grounds should fulfil highest standards and not aim for regime change or geopolitical goals of a group of actors. In my opinion the only body able to have this position as moral agent is the

United Nation Security Council even accepting the problem of possible veto against resolutions.

Political leaders worldwide should adapt their positions to achieve compromises to build up trust and confidence between all nations. International Law should be followed and not only be waived as not binding for strong actors. Each leader has of course first responsibility for his country and citizens but we all have also responsibility for mankind as a whole. Breaking International Law is difficult to sanction but at least it should be addressed from all sides. Blind obedience of so-called partners in international organizations is not helping to build trust and confidence. Breaking International Law is a crime however we put it and it should be addressed neutral against all government acting like this.

References

Swiss Confederation/Federal Department of Foreign Affairs FDFA, Webpage "International Law" https://www.eda.admin.ch/eda/en/home/foreign-policy/international-law.html [accessed 10/05/18]

International Commitee of the Red Cross, Legal Factsheet "What is International Humanitarian Law", published December 2014 https://www.icrc.org/en/download/file/4541/what-is-ihl-factsheet.pdf [accessed 10/05/18]

United Nations, Fact Sheet #5 "Role of the United Nations in International Law", https://treaties.un.org/doc/source/events/2011/Press_kit/fact_sheet_5_english.pdf [accessed 10/05/18]

Jayshree Bajoria, Rober McMahon, "The Dilemma of Humanitarian Intervention", published by Council on Foreign Relations, June 2013 https://www.cfr.org/backgrounder/dilemma-humanitarian-intervention [accessed 10/05/18]

Law, Ethics & Society

Martin Binder, "Why does UN Humanitarian Intervention remain selective?", published by Oxford Research Group, March 2017
https://sustainablesecurity.org/2017/03/07/why-does-un-humanitarian-intervention-remain-selective/ [accessed 10/05/18]

Conor Foley, Interview "How Humanitarian Intervention failed the World", published by FP-Foreign Policy in November 2008
http://foreignpolicy.com/2008/11/01/how-humanitarian-intervention-failed-the-world/ [accessed 10/05/18]

Anne-Sopie Massa, "Does Humanitarian Intervention serve Human Rights? The Case of Kosovo", published by Amsterdam Law Forum 2009
http://amsterdamlawforum.org/article/view/63/120 [accessed 10/05/18]

Fred Aja Agwu, "The Challenge of Humanitarian Intervention Since Rwanda", published by Council of Councils, August 2014
https://www.cfr.org/councilofcouncils/global_memos/p33324 [accessed 10/05/18]

Walden Bello, "The Crisis of Humanitarian Intervention", published by Foreign Policy In Focus in August 2011
https://fpif.org/the_crisis_of_humanitarian_intervention/ [accessed 10/05/18]

Kirthi Jayakumar, "Humanitarian Intervention – A Legal Analysis", published by E-International Relation, Feburar 2012
http://www.e-ir.info/2012/02/06/humanitarian-intervention-a-legal-analysis/ [accessed 10/05/18]

Vaughan Lowe Antonios Tzanakopoulos, "Humanitarian Intervention", published by Oxford Public International Law, May 2011
http://opil.ou-plaw.com/view/10.1093/law:epil/9780199231690/law-9780199231690-e306 [accessed 10/05/18]

United Nations, Charter of the United Nations
http://www.un.org/en/charter-united-nations/index.html [accessed 10/05/18]

International Law Under Attack

Group of 77 South Summit, Havana 2000, Declaration of the South Summit
http://www.g77.org/summit/Declaration_G77Summit.htm [accessed 10/05/18]

Global Policy Forum, Humanitarian Intervention?
https://www.globalpolicy.org/humanitarian-intervention.html [accessed 10/05/18]

Hongju Koh Harold, "Syria and the Law of Humanitarian Intervention (Part II: International Law and the Way Forward)", published October 2013
https://www.justsecurity.org/1506/koh-syria-part2/ [accessed 10/05/18]

Report of the Secretary General United Nations General Assembly Security Council, "Responsibility to protect: timely and decisive response" July 2012
http://www.responsibilitytoprotect.org/UNSG%20Report_t imely%20and%20decisive%20response(1).pdf [accessed 10/05/18]

9 781733 537117